Becoming a Digital Designer: A Complete Career Guide

Becoming a Digital Designer: A Complete Career Guide

Bob Ford

STATES
ACADEMIC PRESS
www.statesacademicpress.com

Becoming a Digital Designer: A Complete Career Guide
Bob Ford
ISBN: 978-1-63989-068-2 (Hardback)

STATES
ACADEMIC PRESS

Published by States Academic Press,
109 South 5th Street,
Brooklyn, NY 11249, USA

Cataloging-in-Publication Data

Becoming a digital designer : a complete career guide / Bob Ford.
p. cm.
Includes bibliographical references and index.
ISBN 978-1-63989-068-2
1. Computer graphics--Vocational guidance. 2. Digital media--Vocational guidance.
3. Graphic arts--Vocational guidance. I. Ford, Bob.
QA76.575 .B43 2021
006.7--dc23

For more information regarding States Academic Press and its products, please visit the publisher's website www.statesacademicpress.com

Table of Contents

Preface

A designer is a professional who can plan, design and create objects according to a specific idea or target. Digital design involves the use of softwares and other digital tools to visually convey an idea or project. Professionals in this area create 2D and 3D images, graphics, typography and cross-screen media. Digital design is especially used in corporate design, product packaging, communication design, web design, editorial design and branding. This book unfolds the innovative aspects of digital design, which will be crucial for the holistic understanding of the subject matter. It will serve as a valuable source of reference for those interested in this field.

To facilitate a deeper understanding of the contents of this book a short introduction of every chapter is written below:

Chapter 1- Graphic design or digital design is the design and creation of ideas, information and messages using visual aids such as symbols, pictures, diagrams, etc. along with technological devices. Scanners, digital image editing software, computers and styluses are common devices that are used in this field. This chapter will provide an integrated understanding of digital design.

Chapter 2- Photo editing is a common practice that is part of digital design. Popular photo editing software include Adobe Photoshop, Picasa and GIMP. Hue, saturation, color, retouching, etc. are the basic elements that can be adjusted by using these software. This chapter has been carefully written to provide an easy understanding of the varied facets of professional photo editing.

Chapter 3- Adobe Photoshop is a popular graphic image editing software that is developed and published by Adobe Systems. Various tools of Adobe Photoshop include cropping, eraser, slicing, shape tools, pen tools, etc. The major components of Adobe Photoshop are discussed in this chapter.

Chapter 4- Adobe InDesign is a software that allows users to use page layout tools to create and design content specific to pages. Newspapers, books, posters, etc. are designed using such software. The chapter strategically encompasses and incorporates the major components and key concepts of InDesign, providing a complete understanding.

Chapter 5- Macromedia Flash is one of the software that is used to create multimedia and animated images. Animation may be in 2D or 3D. Animation process is best understood in confluence with the major topics listed in the following chapter.

Chapter 6- Digital design is applicable in almost all forms of visual communication that is practiced today. Digital flip books, invitations, logos, brochures, etc. are some of the items that are regularly made using desktop publishing and image editing software. The topics discussed in the chapter are of great importance to broaden the existing knowledge on digital design.

Finally, I would like to thank the entire team involved in the inception of this book for their valuable time and contribution. This book would not have been possible without their efforts. I would also like to thank my friends and family for their constant support.

Bob Ford

Chapter

1 Digital Designing Basics

Graphic design or digital design is the design and creation of ideas, information and messages using visual aids such as symbols, pictures, diagrams, etc. along with technological devices. Scanners, digital image editing software, computers and styluses are common devices that are used in this field. This chapter will provide an integrated understanding of digital design.

How to make Digital Art

Digital art is becoming increasingly popular among many artists. With features that are unique to this medium, it's not hard to explain its popularity. To make digital art, you'll need a computer, a program that allows for digital drawing, and a tablet. Then, after learning the basics of digital art, and getting plenty of practice, you'll be well on your way to excelling at digital drawing.

Method 1

Preparing the Illustration

1. Sketch out your idea on paper. Unless you don't have a scanner, this is the best way to start. Try to get the anatomy and physiology of your subject as close as possible, but don't fret, as adjustments can be made later. Don't add too much detail such as fur or clothing texture just yet. Be sure to use pencil if you want to fix mistakes.

    - With the sketch, getting the details right isn't as important as getting the general ideas and feel of the illustration down. The drawing will likely change a lot between this step and the final result.

2. Scan your drawing. Place your drawing face down on the scanner. Close the scanner and then start the scan. Name the file once it's finished scanning and save it as a .PNG or .JPEG for the highest quality.

3. Open the file in whatever program you want to use. GIMP is good for beginners since it is free to download. It's probably not a good idea to use Microsoft Paint because of its limited features and hard to view canvas. A lot of people use Adobe Photoshop for making digital art.

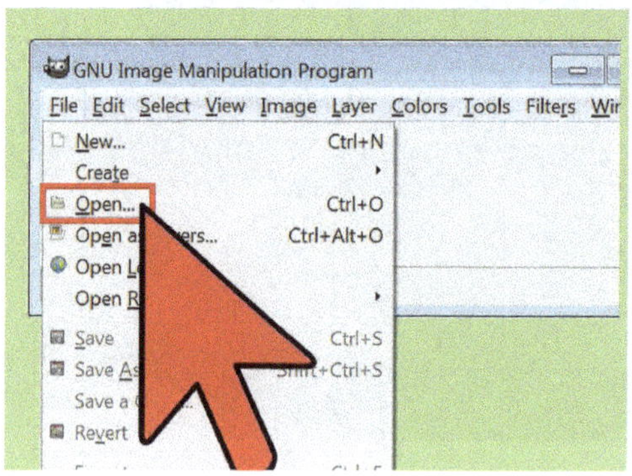

4. Alternatively, sketch directly in the art program you're using. If you do not have a scanner, you can make your sketch directly in the program you're going to use. Plug the tablet into the computer using the cable that came with the tablet, and follow the instructions with the tablet to install the software.

- Open the program you chose to draw with, and connect your tablet. Then create a new file, and start sketching.

Method 2

Outlining and Coloring

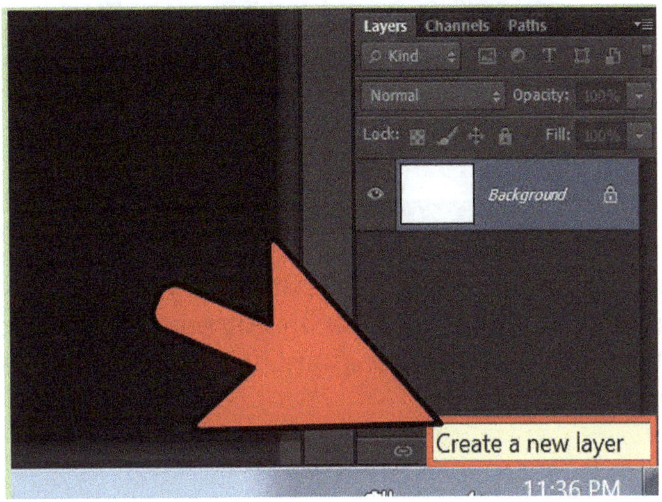

1. Make layers. Right now your sketch is the only layer in the file. First, create a background layer by hitting the new layer button, and using the fill-in tool to fill the transparent layer in white. Then drag that layer to the bottom, so that it's the first layer of the drawing. For each major part of the drawing, like the face, hair, clothes, and background, create a new layer above your sketch layer, and name them appropriately.

- Multiple layers allow for more detail and flexibility without the risk of messing up the entire piece.

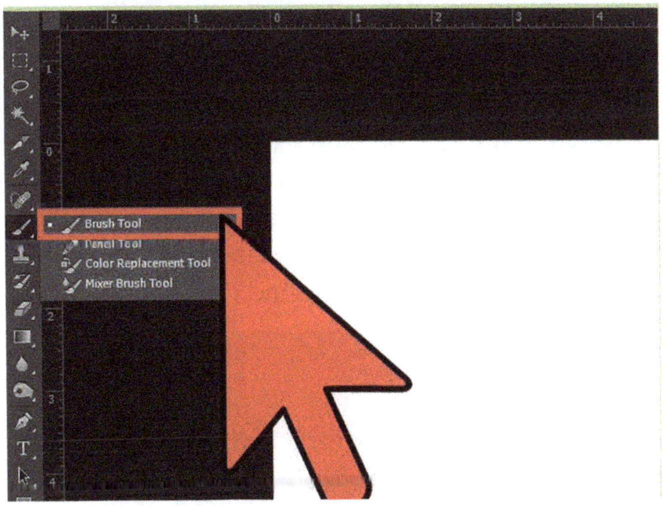

2. Outline the drawing. On each layer you've created, start outlining the sketch with the brush tool. Set the brush to a small size like 2 to 4 pixels. The outline will make things easier to color later on. In this step you can also fix any anatomy mistakes that you made while sketching.

- After outlining the whole drawing. Delete or hide the sketch layer, so you can color in the outline without being distracted by the sketchy lines of your original sketch.

3. Get the basic colors in. After you've outlined your drawing, you'll need to sketch out the colors of your drawing. Use brushes of varying sizes, depending on how big of an area you're filling in, and color in all the different sections of your drawing. Just use a single color for each area, like the face, hair, and each article of clothing.

Method 3

Finishing your Art

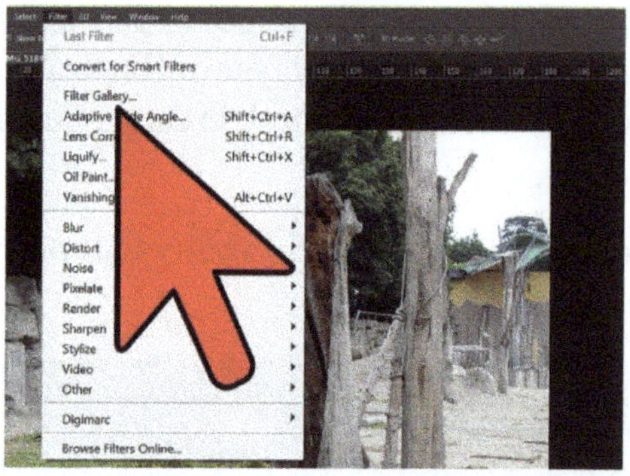

1. Add detail. Depending on your skills, style, and ease with the program, you can do many different things here. You can add more layers and get even more detailed, or skip straight to the shading section. Just remember that more layers are good if you want to fix one aspect of a picture and not the entire thing. This is when you can add things like more detail to the eyes, pockets and creases in the clothing, and structure to the background.

2. Shade your drawing. To start shading, pick the eyedropper tool and use it on the area you want

to shade. Then go into the color picker and drag the color to a darker shade. Use that color and the brush tool to shade the area you're working on. Repeat to add more shading and shade the entire drawing.

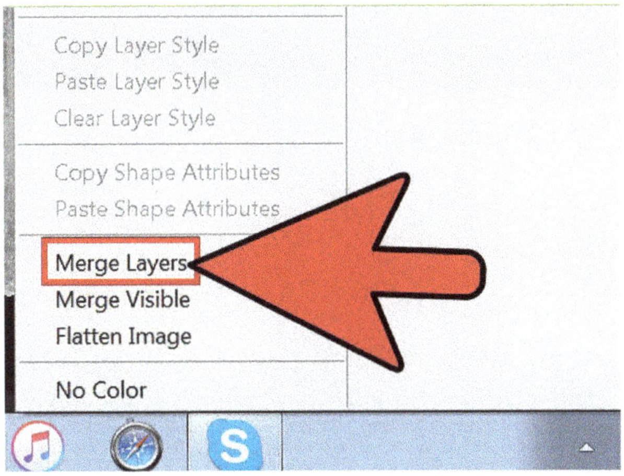

3. When finished, be sure to merge all the layers. First, save a copy of the file so that you can go back and work on it more later if you choose. Since .PNG and .JPEG can't handle them, you'll have to merge all layers into one in order to save in those formats.

4. Export the file. Go to file, and save as. Save the file as a .PNG or .JPEG. If you ever want to go back and change something in the drawing, you can open the .PSD file, or whatever file type the program you have uses.

How to Design a Logo

A great logo is more than images and words, a good logo tells a story about your company--who you are, what you do and what you stand for. That's a lot to ask of one piece of art, which is why it's important that you take the time to do it right. Fortunately, you don't have to do it alone. The steps below will take you through the process of designing a logo that will successfully brand you in the marketplace.

Part 1

Brainstorming

1. Determine the primary function of your logo. A logo represents your brand through the use of shape, fonts, color and images. Being clear on why you need a logo can guide your design.

- Boost recognition. Is your company new or competing in a field with a lot of other players? Having a strong logo can help clients recognize your brand more readily.
- Create memorability. Consumers shop with their eyes and logos can be easier to remember than names, products and services. Over time, a customer comes to associate your logo with your company.
- Create trust. Part of bringing in and keeping clients is based on their willingness to trust you. A solid logo that conveys your honesty and integrity can help put clients at ease.
- Enhance admiration. If clients already have a good impression of your business, you can build on that by creating a logo that is well-regarded for its good looks, cleverness or effective simplicity.

2. Think about your target market. It's important to be clear on who your client is and customize the look of your logo to appeal to those who will be using your services.

- A logo for a florist shop could incorporate a whimsical font and a bright color scheme; this wouldn't work so well for an auto body repair garage.
- A logo for a law firm must communicate integrity and strength; not necessarily the look that would work well for a catering company.

3. Decide whether to incorporate your company's name into the logo. Of course, you want to build name recognition for your business, but making the name part of your logo design may not always be a good idea.

- Include the name if it is reasonably distinctive but not yet a household word or if your marketing funds are limited and your goal is to build name recognition.
- Do not include the name if it is too generic, too long, doesn't translate well globally (if that's a consideration) or lacks personality. Leave the name out, too, if you must put your logo on a product, such as a sneaker or a handbag.
- Think of all the different ways you plan to use your logo. Picture the smallest size you may need; if the company name won't be readable when the logo is the size of a thumbnail, it may be best to leave it out of the design.

4. Follow the company's color scheme. If your company has already established the use of certain colors in its signage, advertising and other materials, it's important that those colors are reflected in the logo.

- Consistent use of colors builds familiarity. You want customers to be able to mentally "link" your logo to the company.
- If your company has branded itself with specific colors, the public will have developed a subconscious association with those colors. For example, color scheme is green.
- If you don't yet have an established color scheme for your business, do some research on the psychology of colors so that you can choose appropriately. For example, red signifies strength, passion, energy and confidence but it can also signal danger.

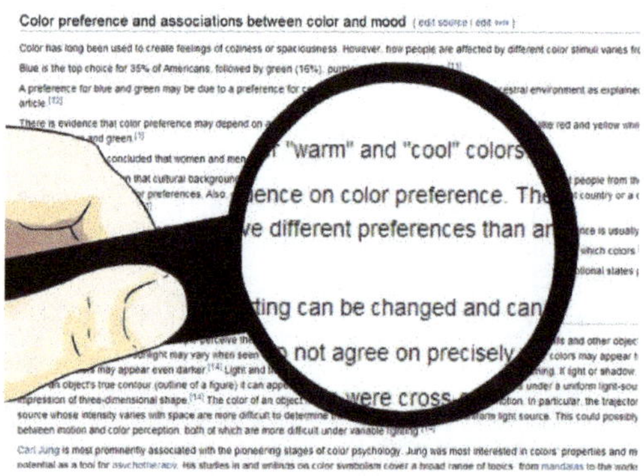

5. Be inspired by but don't copy successful logos. While it might be tempting to create something that looks like your favorite corporate logo, it will communicate an unintended message to your audience—that you're lazy and uninspired.

- Look at logos of other business similar to yours. Ask yourself what you like and don't like about them. What works and what doesn't. Don't get overwhelmed by looking at too many examples—10 or 12 should be more than enough to give you ideas of what to do and what to avoid.

- A successful logo should be simple, memorable, timeless and appropriate. Keep these as goals as you play around with ideas.
- If you're struggling for ideas, trying using different key word to conduct searches online or use a thesaurus to move your thinking in some new directions.

- Doodle. Sketch things out and play around with them. Write key words in different fonts. See if something visual sparks an idea.

6. Keep it simple. Designing a logo is an exercise in restraint. While it may be tempting to try to convey a multitude of messages with your design, trying to do too much will sabotage the success of your logo.

- Avoid too many colors, multiple fonts and layered images. A confusing or cluttered logo won't convey a clear message.
- If there are too many visual elements in your logo, it will be difficult for the customer to process. They won't know where to look or what it means.

- Practically speaking, a simple logo is easier and less expensive to reproduce. Since your logo may appear on a variety of items—from letterhead to advertisements to tote bags—simplicity could save you money in the long-run.

Part 2

Testing the Design

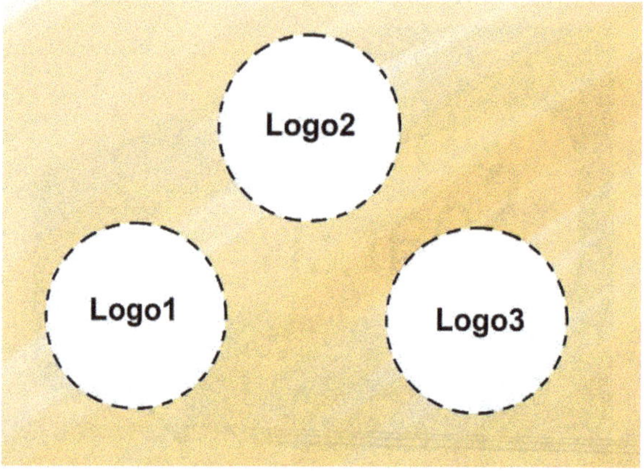

1. Create multiple designs. In the early stage, you may have several ideas that you want to express in your logo design. Commit them all to paper so that you can see what works and what doesn't.

- Even a design that's a dud can spark an idea or offer one element that you want to retain in the next version of your design.

2. Draw a rough sketch of the design. You're better off putting pencil to paper in the initial stages of your logo design process. Sketching is a quick and easy way to get the ideas out of your head and on to paper where you can evaluate them more easily.

- Plain white paper or simple graph paper make good backgrounds for your pencil sketches.
- Don't erase. Designing is not a linear process. Keep the pages with the designs that you didn't like. They may spark an idea or, upon later examination, offer something of value.
- Large design companies will often sketch out dozens of pages of logo concepts before they even touch a computer mouse. Take a tip from the pros and focus on your sketches first.

3. Show the design to a test market. It may be tempting to move forward once you've come up with what seems to you to be a winning logo, but it's important to get feedback.

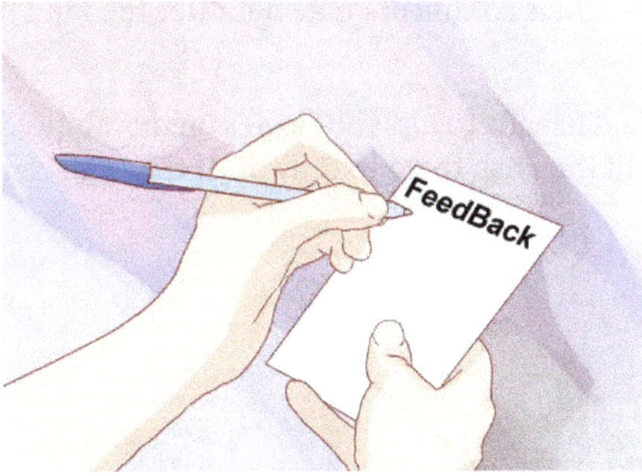

4. Get feedback from people in your target market. Show your design(s) to a sampling of people who fit the profile of your ideal customer. You may show them multiple designs or simply the one you feel to be the strongest candidate.

- Ask key questions that will reveal their reaction to the logo. Do they think it's boring or exciting? Ugly or attractive? Generic or unique? Also check to see what image or message the logo conveys to them, whether they find it easy to read/recognize and if it seems consistent with what they know about your company or about your industry.

5. Be wary of relying too heavily on family and friends. While you may want to informally get the opinion of those close to you, their comments may not offer the kind of feedback you'll find to be most useful.

- You can use family and friends to test your logo's memorability. Let them look at the design for a few seconds and then ask them to draw it. If they can remember most of it, then it's memorable.

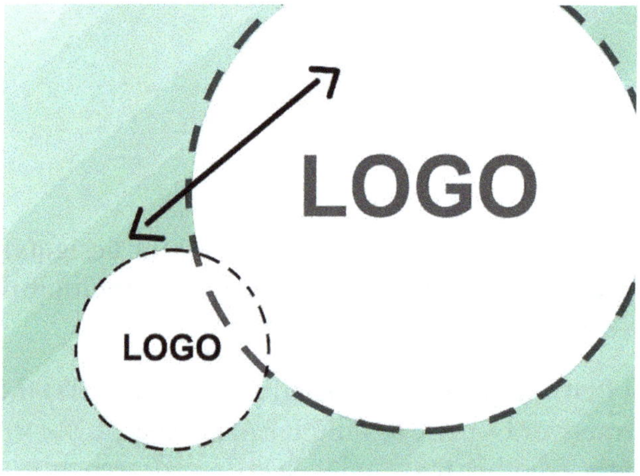

6. Make sure that the design is scalable. Consider all the different ways you may use your logo—in newspaper ads, on signage, on your website. Your logo must function well whether it's being reproduced in a large or a small format.

- If a logo has too much detail or lines that are too thin, those elements may get lost or the logo may look too fussy at small sizes.
- If a logo is drawn to look good only at a business card size, it will tend to appear clunky when reproduced larger.
- Graphic design programs such as Adobe Illustrator or Inkscape will allow you to test the scalability of your design. If you're working by hand initially, try making copies of your design at different size settings.

Part 3

Finalizing the Design

1. Create a final draft. Ultimately, you need to have your logo digitized. You can do this yourself or hire a professional to make it happen for you.

- Learn a graphic design program. The most used program is Adobe Illustrator but Inkscape is another offering, and it can be downloaded online for free.
    - There are a number of instructional books and websites that can help you learn Illustrator. Community colleges and some continuing education programs offer classes in this design program.
- Hire a professional graphic artist. If you already have a background in graphic arts, computer-assisted design or you're a quick study, then you may be able to do it yourself; otherwise, you're better off putting your work in the hands of a professional.

- Visit designers' websites to see their portfolios. You want to choose someone who has experience working with logo design.
- Ask about turnaround time. Depending on what stage your design is in, you may go through another revision with an artist or he or she may simply reproduce your idea "as-is." In any case, find out how long it will take from the time you give them your design until you see a finished product.
- Find out about costs. Again, where you are in your design process will impact the cost of this service. If you need someone to go back to square one with you in your design, that will be more expensive than if you are happy with the logo you've created and simply want to have it professionally computerized.
- Check online services. There are a number of online graphic design services that allow you to pay a set fee and in return receive several logo designs from artists trying to win the job. You choose the design you like best and work with that artist through the completion of the project.

2. Keep listening. Once your logo is finished, it's important that you stay open to feedback on the design.

- Use social media. If your company has an established online presence, run your logo past those who are connected to you and listen to what they have to say.

- Try your logo out on your website first. If the response to your logo isn't positive, it's easier and less expensive to revise and republish it on your website than to redo printed materials.

- Get details. If clients say the logo is "confusing" or "difficult to read," press them for details. The more you can find out before you invest in all of your print collateral, the easier it will be to tweak the design.

How to Design a Website

Designing a great website may seem like a daunting challenge, but as long as you keep the basics in mind, you will find the process interesting and enjoyable. There's more to it than just looking good! We'll show you the basics, and some general guidelines to help you design websites that keep people coming back.

Part 1

Finding your Design

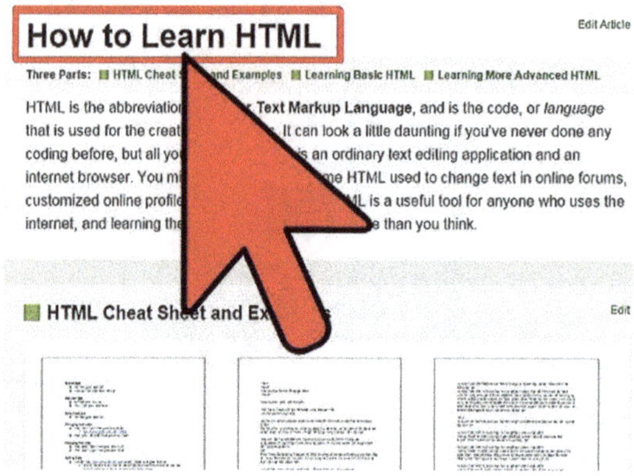

1. Design your own website. if you're new to web coding and design but you really want to build a website yourself, there are many options open to you. You can build a simple site by teaching yourself basic html and CSS coding. Just be sure that you can also make it look nice and professional!

2. Use a pre-made website template. You can purchase or find free pre-made websites very easily on the internet. These are pre-made codes which you simply use and alter to your own needs. There are many reputable providers of templates, but a good one is Wix.

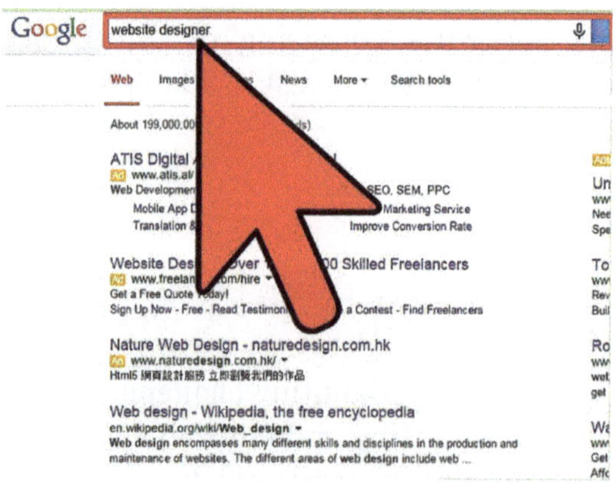

3. Hire a website designer. If you want something tailored to your needs that looks professional

and runs great, it's probably a good idea to hire a website designer. While this will definitely cost you money, it won't be as expensive as it sounds. You can get a designer on the cheap by advertising at a local technical college or university. Their experience will help guide you to a more successful, more professional website.

Part 2

Making Basic Design Considerations

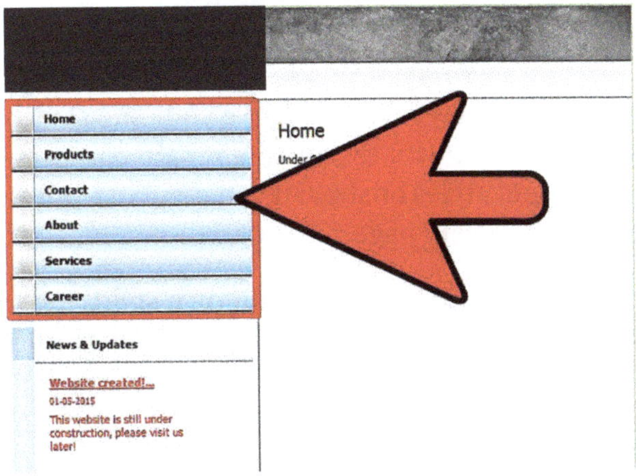

1. Streamline your webpage. You want everything to be as fast and easy to use as possible. Minimize the number of choices that someone has to make, make navigation extremely self-explanatory, and help them get to what they're looking for as quickly as possible.

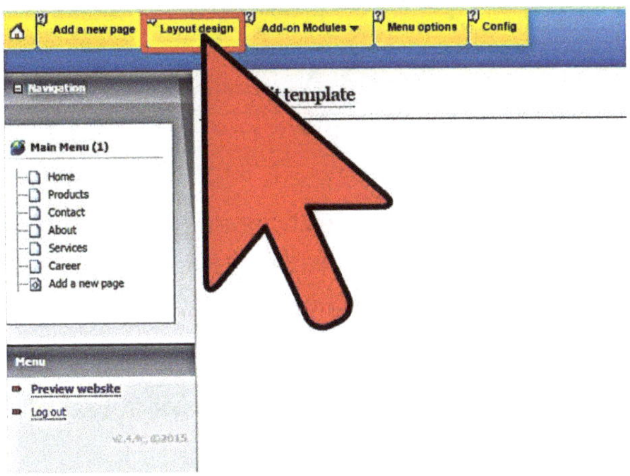

2. Practice good user interface design. Positioning the various elements of the website, such as the title, sidebars, logos, graphics, and text, in the same places on every page will make your site navigable and intuitive.

- Keep the same header at the top of every page. Whether or not your site content lends itself to many repeating elements, making sure that the top of every page is identical is a must.
- Use logic in your design. The elements on a single page should be ordered logically by importance or by topic; the various pages in the site should do the same.

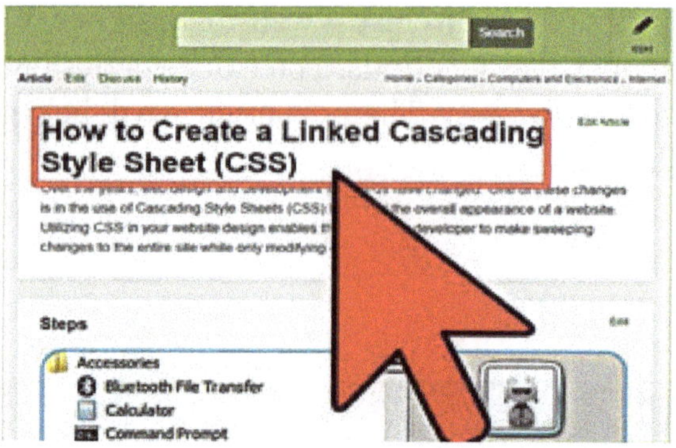

3. Create a consistent style. While the layout should give your site structural consistency, the style should give it thematic harmony. Stick with two or three main colors and make sure they harmonize well. Avoid using too many font styles or sizes; if you do plan to alternate between a few, make sure you use them the same way on every page.

- Use Cascading Style Sheets (CSS) to manage uniform style, and to make it easier to change elements across an entire website without having to go to every individual page.

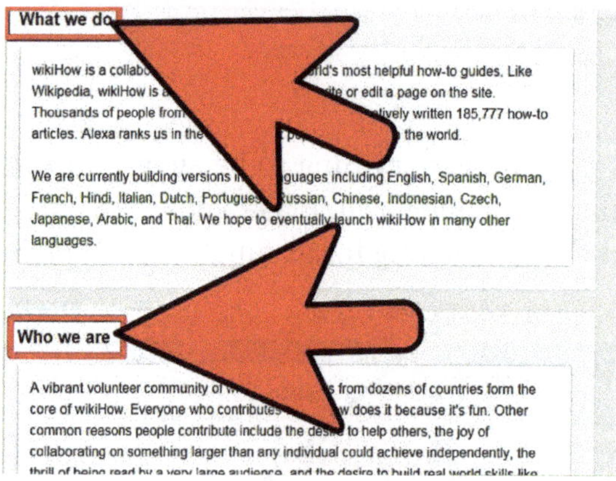

4. Maximize readability. To make your text easier to read, break it into smaller sections. Use subheadings and appropriate spacing to separate each of the sections. Use bold or different-sized fonts to show the hierarchy and importance of the topics.

- Pay attention to text handling. Don't make the font too small, and widen the line spacing to make large blocks of text more readable. Large blocks of text will be harder to read; break these up into smaller paragraphs instead.

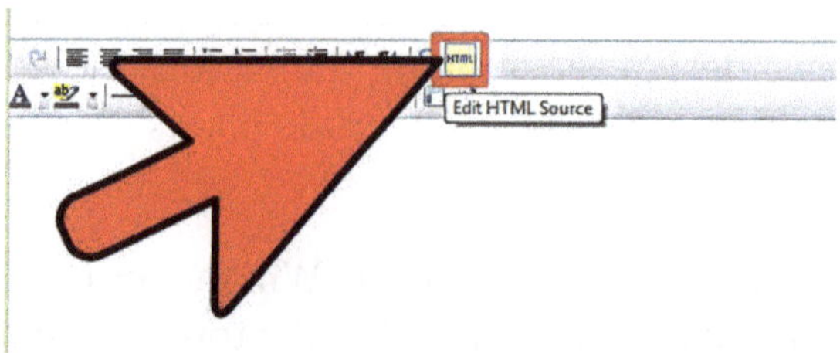

5. Make your website universally readable. Use standard HTML and avoid tags, features, and plug-ins that are only available to one brand or version of a browser.

- Although most modern browsers and computers can handle complex images, everything will be a little snappier if your keep your images smaller in size and optimized for the web. Balance the desire for quality against the need for speed.

6. Test your website. Make sure that every link works as you expect, and that images appear correctly.

- You may want to conduct some usability tests by having members of your target audience test the clarity and ease of use of your design, and give you feedback on your website.

Part 3

Designing for Devices

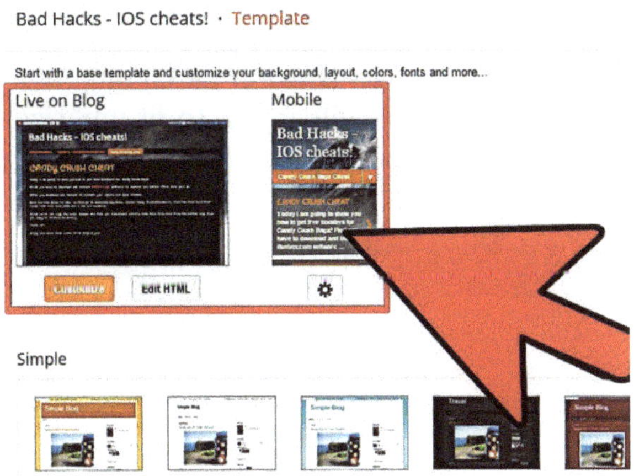

1. Account for mobile browsing. More and more internet browsing is being done on mobile devices these days. If you want your website to attract and keep the highest number of people, you'll need to design your website to be highly usable on mobile devices. The best thing you can do to ensure this is to have a separate website for mobile users but there are other options as well.

- Look for examples of mobile sites. Often, sticking an "m." in the "www" place in a web address for major websites will bring up the mobile version of the site. You'll need to do something similar.

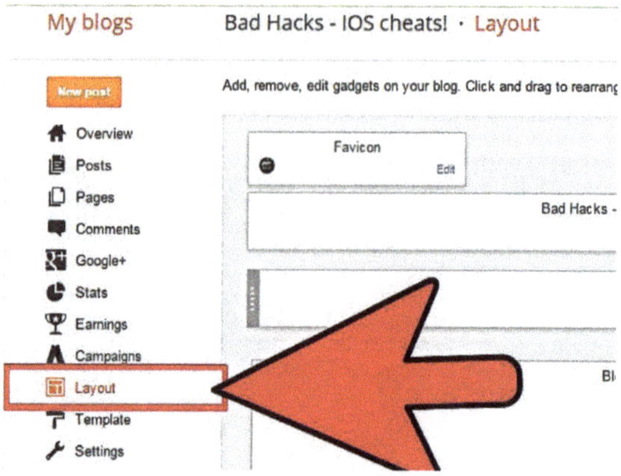

2. Keep your website simple. In general, your design should be simple and to-the-point. Long gone are the days of complex tables and flashing graphics. All users will want something easy to use. This means simple design, minimal columns, and minimal text entry necessary to navigate the site.

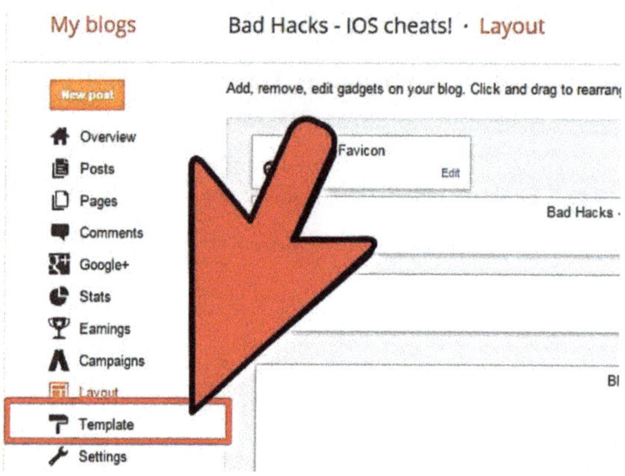

3. Use responsive design. Responsive design is a way of coding your website so that instead of fitting to a few particular sizes of screen, it will adjust to fit any size screen. This is most easily accomplished by setting the column widths to percentages rather than pixels, but more elegant methods also exist.

4. Avoid design features not supported by mobile devices. Many mobile devices can't display things like pop-ups, Flash, Java, or frames. This goes back, again, to wanting to keep your design as simple as possible.

5. Consider making an app. Under certain circumstances it may be easier for you to simply make an app instead of having a mobile version of your site. You don't have to have amazing programming skills to do this, however! Much like there are providers of website templates, there are also companies which will design a basic app for you. Conduit Mobile is a good service to use.

How to Design Posters

Posters are a great visual aid. You can use them professionally for advertisements, announcements, or just to share information. The design of a poster is very important, especially if you're using it as a visual aid to add to a verbal presentation. Using the correct colors, images, fonts, and balance will help you design a remarkable and memorable poster.

Part 1

Choosing your Color Scheme

1. Make it visually appealing. The point of adding color to your poster is to make it visually appealing; it should draw and audience. Too much color is confusing. One or two accent colors that are eye-catching and emphasize your subject is all you need.

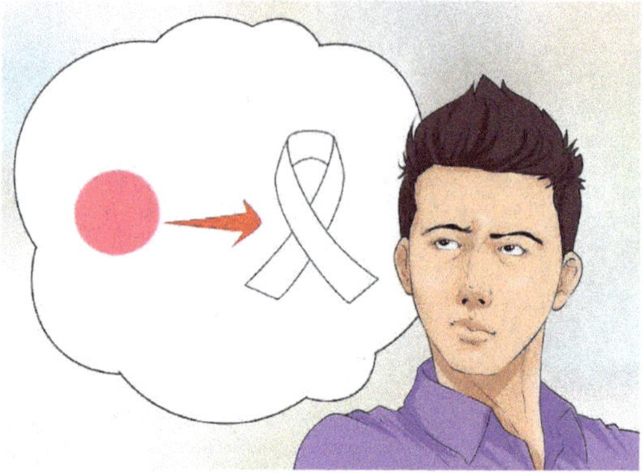

2. Understand the message and audience. If your poster is themed use a matching color. For instance, if you're doing a presentation about breast cancer, be sure to use the correct pink. The audience will see this and be drawn to it because it's familiar.

3. Use dark colored font. Use a poster that has a light colored background and a dark colored text. This not only saves a tremendous amount of ink, but makes it easier for your audience to read.

Part 2

Using Helpful Images

1. Ask yourself if images are helpful. You have limited space on your poster, so use the space wisely. If you're going to use images, they should be figures, diagrams, graphics, or tables that are easy-to-read and help illustrate your ideas.

- Charts are a great visual aid for a poster. They are a good way to add blocks of color while adding a visual explanation of your ideas.
- Clip art rarely illustrates the ideas that you're trying to get across in posters. Choose other images to help with this.

2. Cite your pictures. Make sure the pictures that you're using are public domain. Just because you can copy them from google, doesn't mean they're appropriate to use. If you are going to use a picture from here, be sure to post a citation for it on your poster.

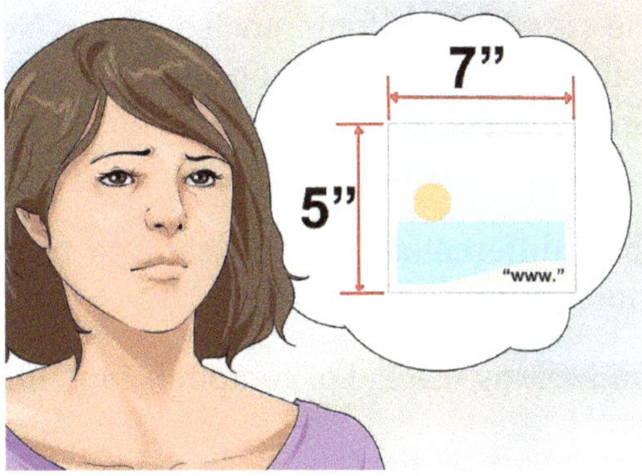

3. Make them a good size. You want your graphics to be easily read from a distance of at least 5 feet.This means they should be no smaller than 5" x 7". You also don't want them to take over the entire poster—your font is the important part of the poster. Create a good balance between the two.

4. Use appropriate placement. Don't overlap your images over your font, but make sure they are

next to any wording that helps explain them. You shouldn't be using these just to fill a giant empty space. All of your images should have purpose.

Part 3

Picking the Fonts

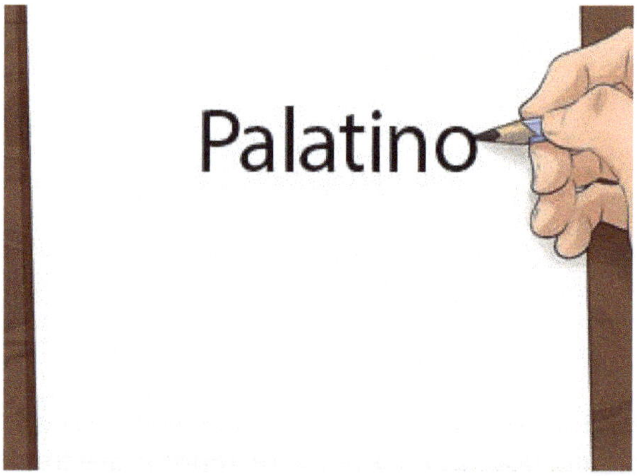

1. Know your styles. You should use a simple, clean and professional writing for the majority of your text. On a computer, these are your serif fonts, such as Times New Roman, or Palatino. These fonts are easier to read, especially at a smaller size. You also have the choice of san serif fonts, such as Arial, Comic Sans, or Helvetica. These fonts can be used sparingly to add visual appeal to your poster.

- Mix them up. It will help differentiate your titles from your informational text—making your titles stand out more.
- If you're using your handwriting instead of computer font, mix up your writing style to add interest to your poster.

2. KISS it. The acronym "K.I.S.S." stands for keep it short and simple. You don't want your poster to be overpowered by words. If you use too many words, many people won't bother reading it all. You want your main ideas to be portrayed on the poster, but you should be going into depth with your verbal presentation rather than with your visual aid.

3. Make your writing the right size. Just as your images, all of your lettering should be legible from at least 5 feet away.

- Title: 72-point or larger
- Names/Subheadings: 48-point type
- Narrative text: 24-point type or larger

Part 4

Balancing your Poster

1. Emphasize the most important information. Highlight the most important aspect of your poster with a cluster of images and color. This will draw the audience's eye to that part of the poster.

2. Connect with your viewers. If your viewers are a younger crowd, you would use more loud colors

and different fonts than if your viewers are an older, professional group. This goes for you images as well. Use charts and graphs to explain things for a work presentation, or use creative characters to help show off safety features for a children's toy.

3. Remember the 1/3-2/3 rule. 1/3 of your poster should be white space. 2/3 of it should be text and images. This creates a balance that is aesthetically pleasing to your audience.

How to Choose the Right Graphic Software for your Purposes

Being able to use graphic software can help you in your work, your play, and can help you express your creativity in many new ways. Software comes with many options and even more price tags. Your options are freeware, shareware, commercial, and open source.

Steps

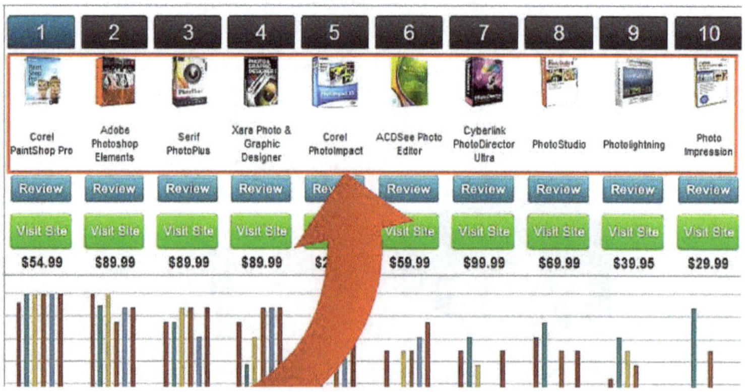

1. Choose your software. You will need to take many things into consideration.

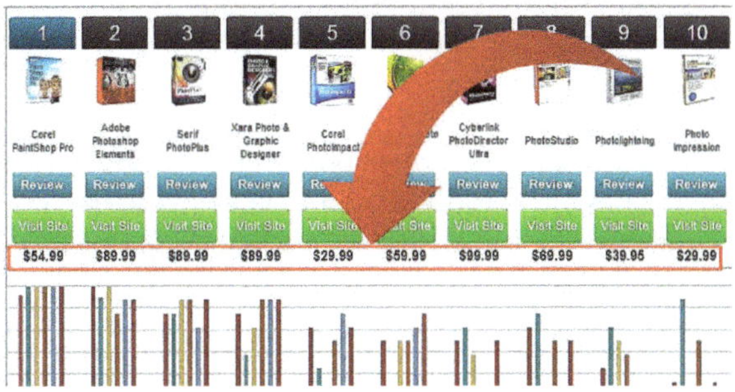

2. Determine your price limits, if any. Do you need to start out with free software, or do you have lots of money to spend. Don't think that you have to be limited by what you can afford. There are basic free options, like IrfanView and PhotoMeister. ' program]]. Other free software is:

- Gimp

- Paint.Net

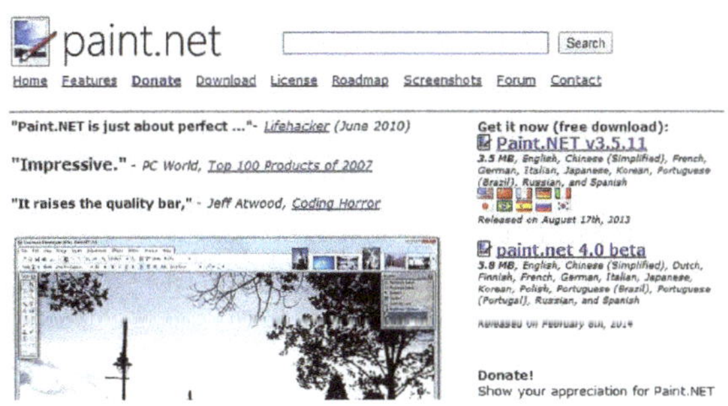

- Inkscape

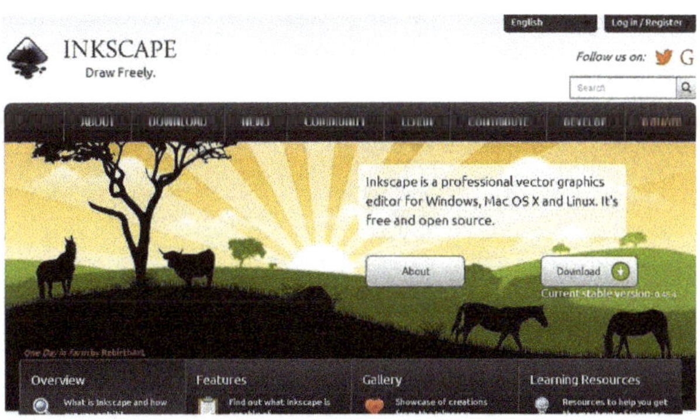

- Project Dogwaffle

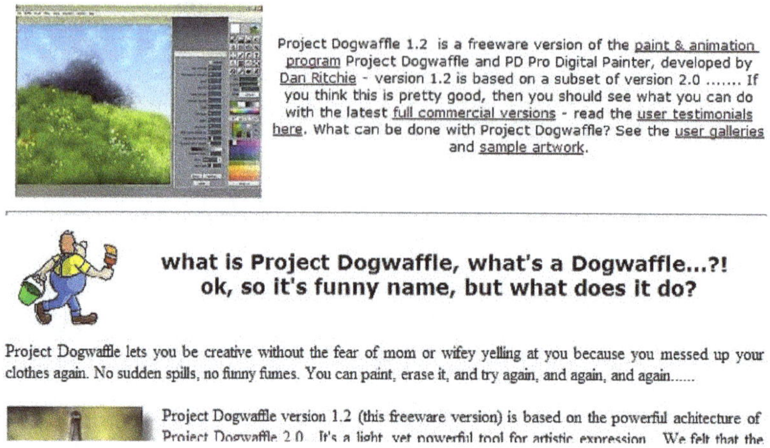

- And a plethora of others. Simply do a search for 'graphic software freeware'.

3. Determine your skill level. Not necessarily with the software, because you are just learning it, but with computers in general. If you are a total newbie to computers, you don't want to start with Gimp or Photoshop or even Paint Shop Pro (unless you are a really quick learner).

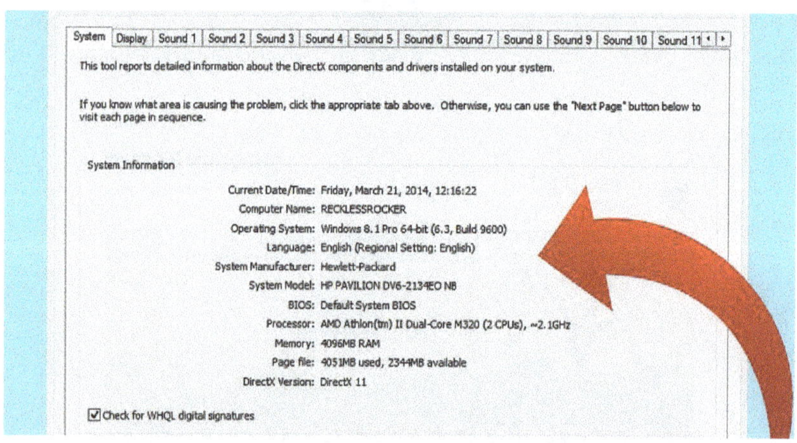

4. Be sure that your computer system is capable of handling the potential software. Regardless of

your skill, if your computer can't run it without slowing way down, you won't want to use it.

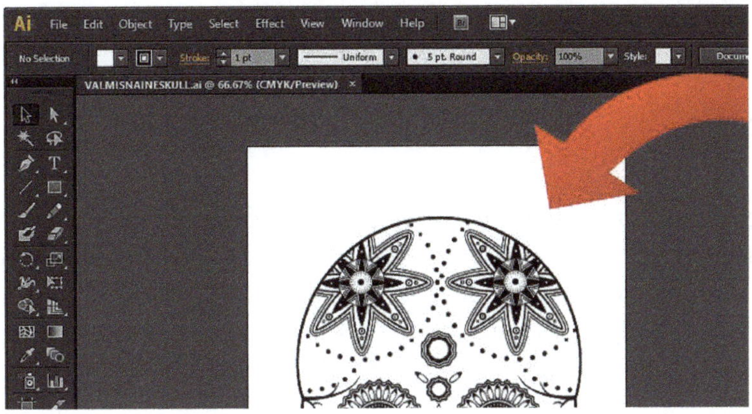

5. Know what you want to do with it. Do you want to just create quick shapes or objects, edit and catalog images, create vector graphics. There are not a lot of software programs that will do all of that. More than likely, you would need different software for different purposes.

Chapter 2

Editing Photographs

Photo editing is a common practice that is part of digital design. Popular photo editing software include Adobe Photoshop, Picasa and GIMP. Hue, saturation, color, retouching, etc. are the basic elements that can be adjusted by using these software. This chapter has been carefully written to provide an easy understanding of the varied facets of professional photo editing.

How to edit a Photo Like a Pro

Editing a photograph like a professional can take a lot of work, trial, and error. There are plenty of programs that allow you to edit photos in varying degrees of complexity. Adobe Photoshop is the most widely used software by professionals, but other applications exist, like GIMP, which are free and offer many of the same tools. The trick to editing a photo like a pro is knowing what aspects of your photo to play with. You don't necessarily need a specific program to make most adjustments. By editing color, hue and saturation, levels, and retouching blemishes on any program, you can turn that decent photo into a great one.

Method 1

Choosing a Photo editing Software

1. Obtain a suitable digital photo editing program, or use an online site for editing. You have a near endless list of options when it comes to your photo editing software. If you're serious about being a professional photo editor, then you should look into the Adobe Creative Suite which offers several programs like Photoshop, Elements, and Lightroom. These programs work in tandem and

offer the largest toolset for photo editing. However, you can find plenty of less expensive or free alternatives.

- Before you spend a lot of money, download a free program or use a trial version of a paid software to see if you like it and to get the hang of basic photo editing.
- Editing a photo to look like it was done by a professional doesn't always involve fancy software as the basic elements are the same. Adjusting white balance, fixing color, reducing noise, and playing with levels are techniques that can greatly enhance your photo and can be done on most photo editing software.

2. Start with free software. If you're new to photo editing, or just need an application to touch up the photos you've taken, don't jump right into paying for expensive software. There are plenty of free options that will still give you plenty of tools to edit and touch up your photos like a pro.

- Picasa is a quick and easy to navigate photo organizing tool that also comes with plenty of non-destructive editing features. Picasa is created by Google, so you can easily save and share your edits. The non-destructive editing means that you can add or undo edits easily, and your original photo is never changed.
- Mac users can try Apple Photos. Your photos and edits can sync with iCloud, and there are plenty of options to edit your photos in terms of color, noise, retouching, temperature, and more.
- Fotor offers a wide array of tools and effects to turn your photo into a professional grade work of art. Fotor will also let you import raw files and even add layers, like Photoshop.
- On1 Perfect Effects is like a free version of Adobe's software. With over 150 one-click photo effects, brush tool, and quick mask tools, and more, On1 Effects allows you to manipulate your photos extensively.
- GIMP is an open source photo editor. It stands for GNU Image Manipulation Program. GIMP offers a lot of the same features that a paid software like Photoshop would offer such as painting tools, color correction, cloning, selection and enhancement.

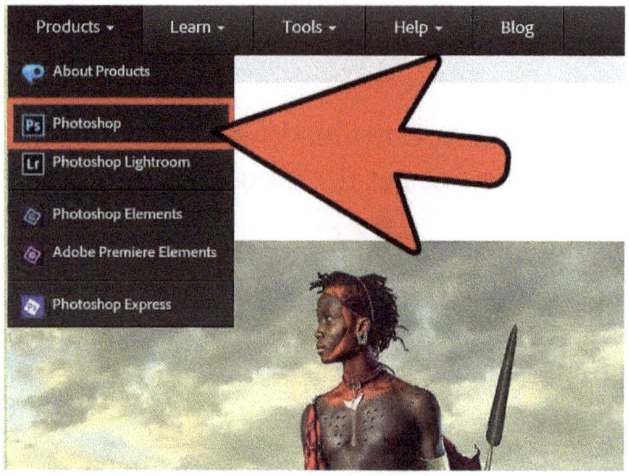

3. Pay for software. If you are serious about editing photos, and may even make a career out of editing, consider paying for software. Paid software typically gives you more tools to use, has better support, and allows you to edit your photos more in depth than a free editor. The Adobe Creative Suite is the most popular software for creating, editing, and illustrating all kinds of digital art from photos to movies. However, other, less expensive options exist that give you plenty of tools to edit your photos like a pro.

- Photoshop is typically the software used by professionals as it allows you to manipulate one or many photos in almost any way you can imagine. However, the learning curve can be steep, and it is expensive.
- Adobe Lightroom is an alternative to Photoshop that also works alongside Photoshop. Lightroom is a bit easier to use and allows you to backtrack on your edits much easier than Photoshop.
- Phase One Capture One Pro is an alternative to Lightroom that is less expensive. Like Lightroom, PhaseOne allows you to upload your photos into a library and make non-destructive edits easily without modifying your original image.

Method 2

Making Basic Adjustments

1. Create new layers. If you have a software that can create new layers, it's always a good idea to

create a new layer for each type of edit. A new layer will allow you to make edits and changes without disrupting the original layer. This way, if you mess up, you can go back without having to start over.

- Not all programs let you create new layers. However, these programs usually offer a way to undo the effect easily so that you can backtrack a step or two without starting over.

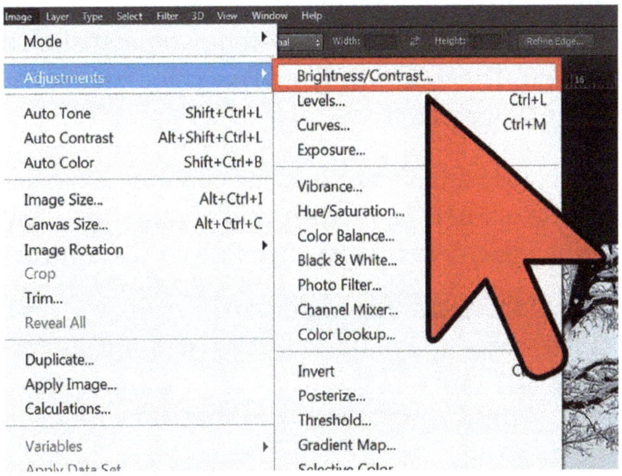

2. Adjust your white balance. Getting the right white balance can be one of the best improvements you can make to a photo. Sometimes, you might not even have to do much else if you adjust your white balance correctly, especially on your camera when taking the photo. Start by adjusting the temperature of your photo, then adjust the tint for smaller corrections.

- If your photo is too cold, showing more blues than you would like, bring the temperature up to counterbalance those blues with more red tones. If your photo is too warm, bring the temperature down.
- The tint slider controls your magenta-green shift. If you need to cool your photo, bring the slider higher into the magenta range. If your photo needs to be warmer, lower your tint to the green spectrum.

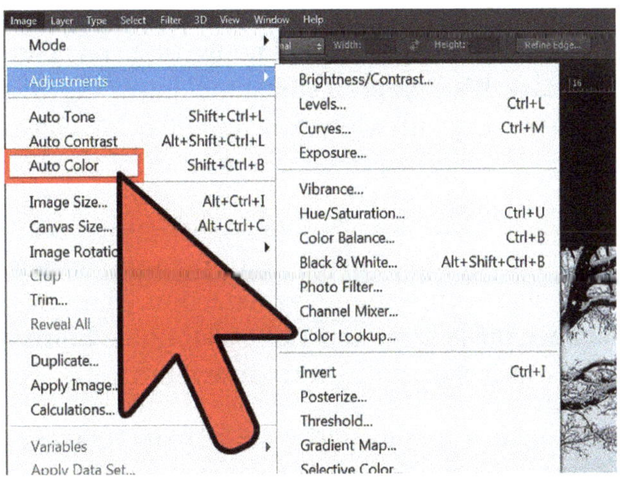

3. Edit your photo's color. Certain colors pair well together, others do not. There are several types

of color, but a basic understanding of how these types work together can help you immensely in the editing room. In the real world your primary colors are red, yellow, and blue. You mix these colors together to get other colors. However, on a computer, we deal with red, green, and blue (RGB) as primary colors.

- Start with a curves layer. Your curves will adjust your color by making your photo warmer or cooler. There's no set answer to playing with color as each photo will require something different. Using a midpoint grey eyedropper tool, you can click on an area of your photo where the color seems off. The tool will change the color balance of that color or area so that balances with the rest of your photo.
- Adjust your light and color with a color overlay channel. Take a single color channel, red, green, or blue, and create a new layer with that channel by copying it over your original photo. Then, adjust the opacity of that layer to find a nice contrast.

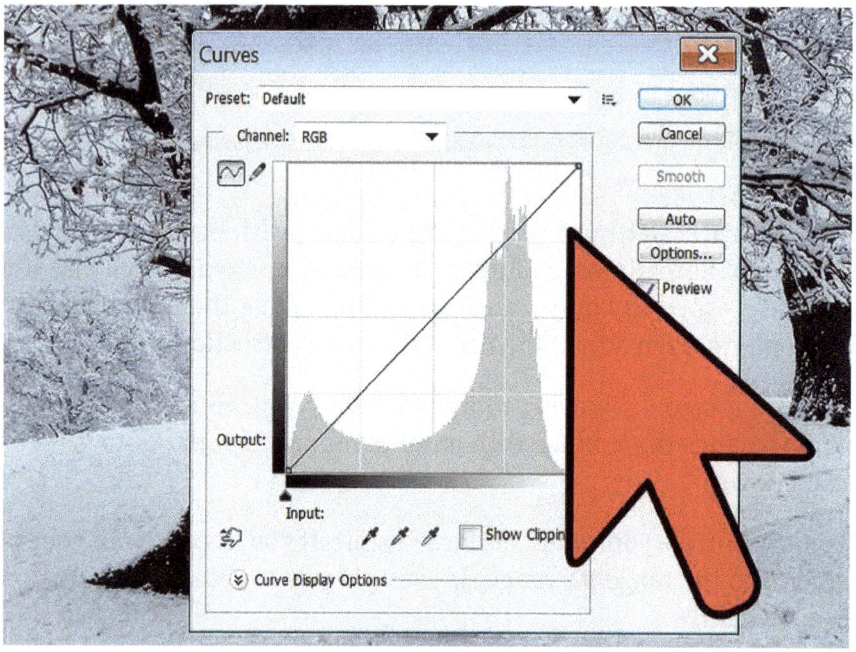

4. Reduce the noise in your photo. Sometimes you'll notice that your photo has a lot of grainy colored dots. This is known as noise. It's easiest to adjust and lower the noise before you make most other adjustments, other than playing with white balance and color. One of the most effective ways to reduce noise in your photo is to sharpen the image. However, too much sharpening can bring back more noise.

- Certain photo editing software like Adobe Lightroom provides a "Detail" panel that provides options for both sharpening and noise reduction. These two tools work together because reducing too much noise alone can make your photo blurry and you have to sharpen it. On the flipside, too much sharpening can cause more noise.
- If you have a noise reduction option, start with that and increase the luminance level. Adjust the slider and pay attention to how far you can go before the photo gets too soft or blurry.

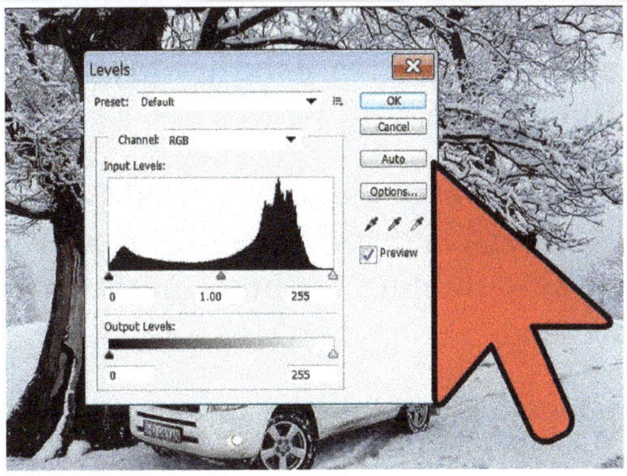

5. Enhance your photo by adjusting levels. If your photo looks like it was shot with an old camera or has a lot of flash, you can adjust the levels of the photo to make it look much more polished. Adjusting levels will counteract the exposure from the camera. Whether your image is underexposed and too dark, or overexposed and too light.

- The ability to adjust your photo's levels isn't the same on every program. On some programs like Apple's Photos app, you can't adjust levels the same way you can in Photoshop, but you do have eight options for adjusting different aspects of your photo. Level adjustment essentially gives you control over brightness in three levels: shadows, midtones, and highlights.
- When adjusting a photo's levels in any program for clarity, the goal is to create the widest tonal range allowing the brightest pixels in your photo to be pure white, and the darkest pixels to be pur black.
- Adjusting your levels allows you to edit your photo so that the darkest pixels convert to black and the lightest pixels convert to white. This enhances the contrast to your photo. If you have the option to adjust the midpoint, the grey area, you want to lighten or darken your midpoints based on the color of the focal point of your photo. For example, if you are adjusting a photo of someone's face, you may want to make the midpoint lighter if your subject's skin tone is lighter. If your subject has a darker skin tone, you want to make the midpoint darker.

Method 3

Making Advanced Adjustments

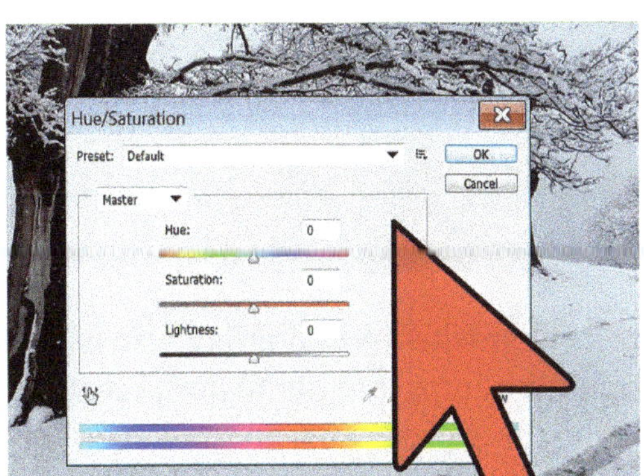

1. Adjust hue and saturation. If you have a dominant color in your photograph that you really want

to stand out, adjust the levels of hue and saturation. For example, to make your greens pop more, if you have a photo that takes place outside, increase the hue to add a bit of blue to make your greens pop out more and turn your saturation up.

- This will add a more vibrant color to your green. Because green and blue are primary and complementary colors, adding a hue of blue to your green will enhance the vibrancy of the green, making it richer. By saturating the hue adjustment you bleed the colors together more creating a vibrant blend.
- To make any photo pop more, adjust the hue and saturation of the most dominant color in your photo.

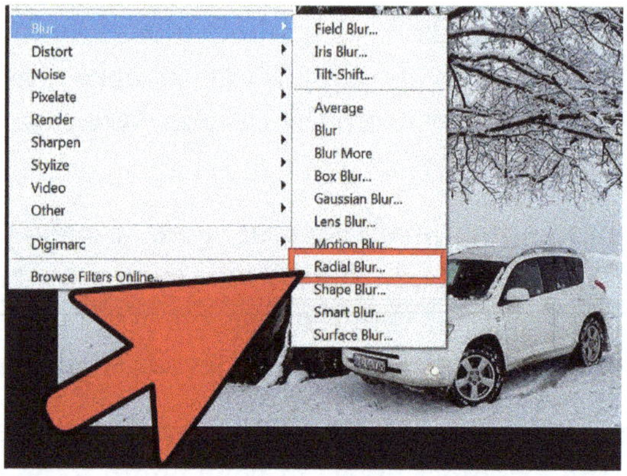

2. Use a radial blur. A lot of professionally edited photos will employ a radial blur which keeps the focal point in your photo in focus while gently blurring out everything outside of the radius.

- The radial blur is great for photos that focus on a person's face, because it will keep the face in crystal clear focus and blur everything around it gently, creating a nice effect and professional looking photo.

3. Create smooth skin and remove blemishes. A major factor in editing photos like a professional is editing your subject's face to remove bumps and blemishes, creating beautiful smooth skin. There are a number of ways to do this on most programs, and not every program allows for comprehensive editing.

- In applications like Picasa or Apple Photos, you can use the Retouch Tool. Select a radius size for your brush that is small enough so that you don't retouch areas that don't need it. On software like these, retouching essentially works by blurring and blending the pixels together to make the area look smooth.

- In more advanced software like Photoshop, you can do more intensive retouching. Use a Quick Selection Tool to select the area of skin that you want to edit. Create a new layer with a Layer Mask so that you don't affect your original layer in case you mess up. Then go to your Filter option > Blur > Surface Blur. This will smooth out the selected area much like the retouch tool works on other programs.
- Then, use a Spot Healing Brush Tool and click on your small selections of blemishes that still show up. The spot healing brush will perform a similar task as the blur, but instead of applying the effect to a larger area, you can pinpoint it to smaller, more specific areas.

4. Use Patch and Fade Tools to fix smaller adjustments. The Patch and Fade Tools are great for fixing larger areas like bags under the eyes. The Patch Tool works by selecting one area and then another. The first area gets patched to look like the second area.

- The Patch Tool is great for skin because instead of just blurring an area of skin to smooth it out, it makes a patch that's taken from another area.
- To smooth out any weird or uneven edges that you may get from the patch tool, use a Fade Tool that fades a patched selection and blends the area.
- Try to match the skin texture on an area you are working on. For example if you are patching an area around the nose, don't draw a patch from the forehead as those areas might be too dissimilar, especially in certain lighting.

How to Resize Digital Photos

The images we take with our digital cameras are pretty, but often far too large to easily send through email or upload to a website. If you need to resize your image, there are a variety of tools available for you to do so, and most of them are free. Check out this guide to learn how.

Method 1

Using Free Web Applications

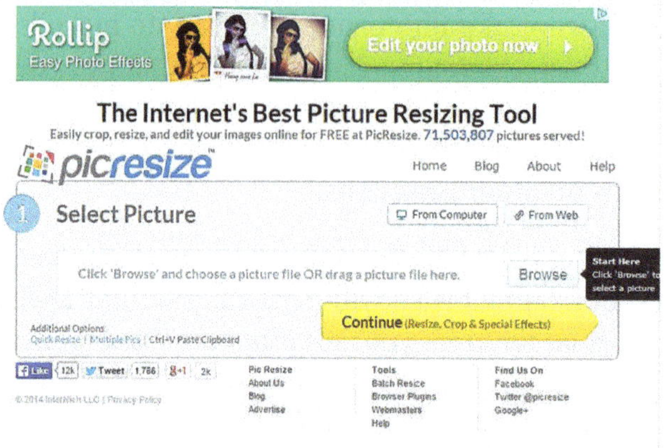

1. Open the web application of your choice. There are many web services that will resize your images for free. You will need to upload your image to the site and then choose your resize options. Most programs offer the same basic features, though some will have extras available that others don't. Several of the more popular sites include:

- picresize
- Resize Your Image
- Shrink Pictures
- Web Resizer
- Resize Pic

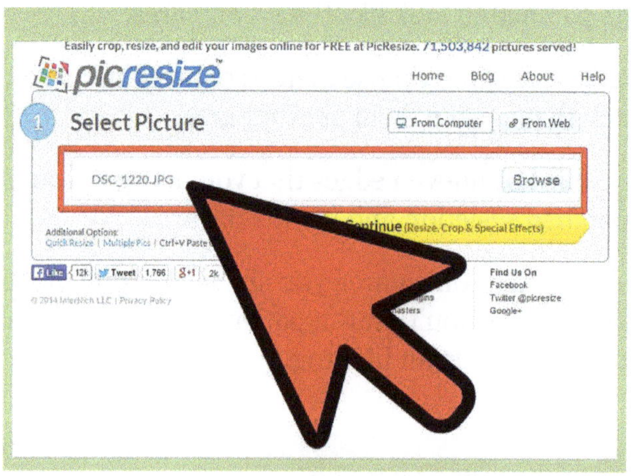

2. Upload your image. You will have to navigate to the image on your computer, and then upload it to the website. Once the upload is complete, the image editing options will appear.

- Most web applications have a maximum file size that is allowed to be uploaded, typically around 5 MB.

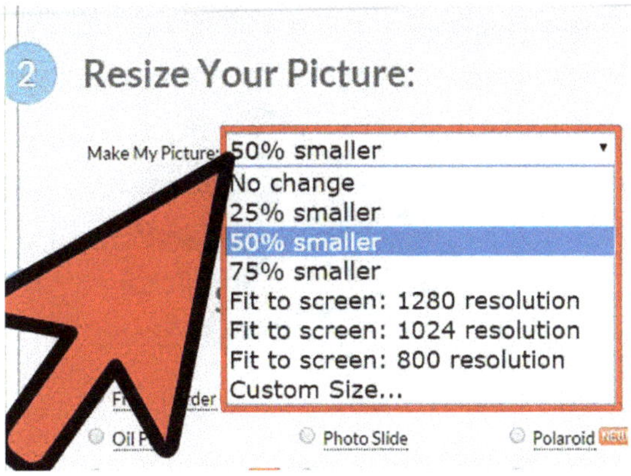

3. Resize the image. Depending on which service you are using, you may have multiple options when it comes to resizing. You may be able to choose a percentage of the original size, or several preset size. Almost all services will allow you to set an exact size in pixels that you would like to resize to.

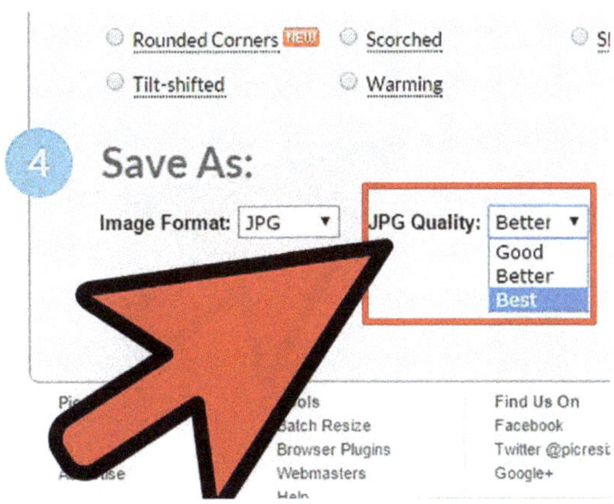

4. Set the quality. Most resize services will let you set how much compression the image will have, which will affect the quality. The higher the compression, the lower the quality and the smaller the file size.

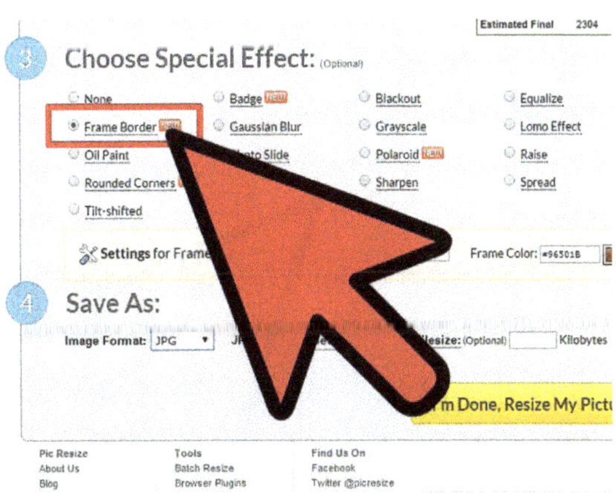

5. Add any other effects. Depending on the service you are using, you may have access to other options such as rotation, color changes, filters, and more. Choose the effects that you want.

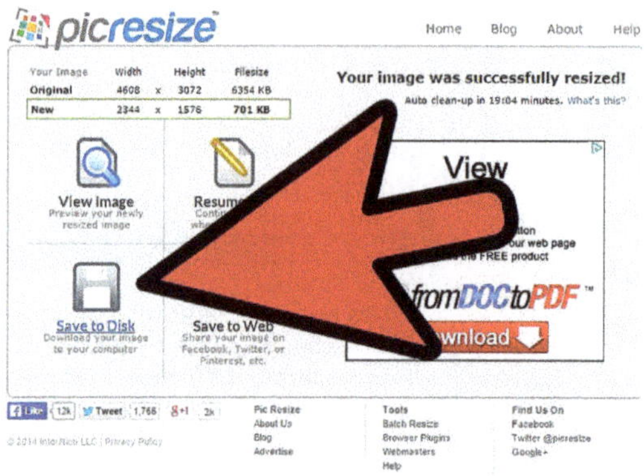

6. Download the new copy. Once you've picked all of your settings and effects, click the Download button. This may be called a Resize button or something similar. The newly-edited photo will be downloaded to your computer, which you can then transfer to wherever you need.

Method 2

Using Microsoft Paint

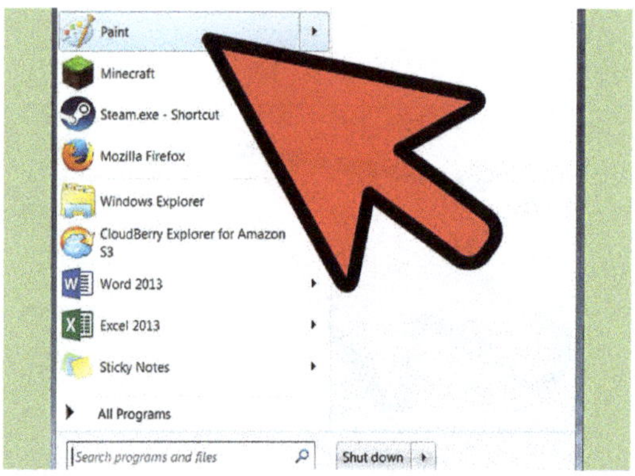

1. Open the file in Microsoft Paint. Click File and then Select Open. Navigate to the file on your computer. If you are trying to resize a photo from Facebook or another online service, you will need to download it first.

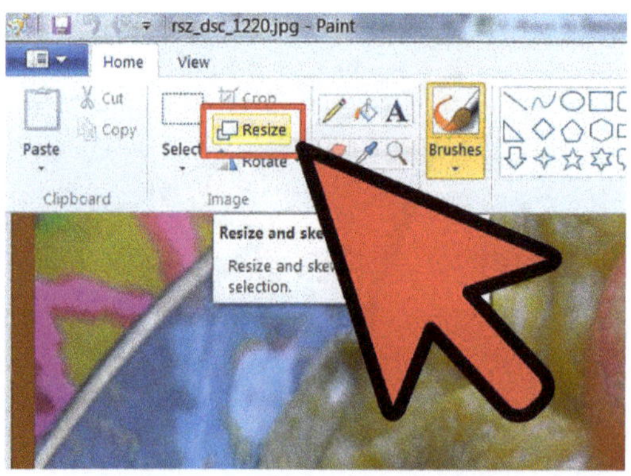

2. Click the Resize button. In newer versions of Paint, the Resize button is located in the Home tab. In older versions of Paint, click the Image menu, and then select Resize/Skew.

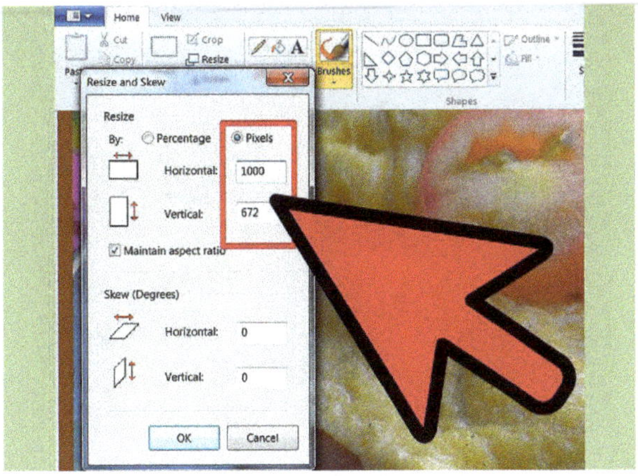

3. Choose your resize method. You can resize by either percentage or by pixel size. If you keep the "Maintain aspect ratio" box checked, both boxes will be filled in automatically when you enter one value, to keep the proportions the same.

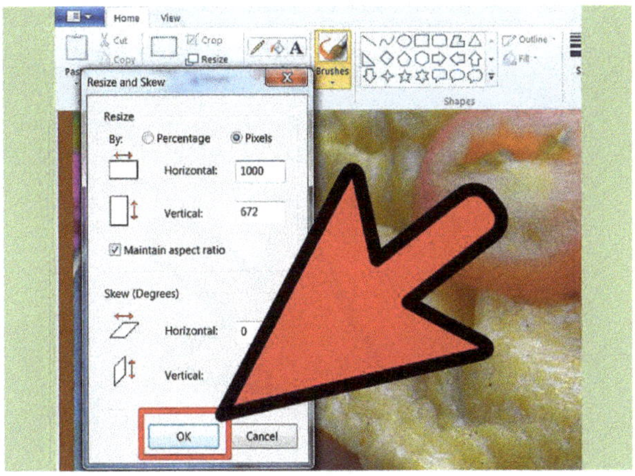

4. Click OK. This will change the image to the size that you specified. If you are unhappy with the changes, press Ctrl+Z to undo the changes.

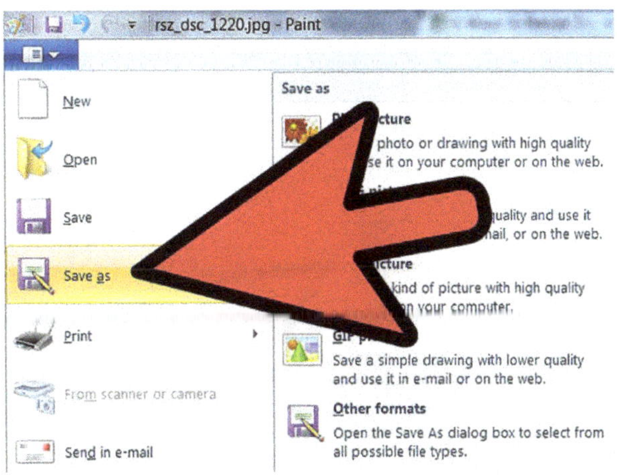

5. Save the resized image. Once you are happy with the resize changes, click File and then select Save As. Rename the image so that you don't overwrite the original.

6. Select a file type. The file type you pick will affect the quality of the image after it is saved. PNG and JPG are the most popular for uploading to the internet and attaching to emails.

Method 3

Using Google Picasa

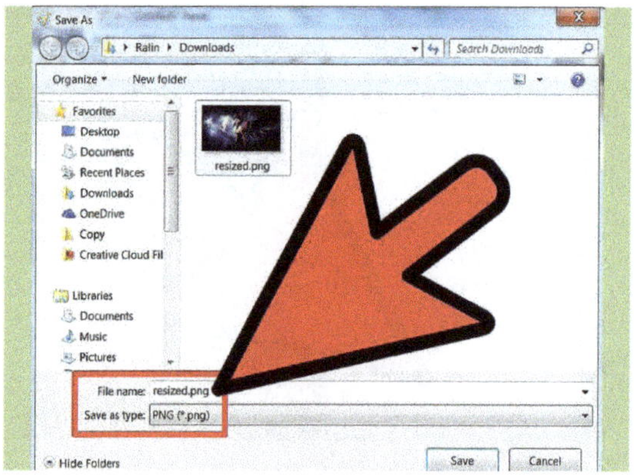

1. Browse for your image in Picasa. If the image you want to resize is not located in your Picasa library, you can add it by clicking file and then selecting Add File to Picasa. Once your file is in your Picasa library, select it.

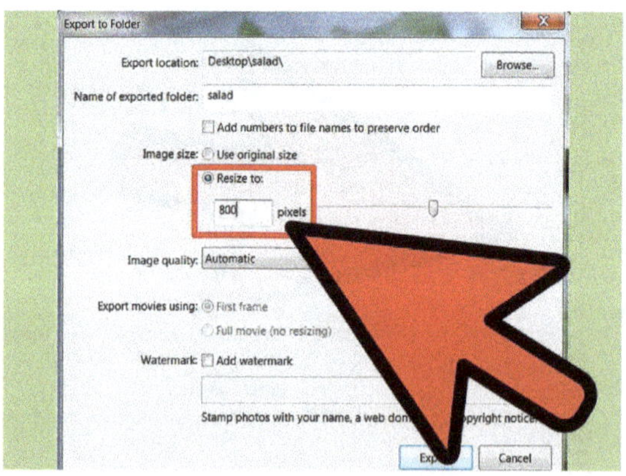

2. Export the image. Click File and then select Export Picture to Folder. This will open the Export to Folder window. You can specify where you want the photo to be saved to.

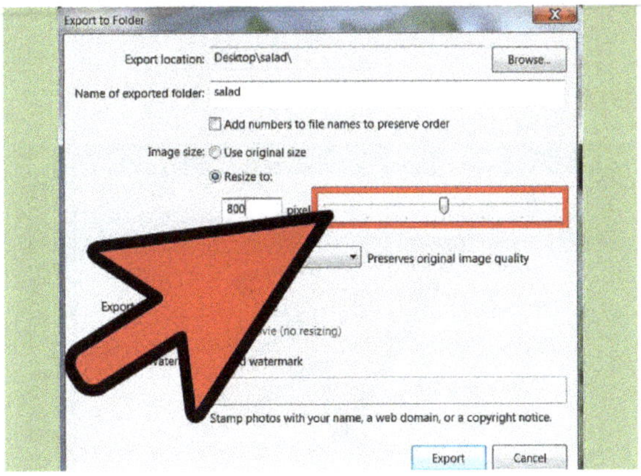

3. Choose your resize options. In the "Image size" section, you can choose to use preset image sizes, or specify an exact pixel size. The pixel size affects the longest edge of the image size, and the other edge will be adjusted automatically.

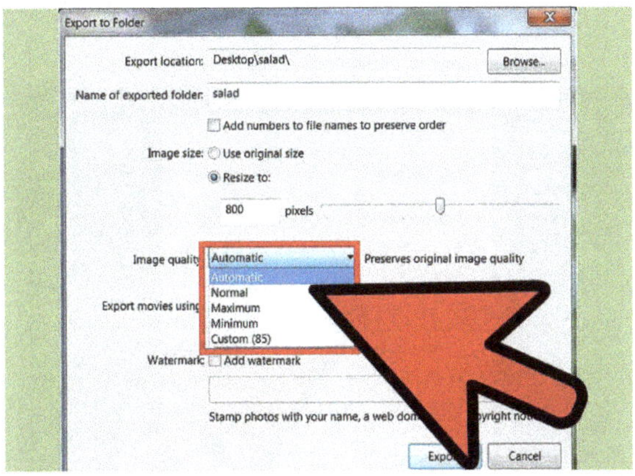

4. Select the desired image quality. Click the "Image quality" dropdown menu. Automatic will attempt to preserve the original quality as much as possible. Maximum will keep as much detail as it can, but will result in higher file sizes. Minimum will result in a much smaller image size at a much lower quality.

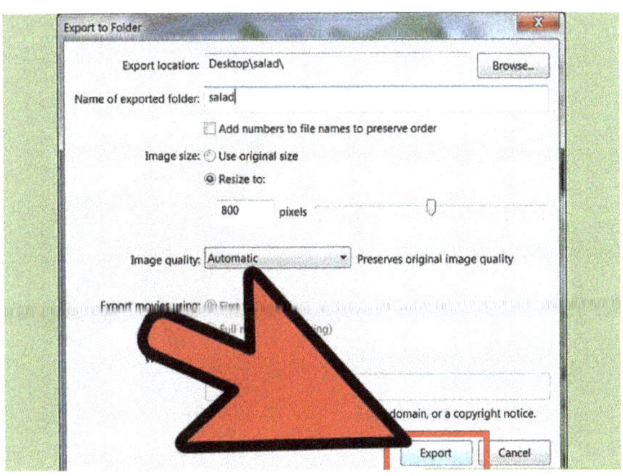

5. Click Export when ready. Your newly adjusted image will be copied to the location that you specified.

Method 4

Using Adobe Photoshop

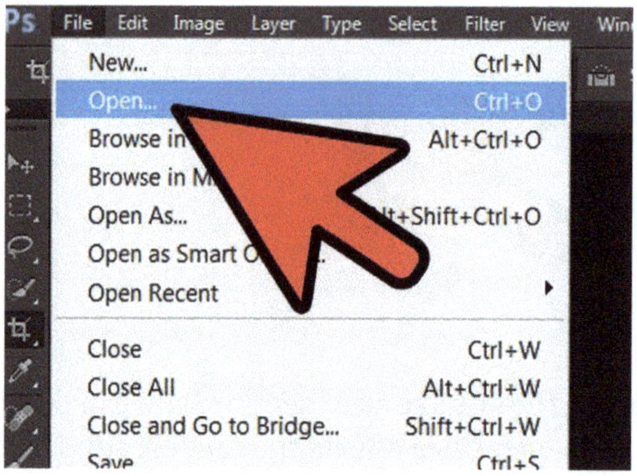

1. Open the image in Photoshop. Click File and select Open. Browse for the image file on your computer or inserted disc.

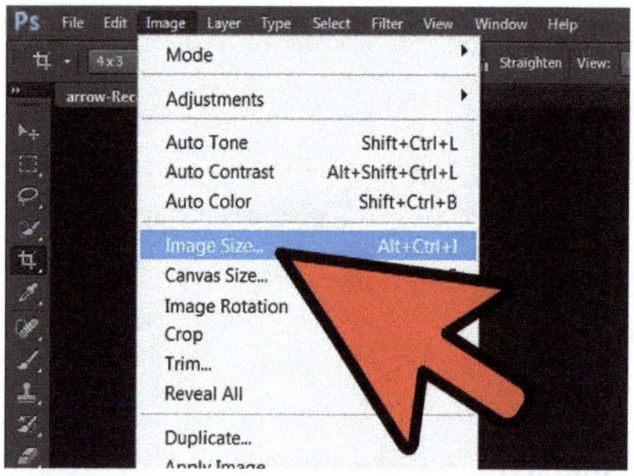

2. Open the Image Size tool. Click on the Image menu and then select Image Size. This will open the Image Size window.

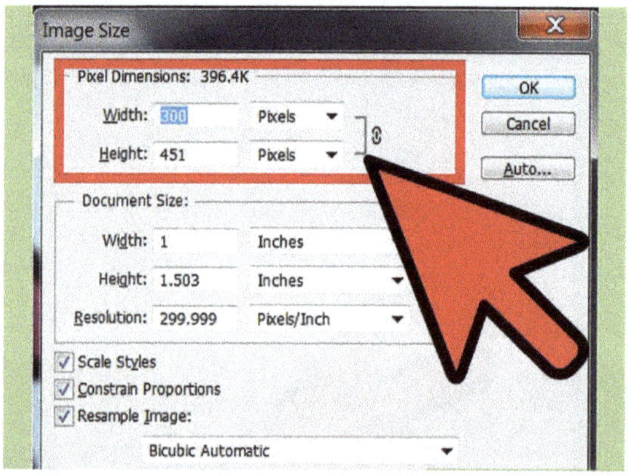

3. Choose your resize method. You can choose to resize in pixels, inches, or percentage. Enter the value you want in one field and the other field will be updated automatically to keep proportions the same. You can keep the proportions the same, or you can unlink them by clicking the Chain icon.

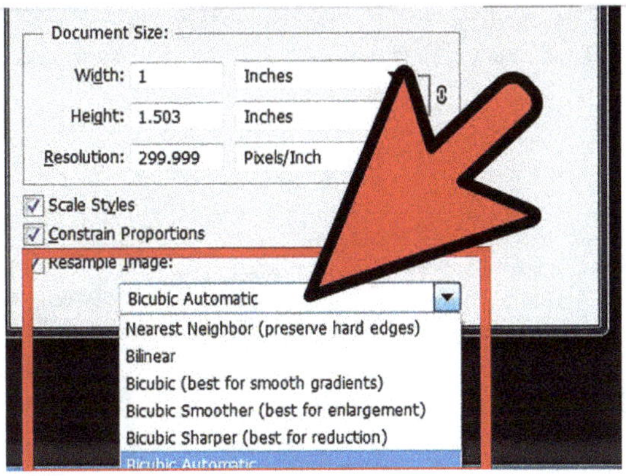

4. Choose your resample options. The "Resample Image" menu will allow you to make adjustments that will affect the final quality of the resize. Pick the one that suits your needs the best.

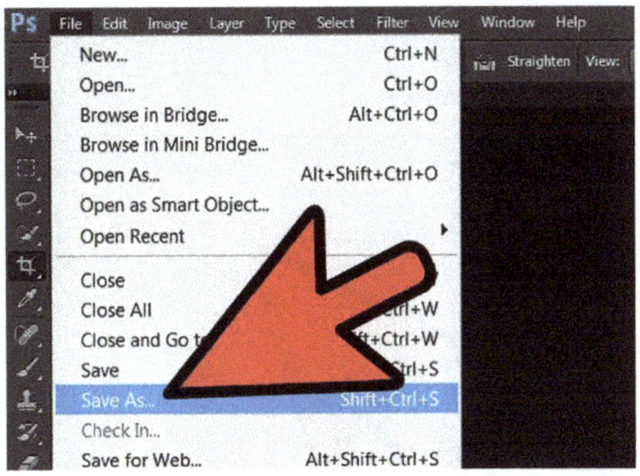

5. Click OK to resize the image. You will see the results in your main window. If you are satisfied with the results, click File and select Save As. Give the file a new name so that you don't overwrite the original.

Method 5

Using GIMP

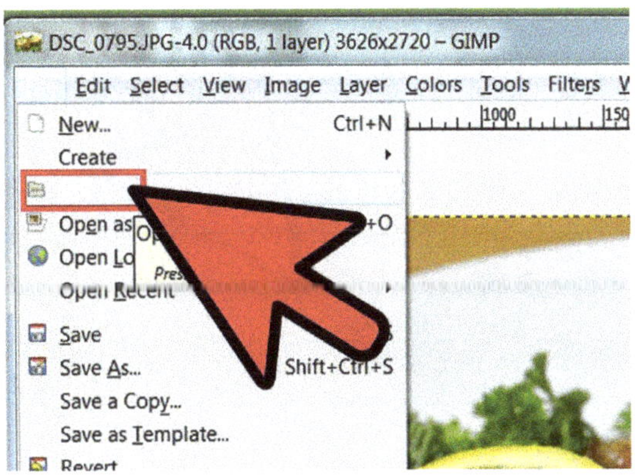

1. Open the photo in GIMP. GIMP is an open-source alternative to programs like Adobe Photoshop. To open your image, click File and then select Open. Browse for your file on your computer.

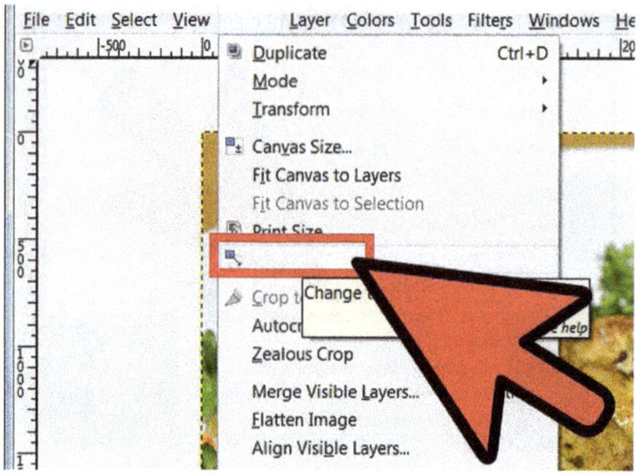

2. Open the Scale Image tool. Click Image and then select Scale Image. This will open a new window.

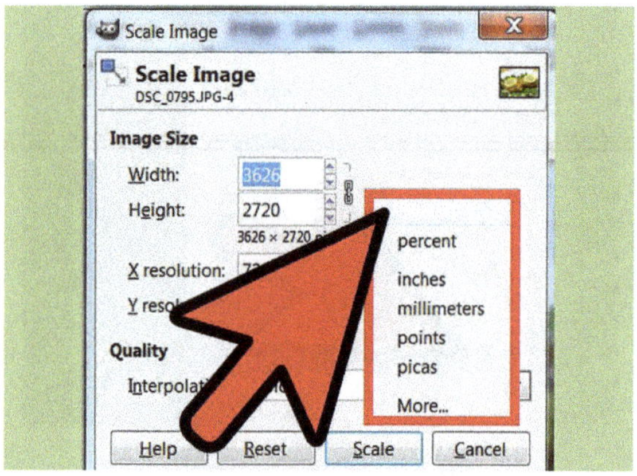

3. Choose your resize method. You can choose between pixels (px), inches (in), or percentage. Use the pulldown menu next to the Image Size fields. Enter the value that you want into one field and the other will be updated automatically to maintain proportions. If you would like to adjust each dimension individually, click the Chain icon to unlink them.

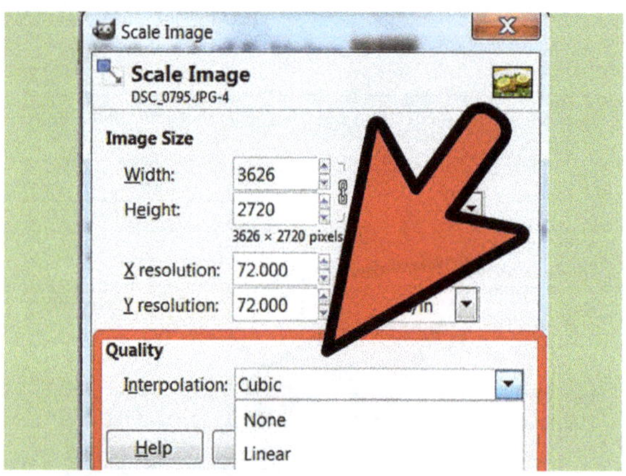

4. Select your quality setting. Click the Quality pulldown menu and select the type of resampling that you want to use. The choice you make will affect the quality of your resized picture. Experiment to find one that works best.

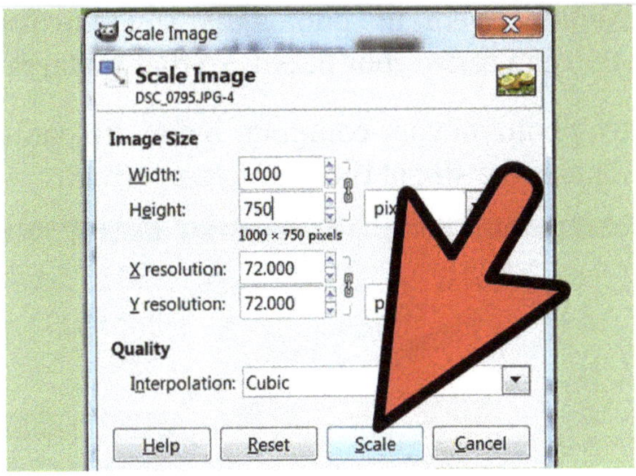

5. Click Scale to resize the image. Once you are set click the Scale button and review the changes to your image. If you are unhappy with the changes, click the Edit menu and select Undo.

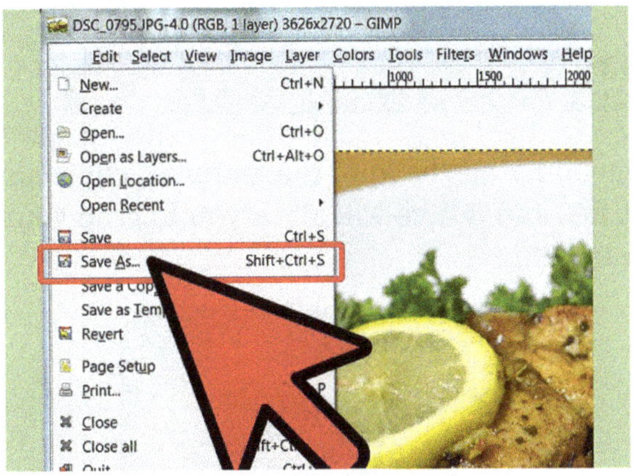

6. Save your changes. Once you are happy with the changes you've made, click file and select Save As. Choose a new file name so that you don't overwrite the original file.

Method 6

Resizing Photos for Instagram

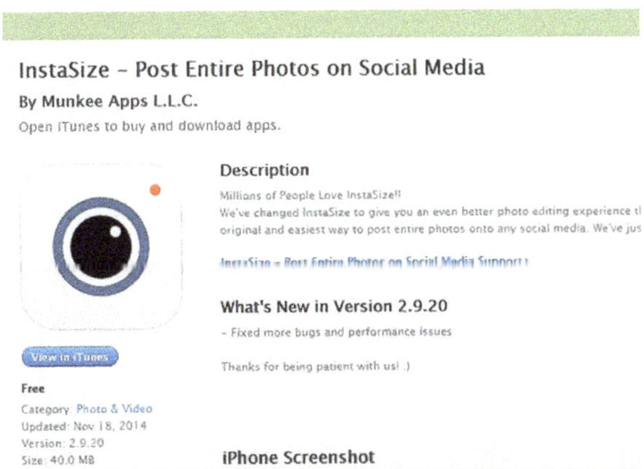

1. Download an Instagram resizer app. Since Instagram uploads take place entirely on your mobile

device, it is much more convenient to edit the photos that you take directly on your phone. There are multiple apps available that can resize your photos so that Instagram does not crop them.

- If you want to resize a photo on your computer before uploading it to Instagram, resize it to 612 X 612 pixels. This is the size of the Instagram format.

2. Run the resizer app. Depending on the app, the features may change. Most will allow you to resize your image so that it fits, and others will allow you to crop your existing image so that the cropped section fits into Instagram.

3. Upload the image to Instagram. Open your Instagram app and browse for your newly resized image. Upload as you normally would and you won't lose any part of the image due to cropping.

How to Change a Digital Picture from Color to Black and White

Everybody loves a great black and white photo, but most digital cameras only take full-color pictures. This article will show you a few simple ideas for turning your color digital photo to black and white.

Method 1

Use Photoshop's Black & White Adjustment Layer

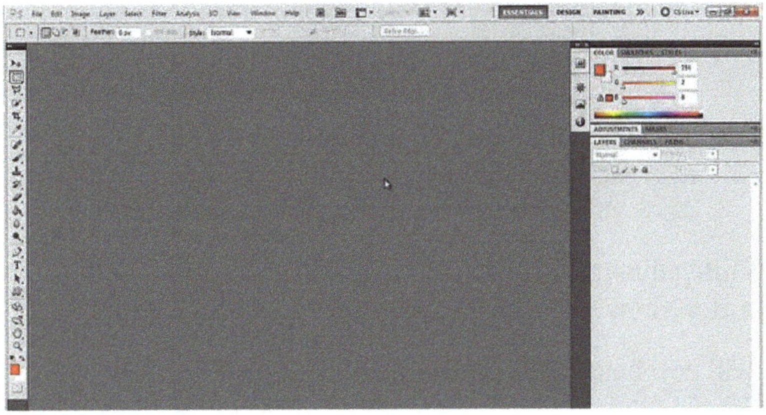

1. Launch Photoshop. You can find it in your Applications folder on a Mac, or from the Start menu in Windows.

2. Open the photo you wish to modify. From the File menu, select Open. Your image will appear on the Photoshop desktop

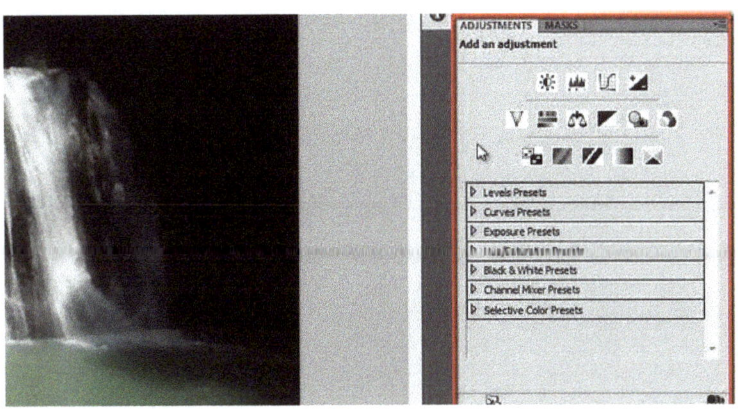

3. Open the Adjustments window. Click on the Window menu, and if it's not checked, select Adjustments. The Adjustments window will open.

4. Add a Black & White adjustment layer. From the Adjustments window, click on the Black & White adjustment button show:

- Your photo will now be in black and white.
- Using the various color sliders, you can alter the black and white balance of your image based on the underlying color information.

Method 2

Use Photoshop's Hue/Saturation Layer

1. Add a Hue/Saturation adjustment layer. Starting from the original color picture, open the Adjustments window and click on the Hue/Saturation button to create a new adjustment layer.

2. Desaturate the colors. Drag the Saturation slider all the way to the left, and your picture will now be in black and white.

- While this lacks the fine tuning of the Black & White adjustment layer, it does offer an opportunity to see what your photo would look like if you left just a little bit of color in, which is sometimes quite nice.

Method 3

Use Photoshop's Channel Mixer Layer

1. Add a Channel Mixer adjustment layer. From the Adjustments window, click on the Channel Mixer button to create a new Channel Mixer layer.

2. Click on the Monochrome button in the Channel Mixer window, and then adjust the RGB sliders or use one of the presets from the menu. Like using the Black & White adjustment layer, the controls give you a great deal of latitude in adjusting the final look of your image. A little can go a long way, so use carefully!

Method 4

Use Google Picasa

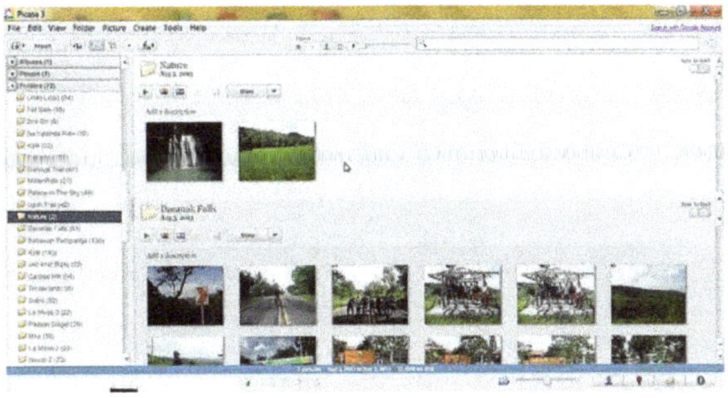

1. Download Picasa from Google.com. Install it as directed, and then launch Picasa.

2. Open your image in Picasa. From the File menu, select Add File to Picasa...

3. In the Picasa window, click on the Image Processing tab in the center (the one with the paint-brush).

4. Filter your photo. Click on any of the B&W options to instantly see the changes.

Method 5

Use other Photo Editors

1. Read the documentation. Most editors will include a filter to make your photos black and white. It might be as simple as a "black & white" button, or it might be a saturation adjustment. Experiment, try out the sliders, and see what happens. No matter what, you'll have a great time doing it!

How to Add a Watermark to Photos

When photos are posted online, they are rarely protected, meaning they can be used by anyone who has access to them. Photos can be protected through copyrights, but a trick often used by photographers is to watermark their photos. Traditionally, watermarks were variations in the thickness of a paper that can only be seen in certain light conditions. Digital watermarks are text or logos that are put on top of the image to establish the owner of the photo. Often, watermarks are opaque and look indented. A great way to ensure that no one is using photos without your permission is to add a watermark with Google's Picasa or Adobe Photoshop. This article will tell you how to add a watermark to photos.

Method 1

Using Photoshop Actions

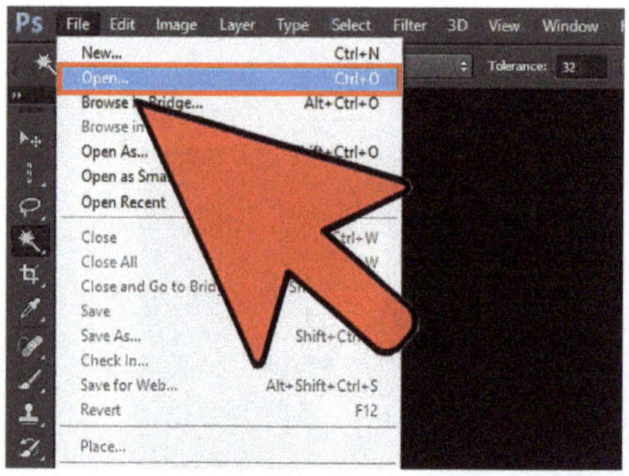

1. Open up your picture in Photoshop. This should be the image that you want to add a watermark to.

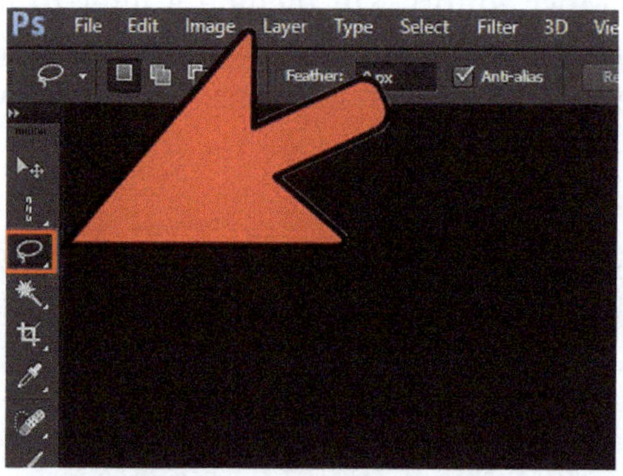

2. Open your logo image file. Open up your logo or design you would like to use as a watermark and save it to a place you can easily access, if you haven't already.

- If you need to remove your logo from a larger image, grab the lasso tool. Make sure your feather is set to the number 0. Click once and draw around the image or text box you want to use as the watermark. When you have outlined it, release your click and save your image or logo.

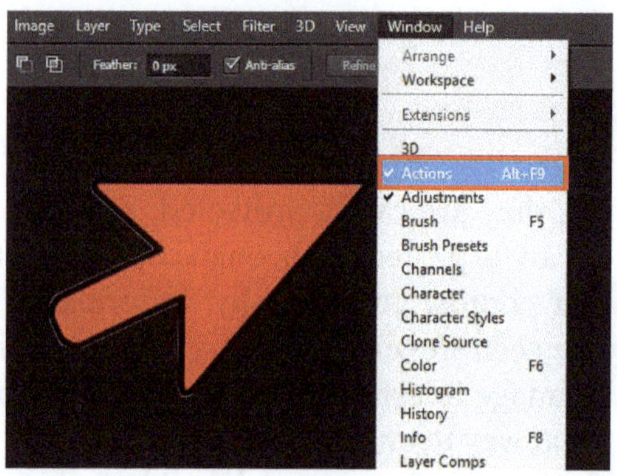

3. Start recording your actions, if you want to. If you plan on adding a lot of watermarks to very

similarly sized and arranged images, then you will want to create an Action. This will allow you to add the watermark to later images with less effort. Go to the "Window" menu on your toolbar. Select "action." Name the action "Watermark." Any actions that you perform from now until you stop the action will be recorded.

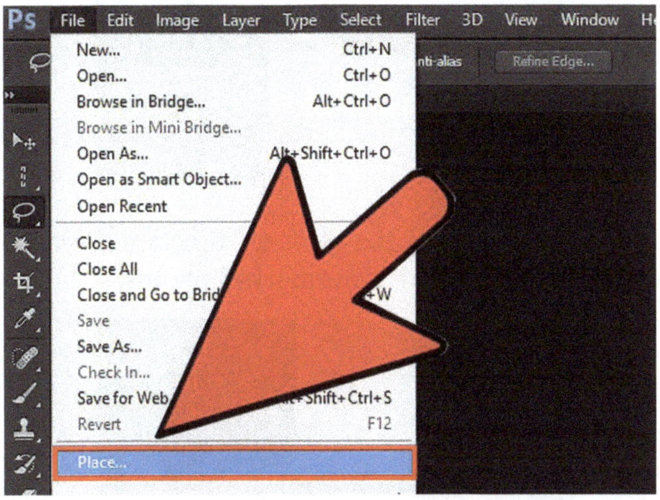

4. Go to "File" and press "Place." Select your logo. Resize the logo until it is the size you would like. Change the opacity if you would like it to be lighter. Align the logo using the right, left, bottom top or center align buttons on the top tool bar.

- Place the logo or text that you have just cut on to your photo in an area that will not obscure the image but will deter people from downloading your picture and using it. Make sure it is not in a place that can be easily cropped off the photo.
- Be sure to use the buttons to align your photo because your Photoshop will be able to record those actions easier than those done only using the mouse.

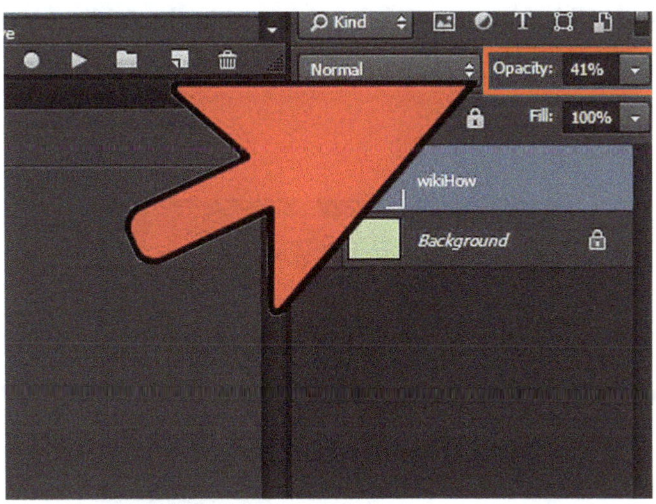

5. Alternatively, make a text watermark. To do a text watermark in Photoshop, make a text box on top of your photo, color it and change its opacity until it is very light in your photo. Do this after you start recording your action.

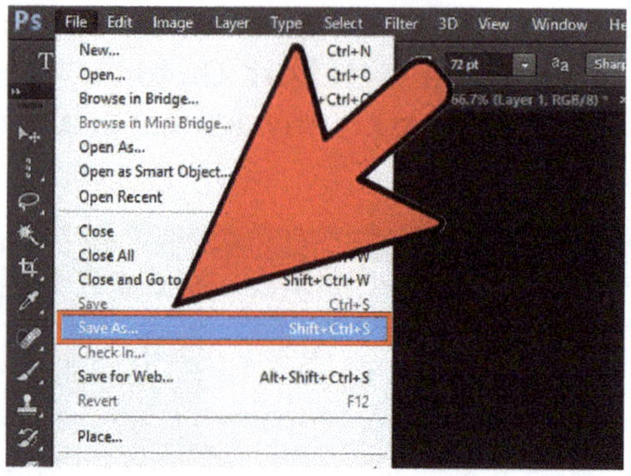

6. Save the photo with the watermark using the "Save as" function. Because you are recording, this will tell Photoshop where to save any future watermarked photos.

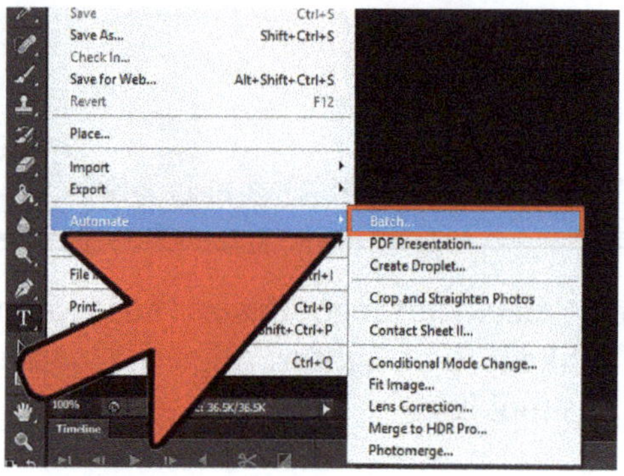

7. Batch add watermarks. To watermark more than one photo, go to "File," select "Automate" and then select "Batch." When the window pops up, choose "Watermark" as the action in the drop down menu. Choose the folder with the images you want to watermark. You will need to have them in a separate folder for this action. Select the destination for all watermarked photos, using the browsing function prompted by the "Destination" button. Check the "Override box." Press "OK" and your folder of photos will be watermarked and saved in the folder you specified.

Method 2

Using Photoshop Layers

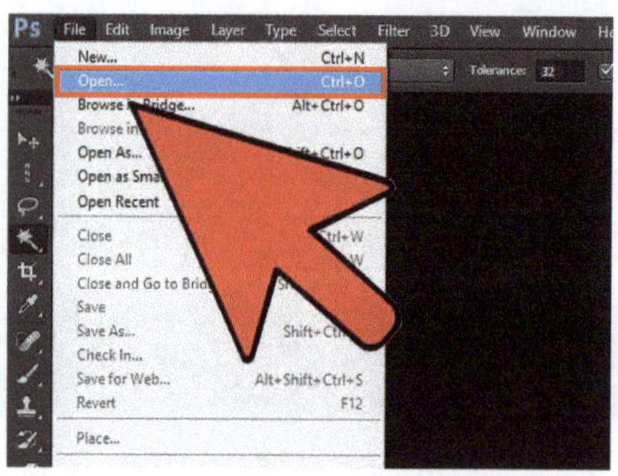

1. Open your image. Save it as a separate file that is just for the watermarked image, so that your original is not lost.

2. Open your watermark. This should contain the logo or image that you want to watermark.

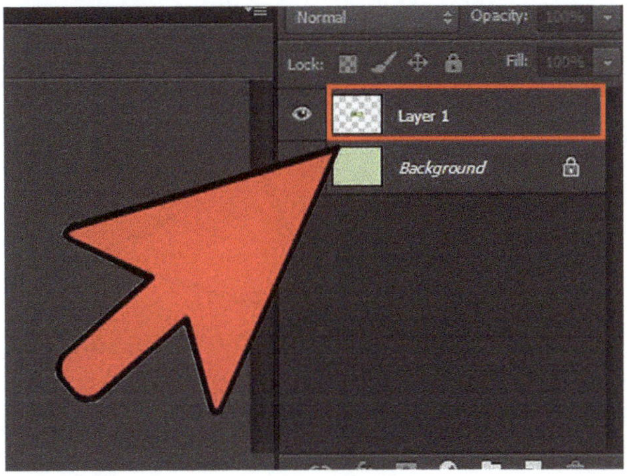

3. Copy the watermark onto a new layer. Copy the image to the file where you want to add the watermark and paste it onto a new layer, above the image.

4. Set the opacity. On the layer that contains your watermark, turn down the opacity until it is no longer as visible.

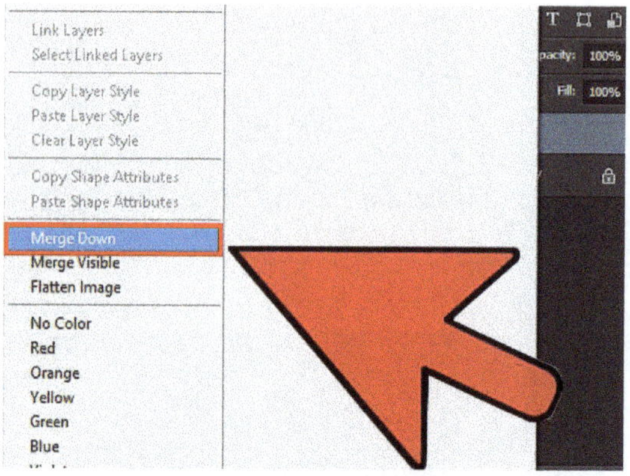

5. Merge the layers. Merge the layer down to join the watermark permanently with image (again, have an unwatermarked version saved somewhere else).

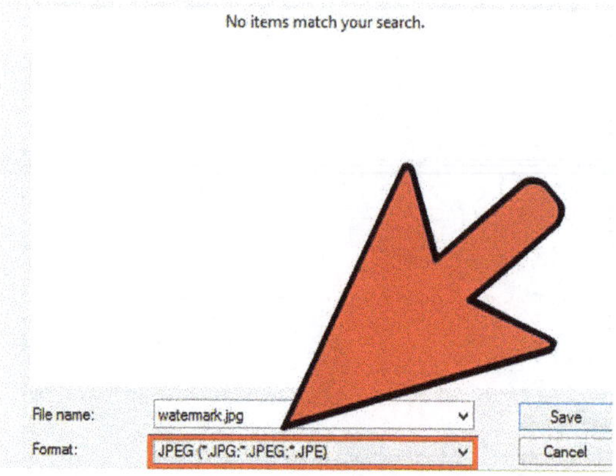

6. Save the file in a non-Photoshop format. Save the file as a jpeg or similar file which will not preserve the layers. This will make it harder for others to remove your watermark.

Method 3

Adding a Watermark in Google Picasa

1. Upload your photos to a Picasa album.

- Picasa is Google's application for handling photos and storing them on the Internet. You can add a watermark in Picasa that is white text. You cannot choose to put a logo as a watermark at this point.

2. Go to your album and select the photos that you want to watermark. You will need to export them to do this.

- On Windows operating systems (OS), hold down the "Shift" button and click on photos to select more than 1 photo to watermark. On Mac OS, hold down the "Command" button and click on photos to select more than 1.

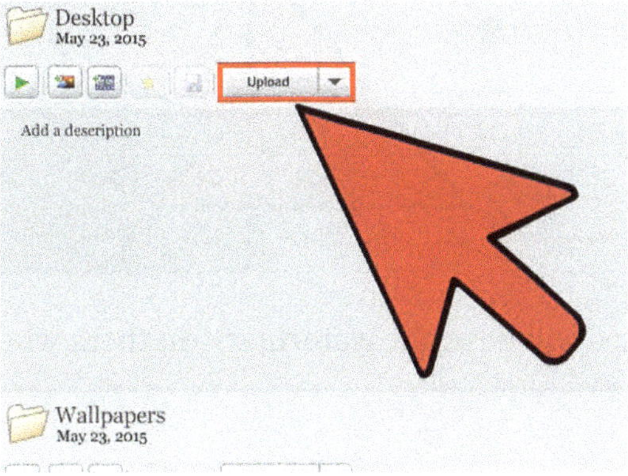

3. Click the "Export" button. This will be found in your photo tray. You will need to have a folder to which you can export the photos.

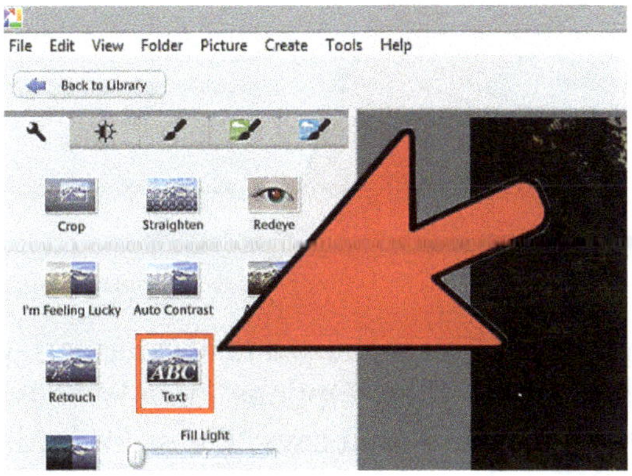

4. Click the "Add a Watermark" option in the menu.

5. Type the text that you want to be displayed as your watermark.

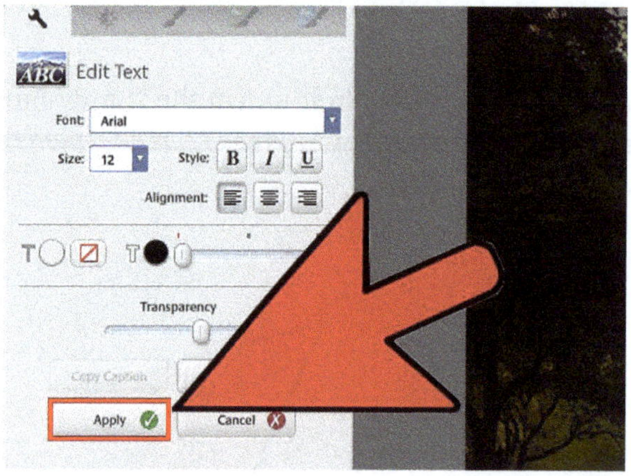

6. Select "OK" and your photos will have the watermark on them when they arrive in your folder.

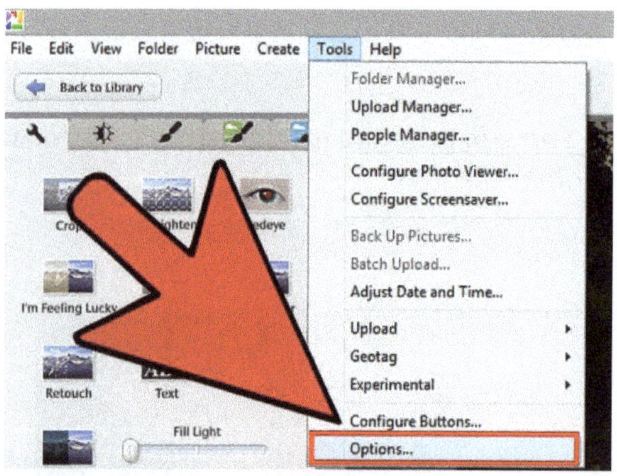

7. Alternatively, add while uploading. You can also add a watermark when you are uploading photos. Before you download, click "Tools" then "Options" on a Windows OS and click "Picasa" then "Preferences" in Mac OS. Click on the tab that says "Picasa Web Albums." Select "Add a Watermark." Type your text. Click "OK" and your albums will arrive in your uploaded album with watermark protection.

How to Remove Cluttered Background on your Photos

In the heat of the photographic moment, it can be very easy to focus only on the subject of the shot and ignore what's happening in the background. It's only when we download the images onto our computer, or get them developed, that we realize that we also managed to capture a whole array of distracting clutter.

Steps

1. Crop the background. Cropping out as much of the background as possible is a simple easy, short-cut. Just make sure that you don't detract from some of the basic rules of composition and symmetry.

2. Select your subject. Use the lasso tool from our toolbox to very roughly select around our subject. Make sure that you leave a little bit of space around his body. Eliminate some of the extraneous space by feathering our edge. In Photoshop, go to Select - Feather. The value will differ depending on the final size of our image. You want to choose a number of pixels that brings the marquee selection closer into your subject without crossing over any of their edges.

3. Blur the background. To blur the background use the Gaussian blur tool. Go to - Filter - Blur - Gaussian Blur. Choose a value that blurs the background without totally eliminating our perception of the subjects. If you have the preview button ticked you can keep trying until you get something that works perfectly.

4. Saturate/Desaturate. In the final stage, desaturate the background slightly to further increase the emphasis on the main subject. Select your sponge tool and set it to desaturate 15%, then brush over the majority of the background.

5. After de-saturating the background, change the sponge tool to saturate and set it at a smaller value (7-8%) Paint over the subject to slightly bring out the colour. The final effect should be subtle - but should help the subject of your image - just pop a little out of the background.

How to Blur the Background of a Photograph

How do professional photographers make those stunning candid portraits, where the subject is in perfect focus, but the background is a blur? Well, there are several techniques you can use to blur the background of a photograph from adjusting your camera's aperture and shutter speed, to manipulating its portrait and autofocus settings, to editing the photograph in Photoshop.

Method 1

Blurring the Background by Adjusting Aperture

1. Set your DSLR camera to the aperture setting. You will find a circular dial, usually on the top of your camera, that has several shooting options such as "Auto". Turn the dial so that the aperture priority setting is selected.

- The aperture setting is identified by an "A" and sometimes an "Av" on certain Canon models.
- Aperture is the size of the hole in the lens through which light travels, similar to the pupil of an eye.
- Aperture is measured in f-numbers (Ex: f/1.4), known as "f-stops". And while it may sound confusing, the larger the f-stop, the smaller the f-stop. So a f/1.4 will have a larger aperture (hole) than a f/2. A smaller f-stop will create a larger depth of field and be able to separate the foreground and background better, blurring the background.

2. Create distance between the camera, subject, and background.

- To better blur the background of your photograph you want to create enough distance between the camera and the subject so that you can zoom on your camera to better focus it on your foreground.
- In addition, the further your subject is from the background, the easier it will be to get a nice blurred look. Depending on your lens, play with this distance having your subject stand 5, 10, or 15 feet away from the background.

3. Fill the frame with the subject in a medium shot. This is a shot that has your subject in the frame from about the waist up. For a great portrait photo you may then want to get a bit closer, or zoom on your camera so you can really focus on the shoulders and head. But starting further out can help you adjust at the beginning.

- Focus directly on the eyes.
- Note: The nose, ears and hair will be in varying degrees of focus. At smaller apertures, the background of a shot will be in focus. At larger apertures, the background will be blurred.

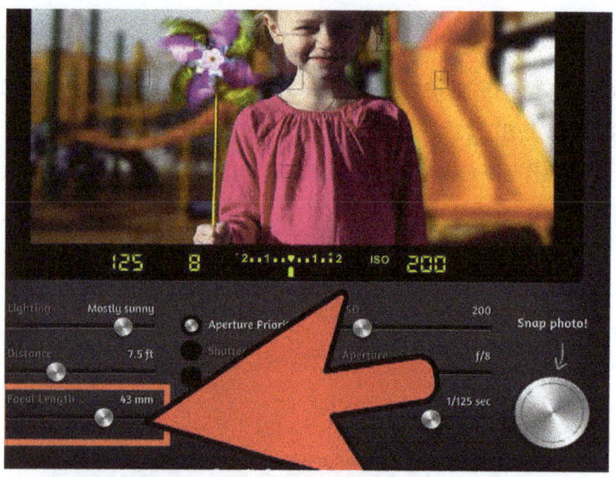

4. Zoom in. Narrow the depth of field further by zooming in. To make as shallow a depth of field as possible, use a long/telephoto lens set on maximum zoom. Stand as close to the subject as possible.

- If you have a very long lens, this might still be quite far away from your subject.
- If you only have the lens your camera came with, you may have to stand closer to the

subject. You should still try and get a fair amount of zoom on your camera, and in general, you will be closer to your subject than your subject is from the background.

- Play around with zoom and snap a couple of test photos to see if you're getting close to the desired results.

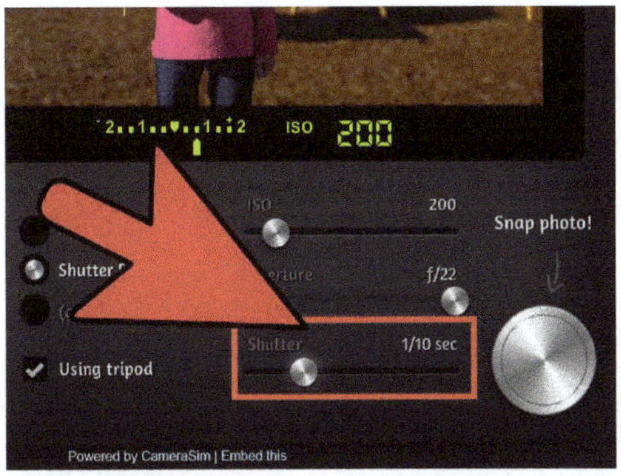

5. Pan with a moving target. If the subject is moving, move your camera to follow the subject and keep it sharp while blurring the background.

- Try different shutter speeds to balance the background blur you want against the subject blur you don't want.
- Try a 1/125 second shutter speed to begin.
- Keep your body and the camera as steady as possible. Track the subject through the viewfinder and ensure your camera is focusing properly on the subject. Take the photo with confidence.
- This technique uses the blurred background to highlight the motion of the subject, whereas background blurred solely through a shallow depth of field is used to make the subject stand out from its surroundings.

Method 2

Using your Camera's other Settings

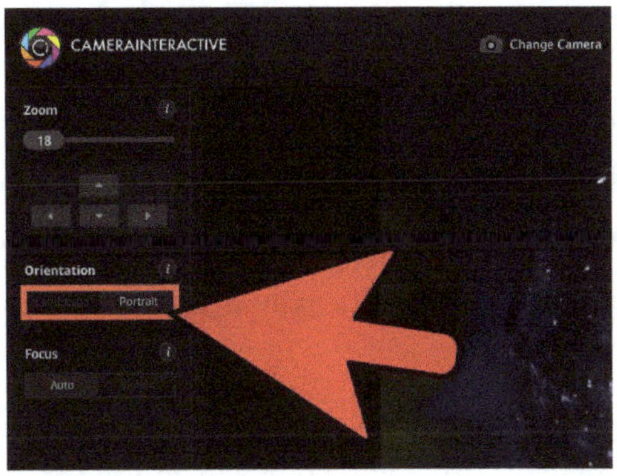

1. Set your camera to the auto setting and use portrait mode. If you don't have a particularly advanced

camera you can still blur the background of a photograph by using your camera's other settings like portrait mode which will adjust the camera automatically to help you with the desired effect.

- The portrait mode is found on the dial usually under the "P" or the little image of a woman. Switch your dial to Portrait mode to have your camera automatically adjust your aperture and shutter speed.

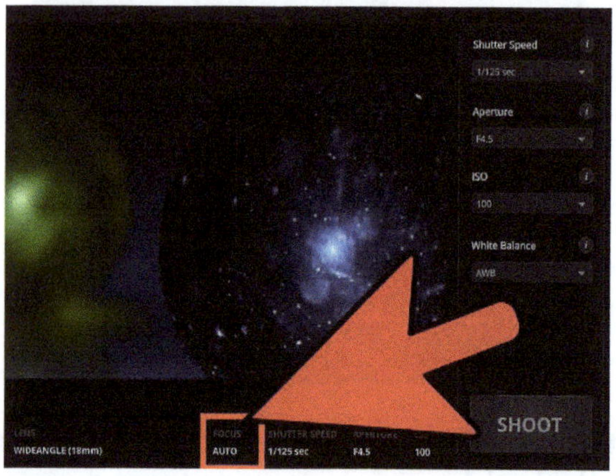

2. Adjust your auto focus settings in the menu. You can hit the "Menu" button on your camera and navigate to the focus selection. In a lot of cameras you will see several boxes with the center one filled in.

- Move your cursor to fill in one of the other boxes that will be closest to where your subject's eyes are.
- This will allow the camera to automatically focus the most on your selected area, blurring the rest out the further away from the focus area an object is.

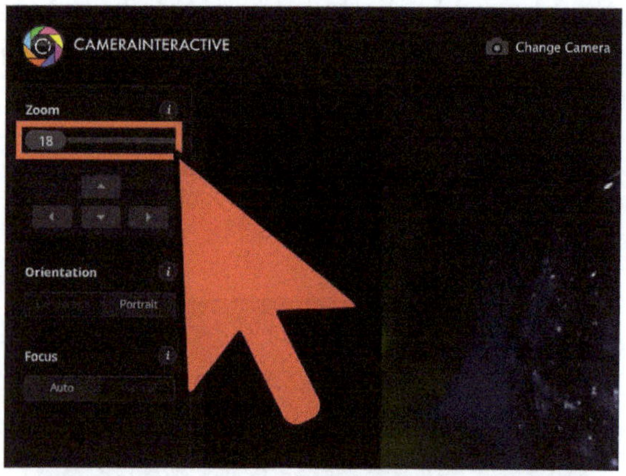

3. Place your subject as far away from the background as possible. You can manually narrow your depth of field if you don't have a lens that will easily do it for you by creating a large distance between the foreground and background.

- If you are taking a photo of your subject in front of say, a wall, then try and move them 10 or so feet away from the wall. With your portrait mode set, your camera should be able to blur the background on its own.

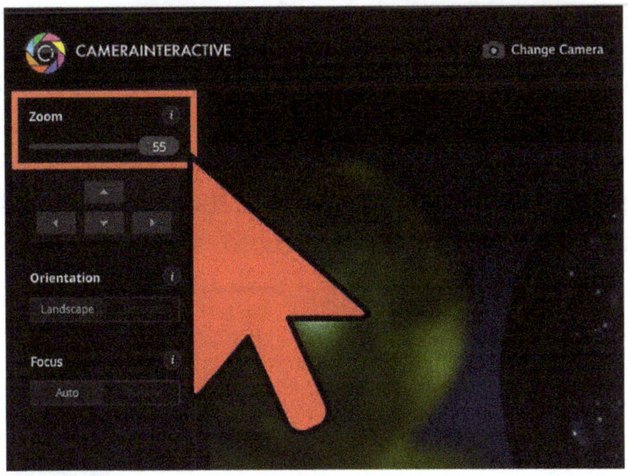

4. Zoom in as far as you can.If you are using a kit lens (the default lens that comes with your camera) then you want to zoom to get a longer focal length, or the distance between the lens and the subject.

- You'll have to play with distance here depending on how far your lens can zoom. You want to be able to zoom in as far as possible while still getting both your subject and some background in the shot.
- This method will mean that there will be less background in your photo, but it will help you get the desired effect. Your subject will remain the same and only the background will shrink if you zoom correctly. But it will help to blur the background.

Method 3

Blurring in Photoshop

1. Employ Photoshop's Blur tool to blur the background of a photograph. Select the raindrop looking icon from the toolbar, this is the blur tool.

- At the top of your screen will see options for brush size, and strength of your stroke. You can adjust these to your liking. For a portrait style photo with a fair amount of background you can select a larger brush size.

- Hold down your mouse and move it over the background of your photo to blur it.
- Keep in mind that this technique does not create true depth - it blurs everything in the background uniformly rather than independently based on distance from the lens. An image blurred "in camera" collects visual information from a scene that a Photoshop blurred image can never obtain because the data is not there in a Photoshop file. The "in camera" image is a much truer and organic image/record.

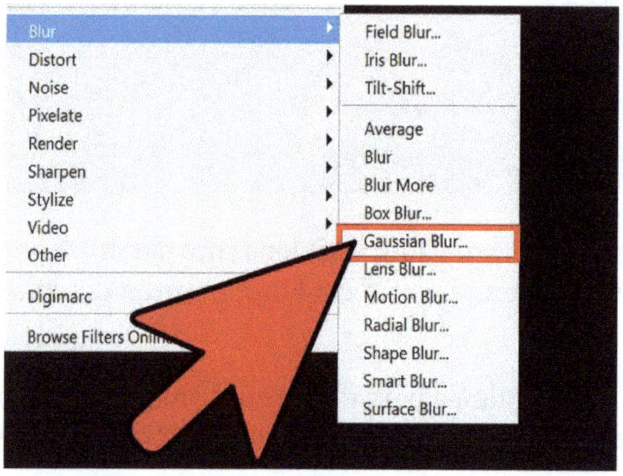

2. Blur using layers. For this option you'll want to create a duplicate layer going to Layers > Duplicate layers. With your duplicate layer, click Filters > Blur > Gaussian Blur.

- Now your entire image will be blurred out. But because you have the original image as a layer under this one, you can use the erase tool to erase the blur over the part of your photo you want in focus.
- Once you have done that, go to Layer > Flatten Image. This will flatten the two layers into one, with your blurred background.

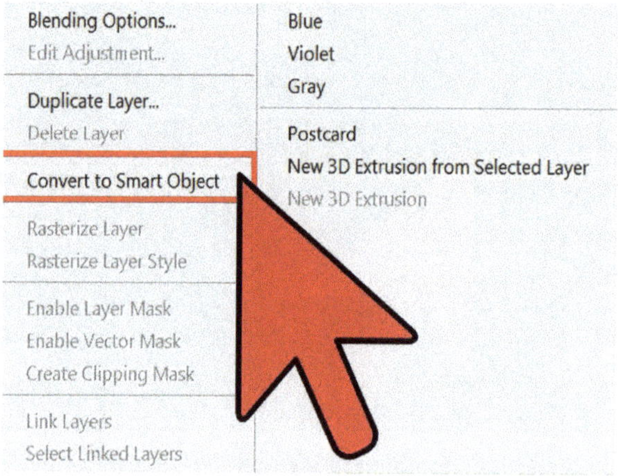

3. Blur the background of your photograph by making your image a "Smart Object". This will allow you to use an iris blur to keep your subject in focus while blurring the background.

- In your Layers panel right-click on your background layer, the image, and select "Convert to Smart Object".

- From your top menu click Filter > Blur Gallery > Iris Blur. Now drag your iris over your subject. You can adjust the size and shape of the iris by clicking and dragging on the different boxes you see. You can also hold shift while you drag to convert the rectangular iris into a circle, adjusting it to the proper size.

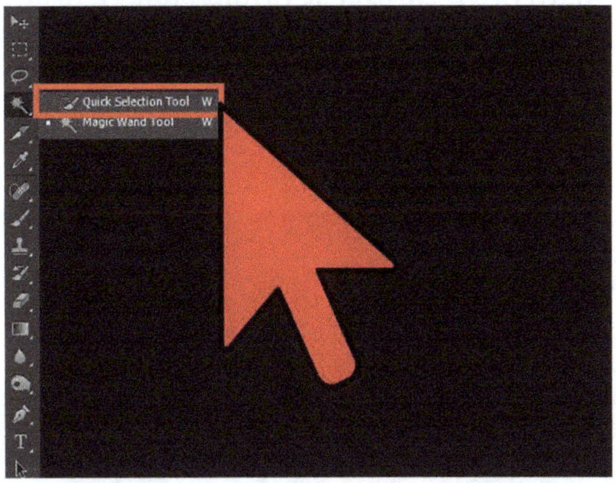

4. Use the Quick Selection tool to blur a background. Find the Quick Selection tool in your toolbar, it looks like a paintbrush with a dashed oval shape next to it.

- Hold and drag it around your subject that you want to remain in focus. This tool uses distinctive edges to select your image, and is much easier to use if you were able to blur your background on your camera even slightly when taking your photo.
- Use the Refine Edge button in the "Options" bar to further refine your selection to make sure everything you want is selected.
- From your top bar menu go to Select > Inverse. Now everything that is not your subject will be selected. From here you want to go to Filter > Gaussian Blur. Simply adjust the Radius slider to your preferred blur setting and click "OK".

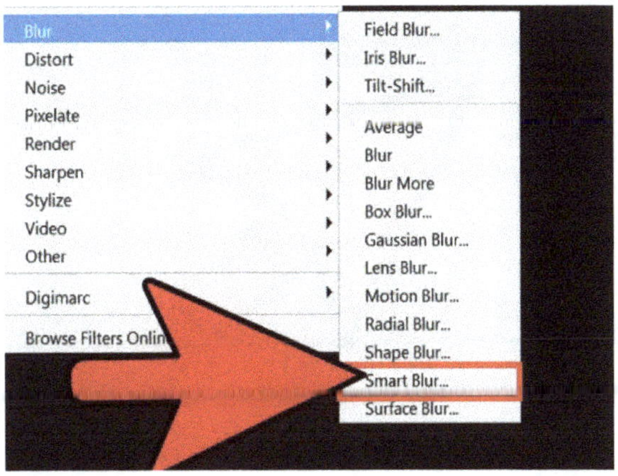

5. If you are using an updated version of Photoshop, try using the "smart blur" option. This filter evaluates the range of pixels in the background and foreground, and gives you more control over the image. The filter is also adjustable which enables the photographer to manipulate the photo even more.

How to Organize your Digital Photos

Taking photos with your digital camera is fun, easy, and addictive. Suddenly you find yourself with hundreds of photos on your hard drive, as well as printed out all over your desk, room, and walls. What should you do to organize and catalogue your photos? Here are some tips to help you clean up the clutter, and enjoy your digital memories.

Steps

1. Download a free image organizer. Fast small ones include Xnview (open source) and Irfanview (popular). Picasa from Google is an easy-to-use photo management tool. However, read the fine print on the agreement you sign with Picasa/Google. It gives Google the rights to all of the photos you put on the site, for their unrestricted use.

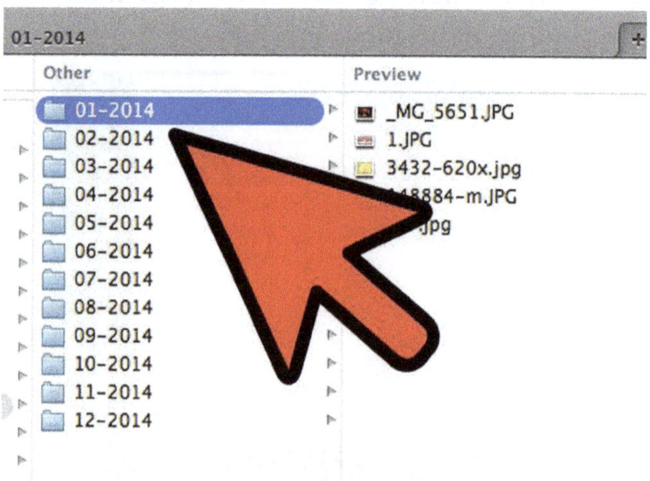

2. When you transfer your photos from your camera to your computer, immediately put them into a folder on your hard drive -- not just My Pictures, but create a subfolder by date (use reverse date format e.g. 2007-06-26 which is listed better by computers ordering files by name), event name or both. After the date you could give your shoot a name

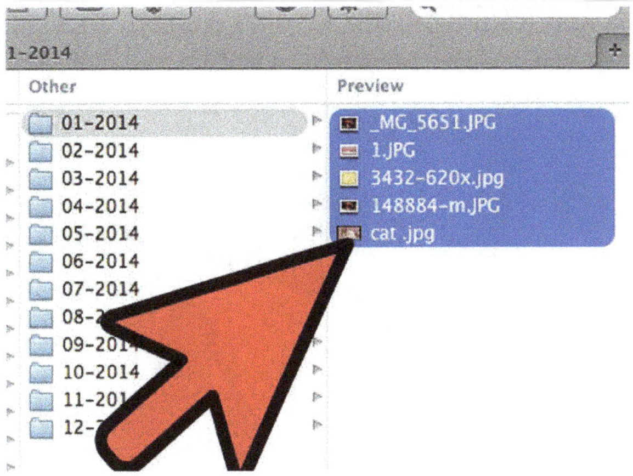

3. If you already have copious numbers of photos dumped into your My Pictures folder, take some time to create sub-folders as described above, and sort them into the appropriate folder.

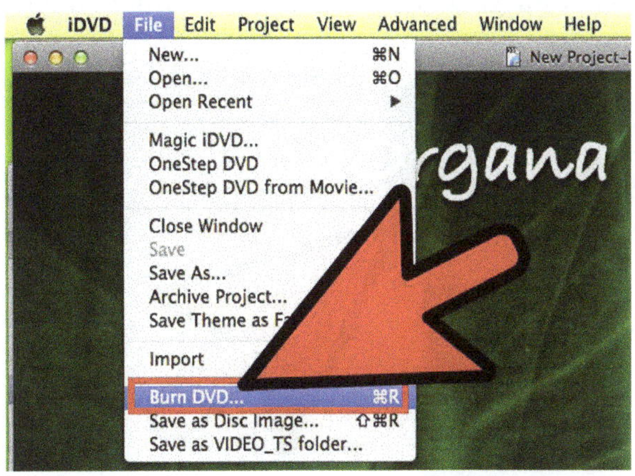

4. Regularly back up your photos by burning them onto a CD or DVD. Nothing is worse than having a hard drive crash and losing all of your pictures. Then, put your CD or DVD into a box, holder, or album (you can find 'photo albums' for picture CDs in photography shops) so you know where it is and have easy access. You can also use Online file backup services like Dropbox, Sugarsync or SkyDrive or use a dedicated Photo Share site that offers file synchronization like InmyPhotofolder.

5. Log your best shots. Open all your images from a shoot. On a mac you can do this in preview.

Scroll through these images and jot down your favourite shots. By doing this you can reduce 200 images down to 20.

6. Import these images into a library. On a mac you could import them into iPhoto.

7. As soon as the ink is dry, organize your photos into albums. The sooner you do this, the fewer photos you will have piling up and cluttering your space, not to mention getting damaged.

8. Do the above step for all of the photos you already have printed out. Use different albums to catalogue and categorize -- for example, you can keep separate albums for friends, events you attend, and 'artful' shots that you take.

9. Remember that if you back up your photos onto a CD, and leave them on the computer as well, you will eventually find you have multiple copies of the same photo in different folders. In Picasa2, when you back up pictures, Picasa will remember not to double up on the same CD.

10. One good method of organizing is to put only photos about a particular subject on each CD and label it as such, such as "grandkids" or "reunion 98" then if you want a particular subject you can find it easily because you don't have "sewing projects" on the same CD as "Reunions".

Chapter 3 Fundamentals of Photoshop

Adobe Photoshop is a popular graphic image editing software that is developed and published by Adobe Systems. Various tools of Adobe Photoshop include cropping, eraser, slicing, shape tools, pen tools, etc. The major components of Adobe Photoshop are discussed in this chapter.

How to use Adobe Photoshop Elements

Adobe Photoshop Elements isn't quite the program Photoshop is, but it has quite a lot of power, does a lot of what Photoshop does, and is considerably less expensive. Unless you are a hard core graphic designer, Elements will be more than enough for you. If the cost is still too high, check out some of the free graphic software out there.

- Any screenshots made here are made with Photoshop Elements 9.

Steps

1. If you haven't already done it, or don't already own it, go to Adobe.com and download it. You will need to give them your email address for them to send in the link.

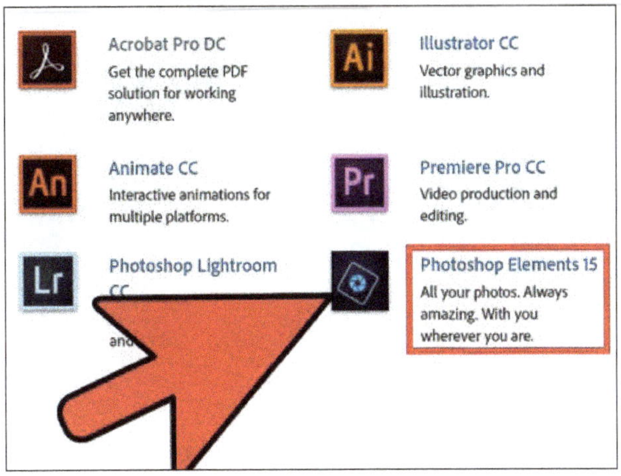

2. Download the 'downloader'. Yes, you download a tiny program that will download the big program for you. It is an EXE file, so you won't need an unzip program for it.

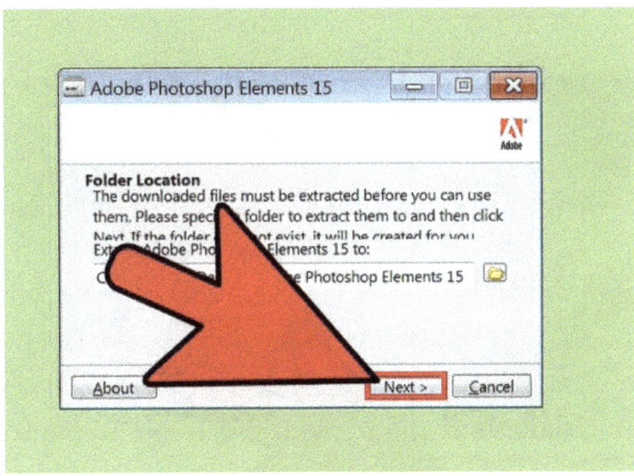

3. Install the program. The downloader will take care of most of the work for you. You just have to wait for it to do it.

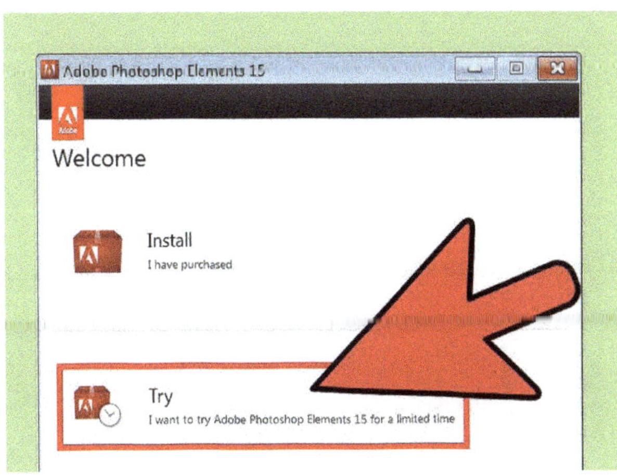

4. 'Inform' the software that you are using it for a trial or enter in your program key that you would get when you buy it.

5. Decide whether you want to 'Organize' or 'Edit'. This screen, and a few following ones, tell you some of the things that PS Elements can do.

6. Click on Edit. For this article, the subject will be the editing part of Elements.

7. Wait. Elements is a good size program and will take a little while to start up.

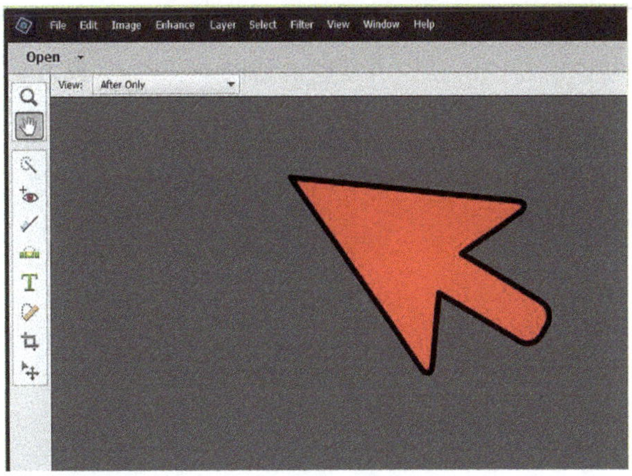

8. Look at your workspace. Right off the bat, you can see that there is a lot that Elements can do.

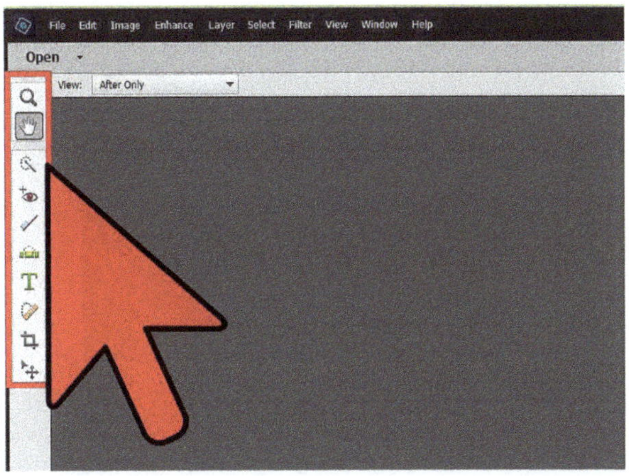

9. Look at the toolbar on the left. From top to bottom, left to right, the tools are: Move Tool Zoom Tool Hand Tool Eyedropper Tool Rectangular Marquee Tool Magnetic Lasso Tool Magic Wand Tool Quick Selection Tool Horizontal Type Tool Crop Tool Cookie Cutter Tool Straighten Tool Red Eye Removal Tool Spot Healing Brush Tool Clone Stamp Tool Eraser Tool Brush Tool Smart Brush Tool Paint Bucket Tool Gradient Tool Custom Shape Tool Blur Tool Sponge Tool

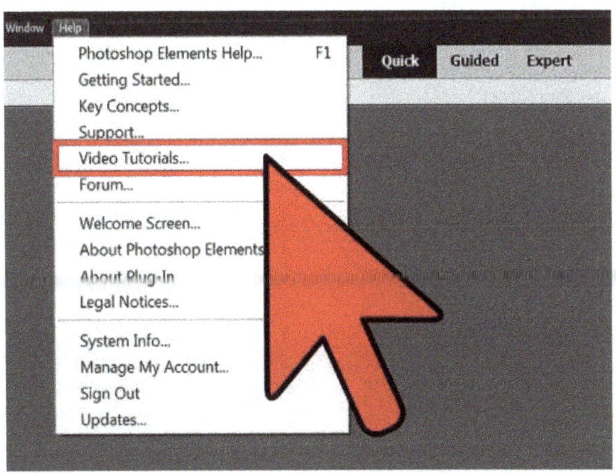

10. Check out the other articles on how to do certain tasks with PS Elements.

How to change Text Color in Photoshop

Adobe Photoshop is a very powerful image editing application. This article will show you how to change the color of text in Photoshop. Photoshop makes it incredibly easy to change the color of text, whether or not you can edit it.

Method 1

Editable Text

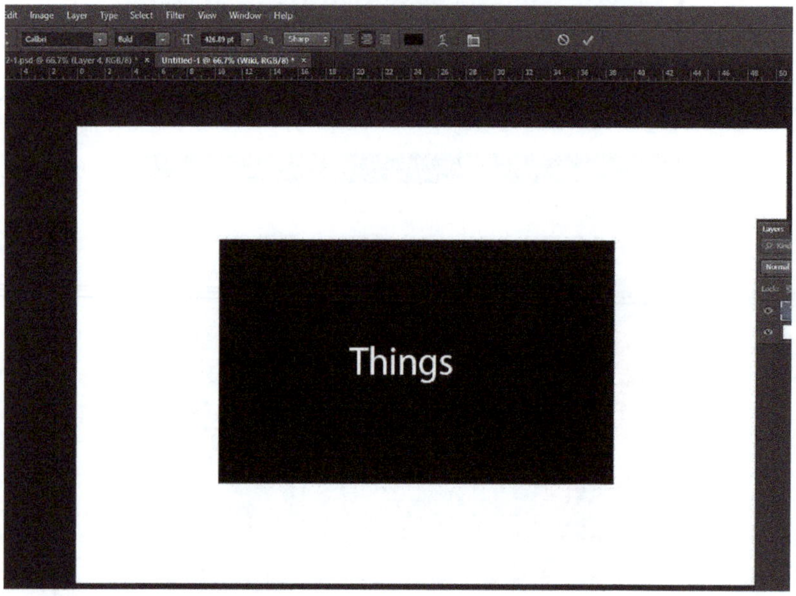

1. Choose the Type tool and select the text.

2. Click the foreground color chooser.

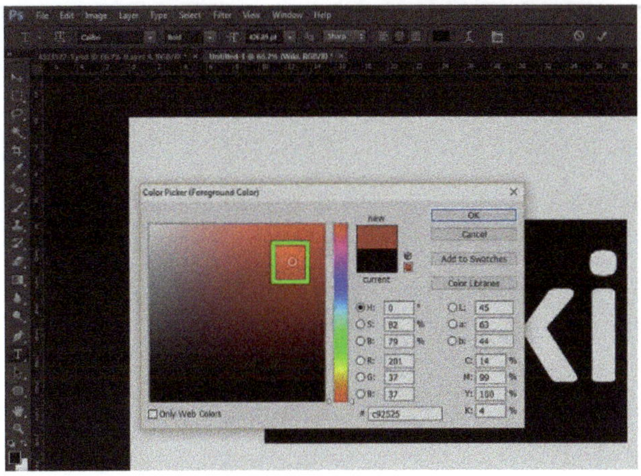

3. Choose the color you want and press OK.

Method 2

Rasterized text

1. Click the foreground color chooser.

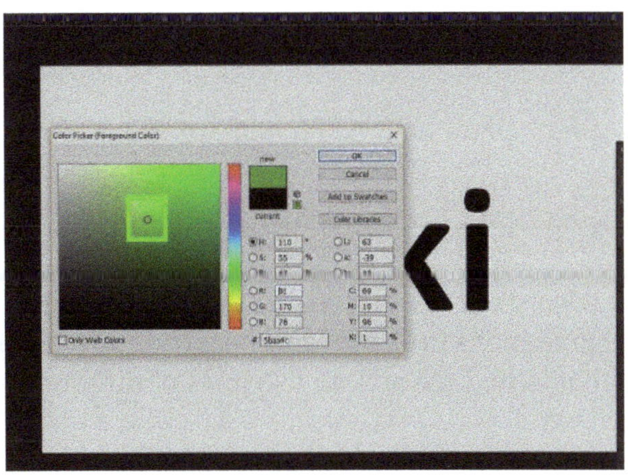

2. Choose the color you want and press OK.

3. Choose the Paint Bucket tool and click one letter of the text.

4. If it worked, click each other letter. If the edges of the text are still in the original color, take a Step Backwards (Edit>Step Backwards) and increase the tolerance of the Paint Bucket tool. Repeat step 3.

How to create Line art with Photoshop

"Line art is any image that consists of distinct straight and curved lines placed against a (usually plain) background, without gradations in shade (darkness) or hue (color) to represent two-dimensional or three-dimensional objects. Line art can use lines of different colors, although line art is usually monochromatic."

This tutorial was done with Photoshop, but other advanced image editing programs such as Gimp are acceptable and compatible with this tutorial.

Steps

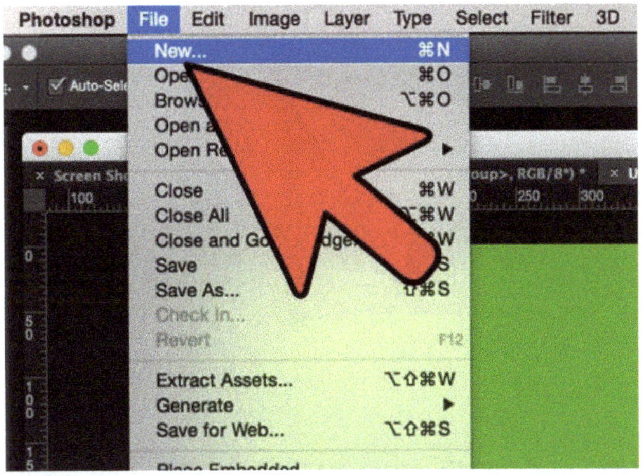

1. Create a new document. Go to File -> New.

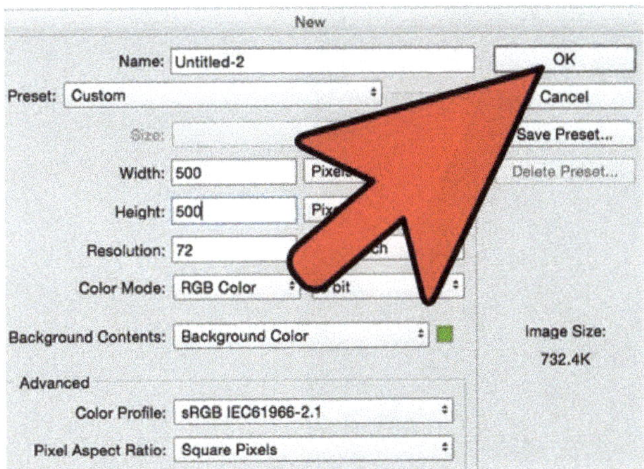

2. Set the canvas size. Here it's shown as 500x500 pixels, but adjust the size to fit what you want to draw. Press "Ok".

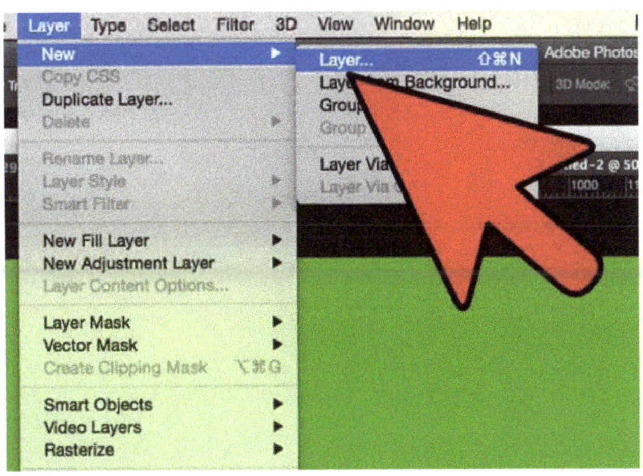

3. Create a new layer. Click Layer -> New -> Layer.

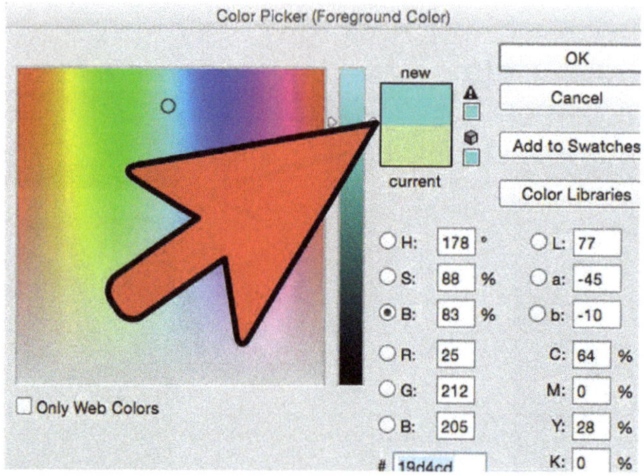

4. Pick a color. Choose any color except what you want your final color to be. Preferably a light color.

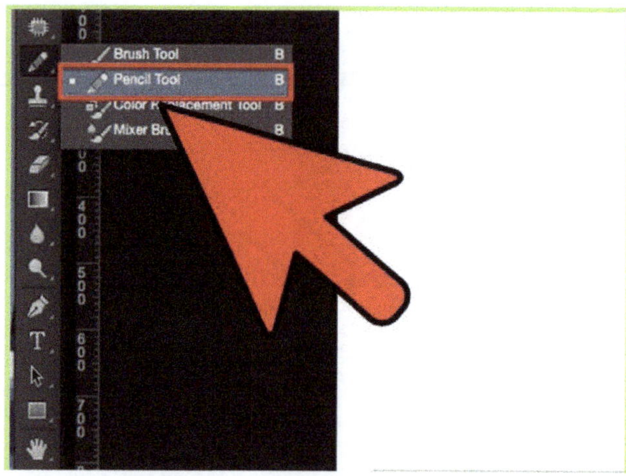

5. Draw. Use the pencil brush to sketch out your drawing. Don't worry about neatness or making solid lines.

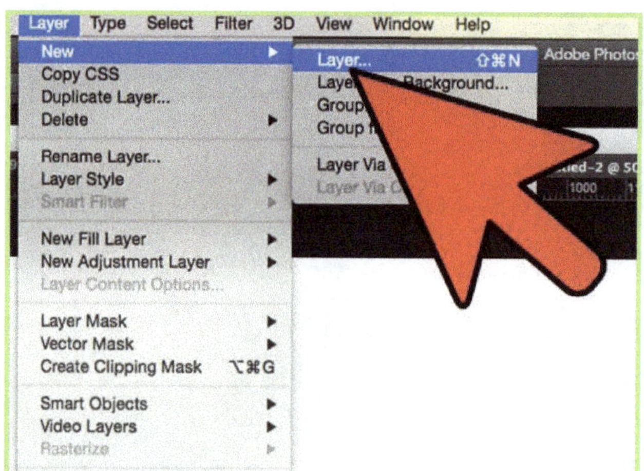

6. Create a new layer. Click Layer -> New -> Layer.

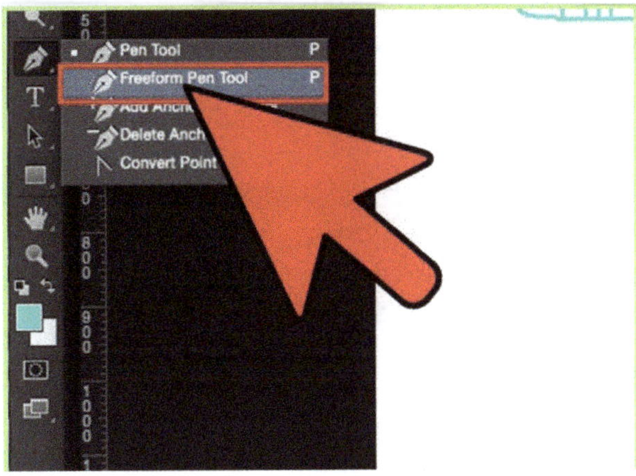

7. Select the Freeform Pen Tool. However if you are experienced with the conventional pen tool, it is the faster and better quality option.

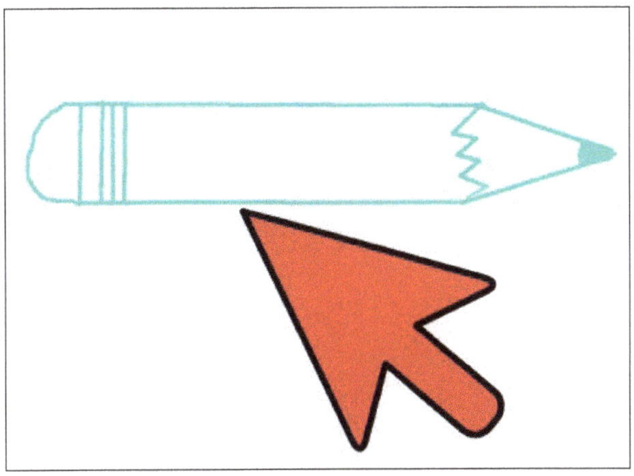

8. Trace your sketch. Only trace one line at a time, then do the next two steps, then trace the next line.

9. Stroke path. Right click the pen tool outline and click "Stroke Path". Select "paintbrush" for the tool to stroke the outline. Make sure your paintbrush tool is set to a 1 px brush (unless you have a very large image or are going for a different style), and your final color is selected.

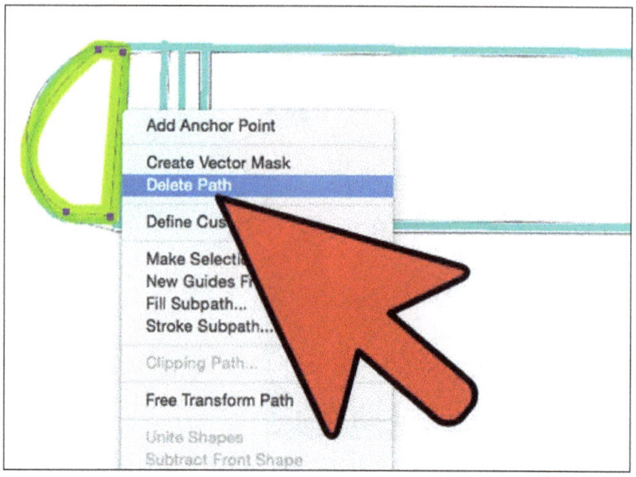

10. Delete Path. Right click the pen tool path and select "Delete Path". Only the paintbrush line should remain.

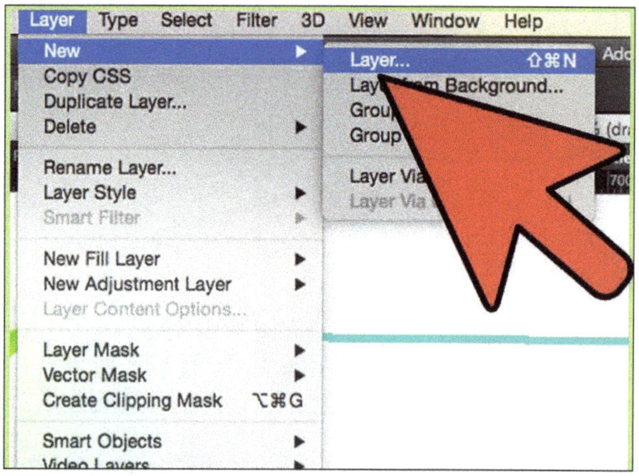

11. Repeat until your entire drawing is outlined.

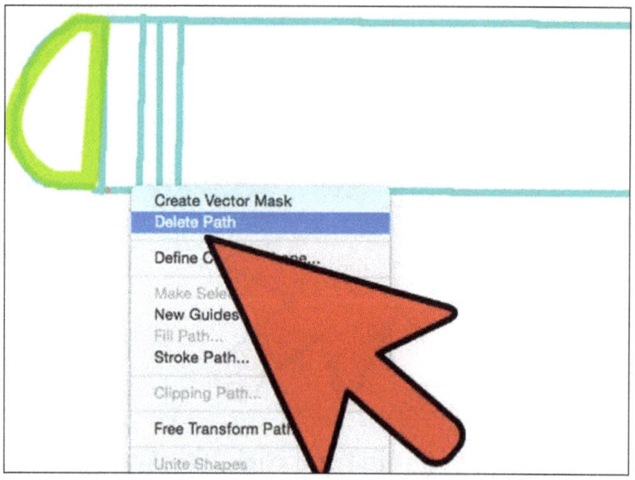

12. Delete or hide the sketch layer and view your final product.

How to Trace an Image using Photoshop

This teaches you how to use Adobe Photoshop to trace the lines of an image in Windows or on Mac.

Part 1

Setting up the Image to Trace

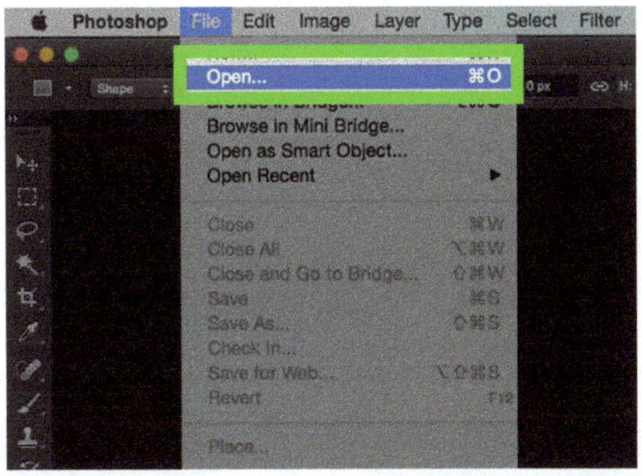

1. Open the image you want to trace in Photoshop. With Photoshop open, click on File in the menu bar at the top of the screen, the click Open... and select the image.

2. Click on Layer in the menu bar.

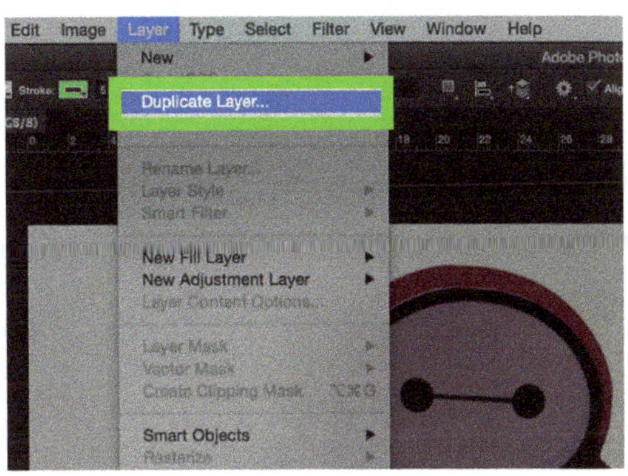

3. Click on Duplicate Layer... and click on OK.

- You can give your new layer a different name otherwise it will be called "[Name of your first layer] copy."

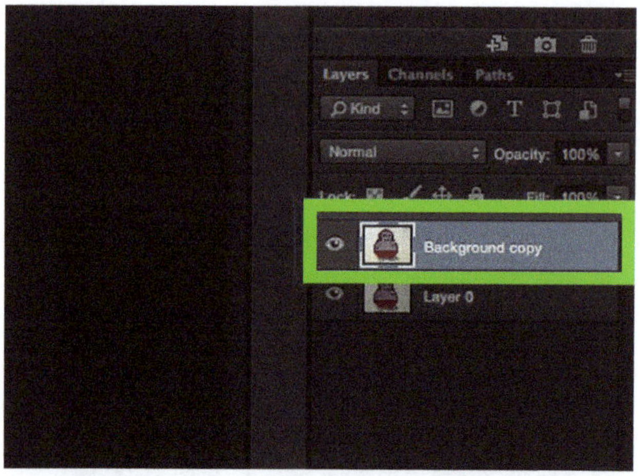

4. Click on the duplicate layer in the "Layers" window. It's in the lower-right part of the screen.

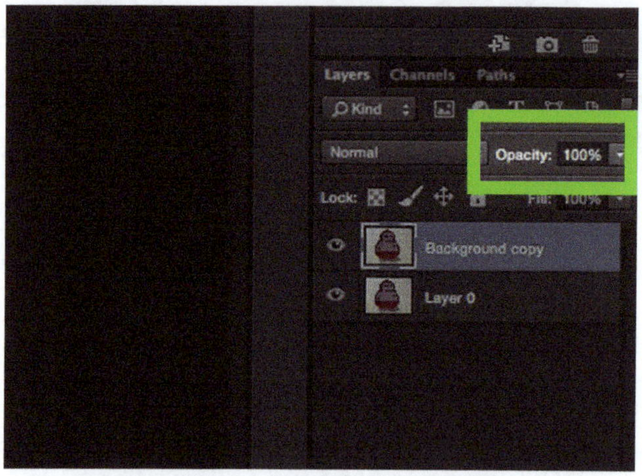

5. Click in the "Opacity:" field in the upper-right of the Layers window.

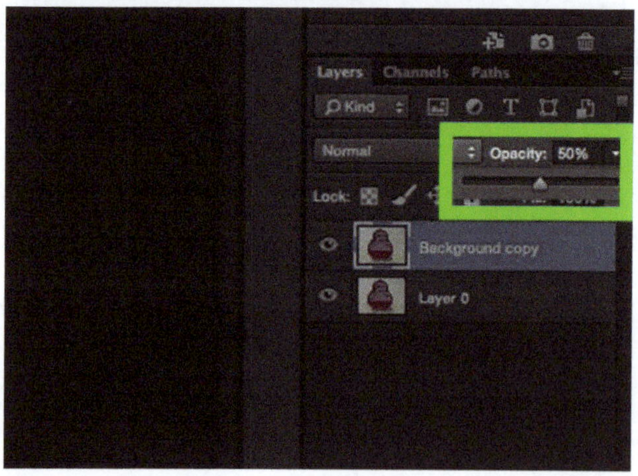

6. Set the opacity to 50%.

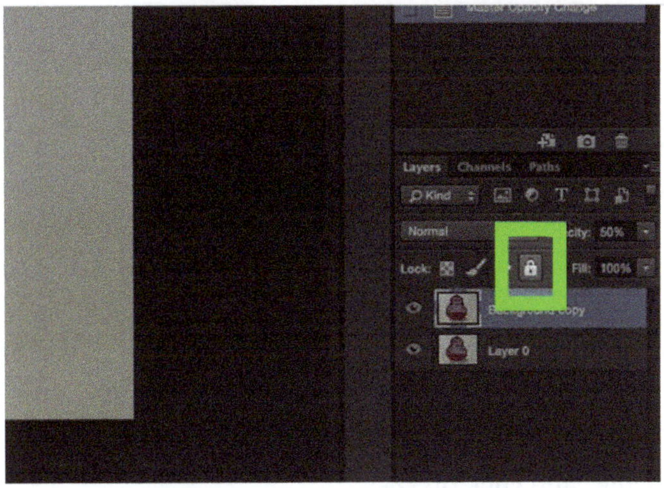

7. Click on the padlock icon at the top of the Layers window to lock the layer.

8. Click on Layer in the menu bar.

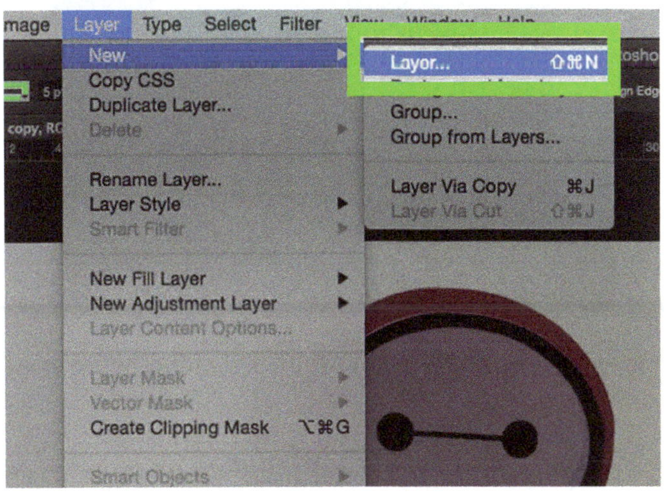

9. Click on New and click on Layer.

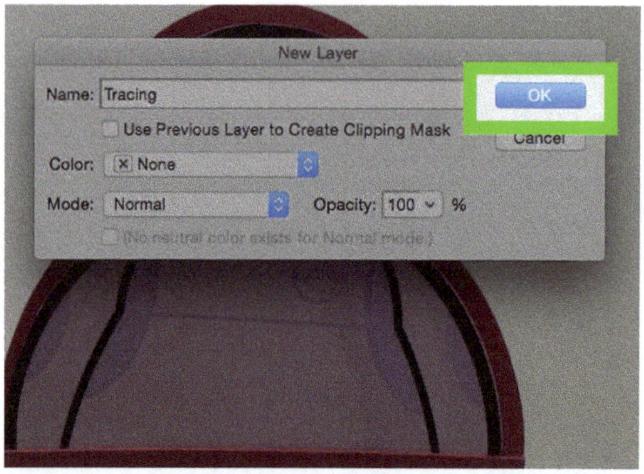

10. Name the layer “Tracing” and click on OK.

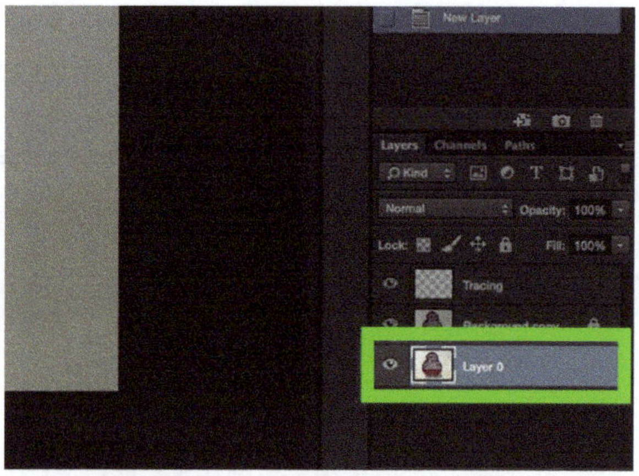

11. Click on the layer labeled “Background” in the Layers window.

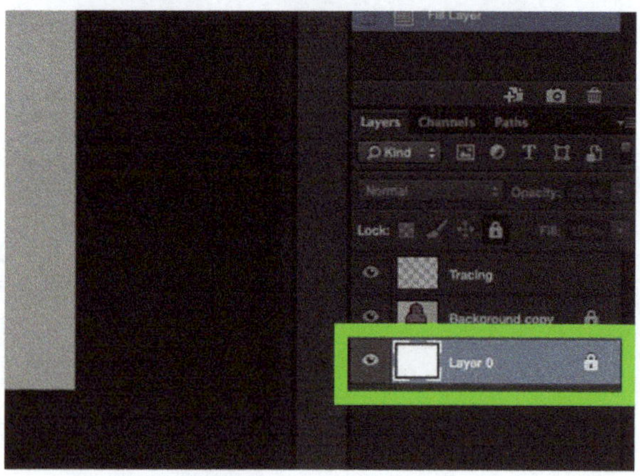

12. Press Ctrl+← Backspace (PC) or ⌘+Delete (Mac). This fills the layer with a white background color.

- You should now have three layers in the layer window: A “Tracing” layer at the top; a locked layer with your image in the middle; and a locked, white background layer at the bottom. If they’re not in this order, drag them to arrange them as such.

Part 2

Tracing the Image

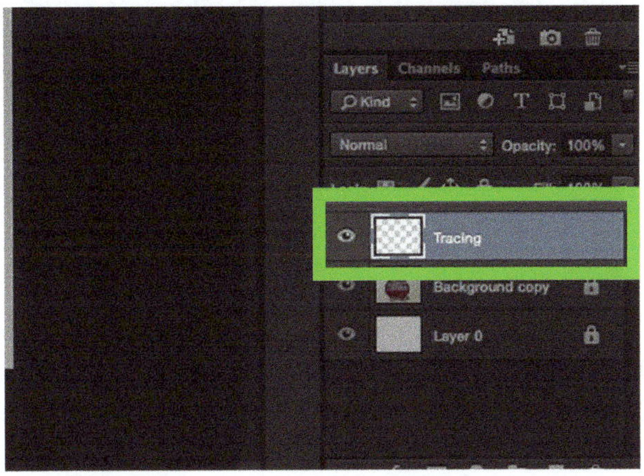

1. Click on the "Tracing" layer at the top of the window.

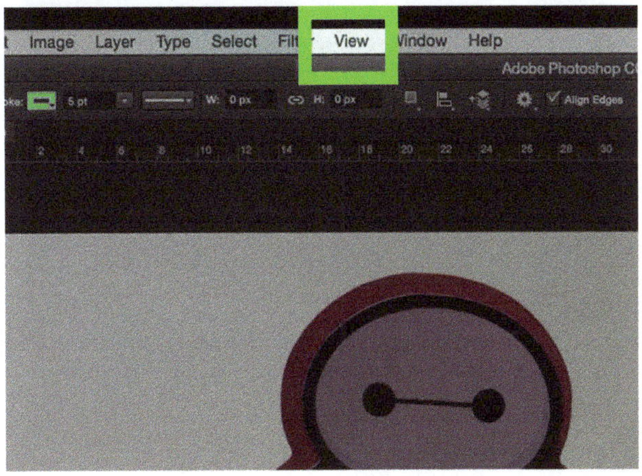

2. Click on View in the menu bar.

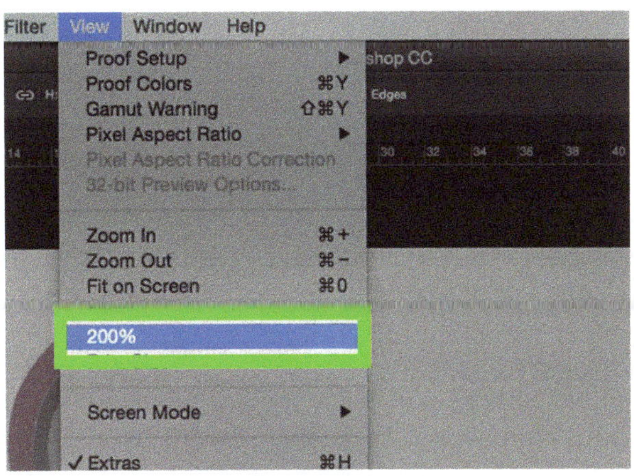

3. Click on 200% to enlarge the image. Click on Zoom In or Zoom Out in the View drop-down to adjust your image to a size that's comfortable for you to trace.

4. Choose a color to start tracing in. To do so, click on one the overlapping squares in the color menu in the upper-right part of the screen, then click on a color in the spectrum below the squares. Click on the other square and then click on the same color.

- Black and white are at the far-right end of the spectrum

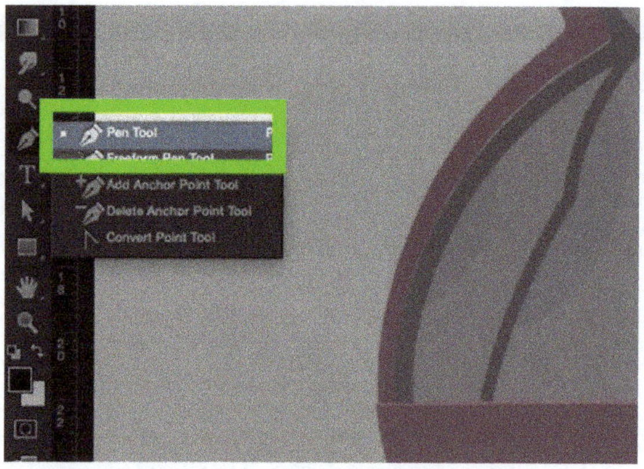

5. Choose a tool in the tool menu at the left-side of the window.

- Pencil Tool: creates even, untapered strokes that are the same width in the middle as they are at both ends. This tool works well if you're going to trace using several small strokes that meet at the ends. The Pencil Tool is a pencil-shaped icon near the top of the second section of the tool menu. If you see a paintbrush icon but not a pencil icon, long-click on the paintbrush icon, then click on Pencil Tool.

- Brush Tool: creates tapered strokes that are thinner on the ends and thicker in the middle. This tool works well if you're want to create a softer, brushstroke appearance with your tracing. The Brush Tool is a paintbrush-shaped icon near the top of the second section of the tool menu. If you see a pencil icon but not a paintbrush icon, long-click on the pencil icon, then click on Brush Tool.

- Pen Tool: creates editable paths with anchor points that can be moved or adjusted. The Pen Tool works well for tracing objects that you'd like to change or alter considerably when you're done tracing. Click on the fountain pen icon below the T in the tool menu to select the Pen Tool.

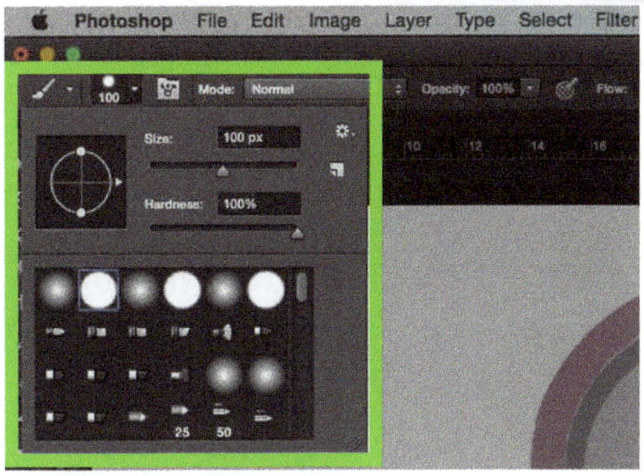

6. Adjust the Pencil and Brush Tool settings. They're in the upper-left part of the window.

- Click on the drop-down next to the tool's icon to adjust the heaviness of the strokes and they're level of gradient (hardness) they have. Strokes with higher gradients appear more like a real pencil or brushstroke.
- Click on the folder-shaped icon to the right of the size drop-down to adjust the shape and qualities of the brush or pencil.

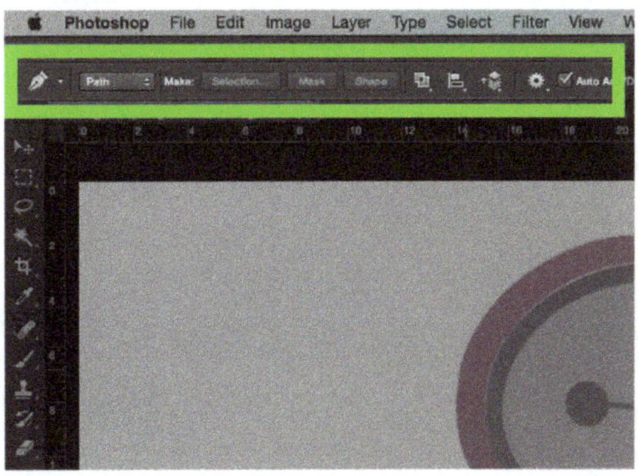

7. Adjust the Pen Tool settings. They're in the upper-left part of the window.

- If you want to use the Pen Tool to create paths as you trace, click on the drop-down to the right of the icon and click on Path.

8. Begin tracing. Use your mouse or track pad to move the tool over the lines you want to trace.

- To use the Pencil and Brush Tools, click and hold as you drag the tool over the lines. Release the click to move the tool and start a new stroke.
- To use the Pen Tool, click and release along the lines of the image you're tracing and a line will appear between each set of points. Curved lines and greater detail require more clicks.

9. Hide the original image. To see how your work is progressing, click on the eye icon next to the middle layer that contains the original image. The image will disappear and you'll see your tracing on a white background.

- When you're finished, click on View in the menu bar, then click 100% to view your image at its actual size.

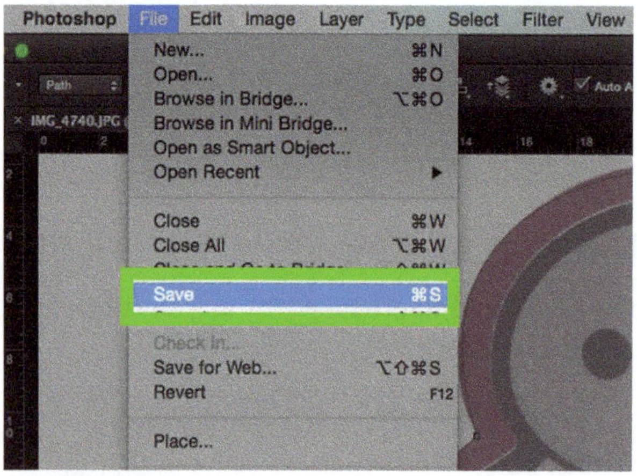

10. Save your image. Do so by clicking on File in the menu bar and Save As.... Name your file and click on Save.

How to make a Fire Effect in Photoshop

If you've ever wanted to add a touch of fire to your images, Photoshop is a great place to go. We'll show you a few ways to get the look you want. It's easy to do, and fun to play with.

Method 1

The Basics

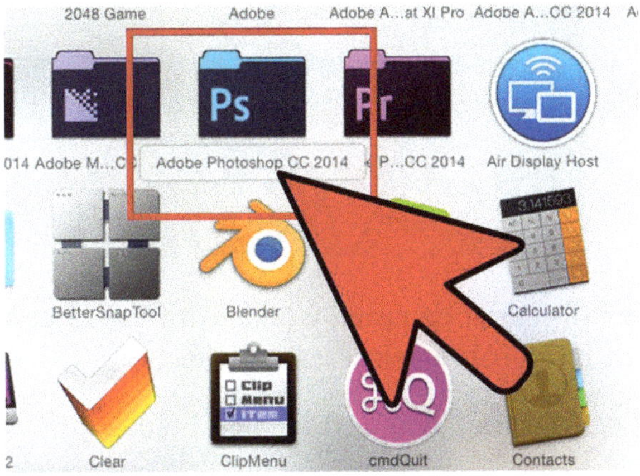

1. Open Adobe Photoshop. Set the background color to black, and the foreground color to orange.

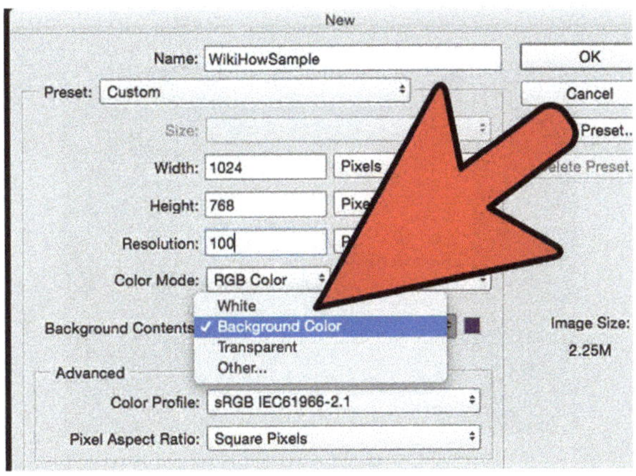

2. Create a new document. Set it to whatever size you desire, and in the Background Contents: popup, select Background Color. Click OK.

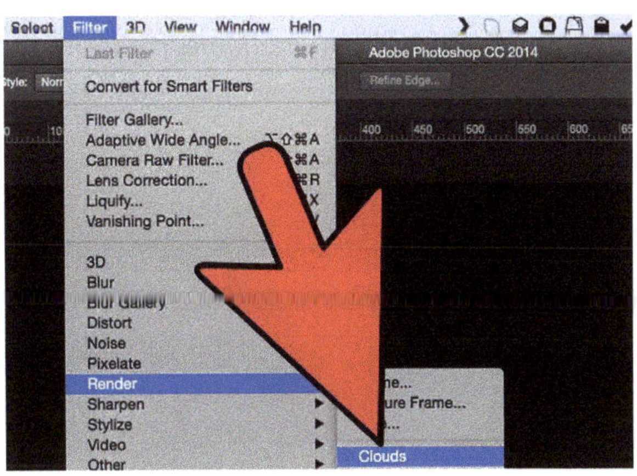

3. Render clouds. From the '"Filters"' on the top toolbar and go down to '"Render"' and select Clouds.

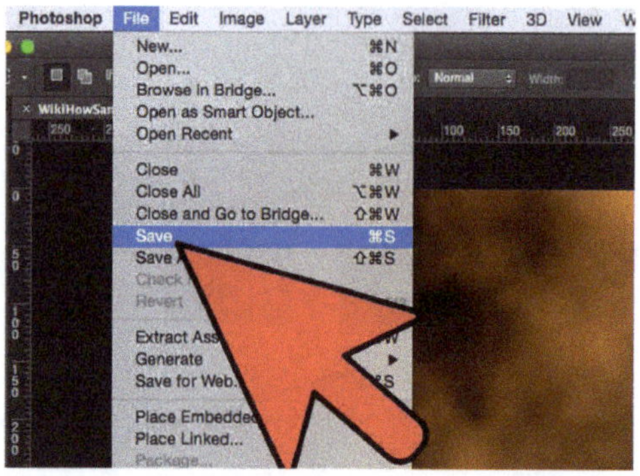

4. Save your fire. This filter will render gaussian clouds with the foreground and background colors. Using different colors can lead to some interesting effects.

- Ready for more? Check out the Advanced method below.

Method 2

Adding Fire to Text

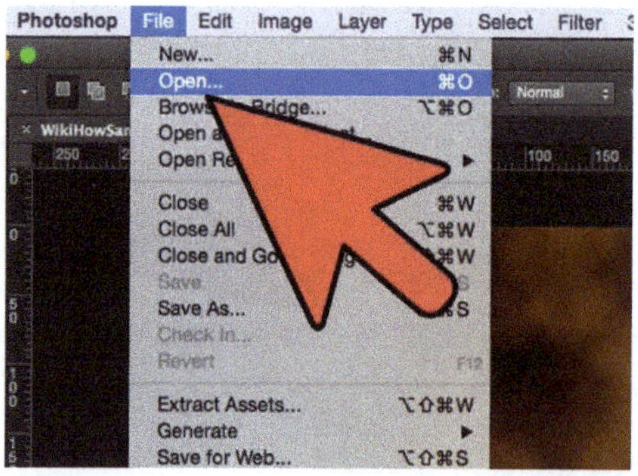

1. Open a document with a text layer, or create a new one. For this example, we used a simple black background with the word "FIRE!" in Arial Black on a second layer. It's important that the text be on a different layer than the background.

- If you're using an existing document, work with a copy of the original.

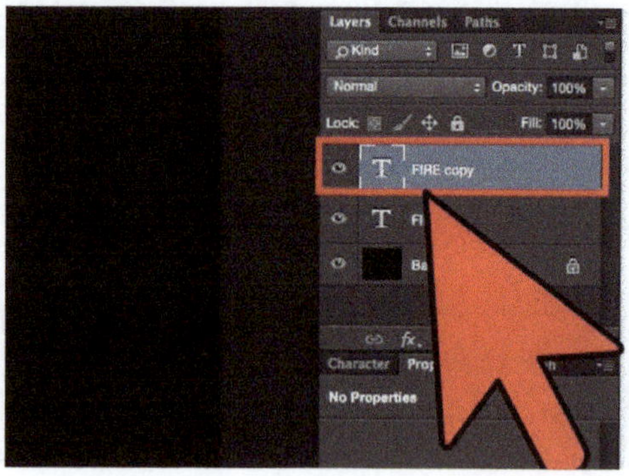

2. Duplicate the text. Drag the original text layer to the New Layer icon at the bottom of the Layers window.

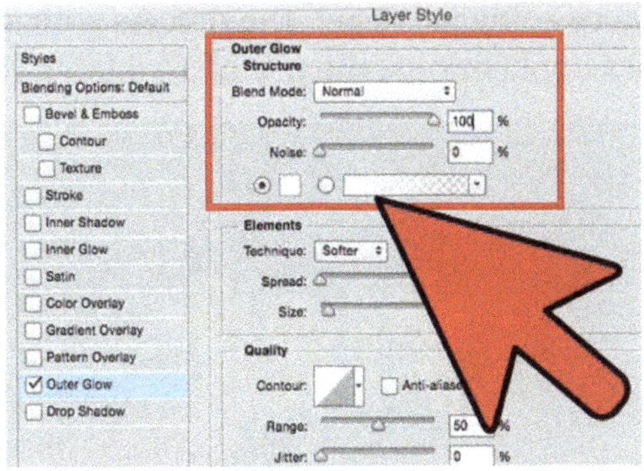

3. Add Outer Glow. Once duplicated, click on the Fx menu at the bottom of the Layers menu, and select Outer Glow. In the resulting Layer Style window, change the glow color from yellow to white, and Opacity to 100%, as shown:

- Click the OK button. Your image should now look like this:

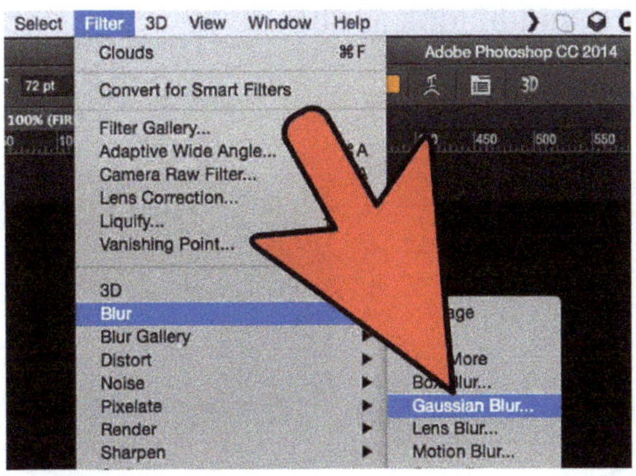

4. Apply Gaussian Blur. From the Filter menu, select Blur > Gaussian Blur... Photoshop will prompt you with a warning that this action will rasterize the type layer, and that you will not be able to edit the actual text if you proceed. OK the warning, and set the blur so that it looks something like this:

- Note that if your text layer is larger or smaller than our example, the actual Radius setting will vary. The example was done using 72pt type.

5. Set up the Smudge tool. Click on the Smudge tool (below the Gradient tool), then click on the brush settings at the top of the window. In the resulting smudge tool adjustment window, use these settings:

- With these settings, you're going to "draw" the fire. As with any kind of brush work in Photoshop or other graphics applications, the use of a tablet is recommended.

6. Create the flames. Using the smudge tool, brush from the letters outward, to give the appearance of flames. Short, quick strokes will give you the best result, and if you're using a brush, vary the thickness by pressure. Your fire should look as shown:

- When done, duplicate the smudged layer.

7. Apply radial blur. From the Filter menu, select Blur > Radial Blur..., and in the resulting window make the following settings:

- While subtle, this will give your fire an additional burst of energy

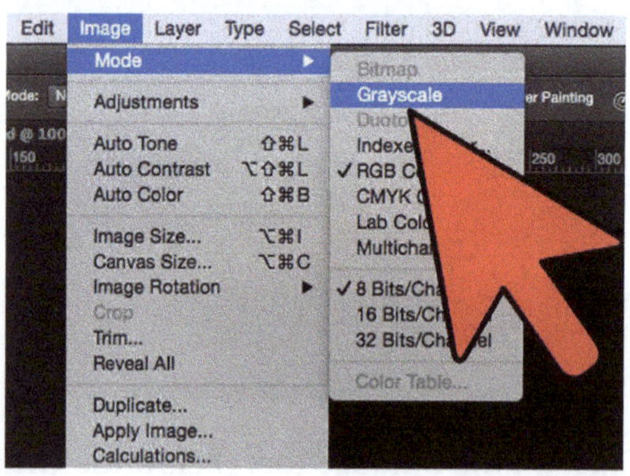

8. Make your image grayscale. From the Image menu, select Grayscale. Once again, Photoshop

will issue a warning that this will flatten the image, and can have an effect on your image. Click the Flatten button to continue.

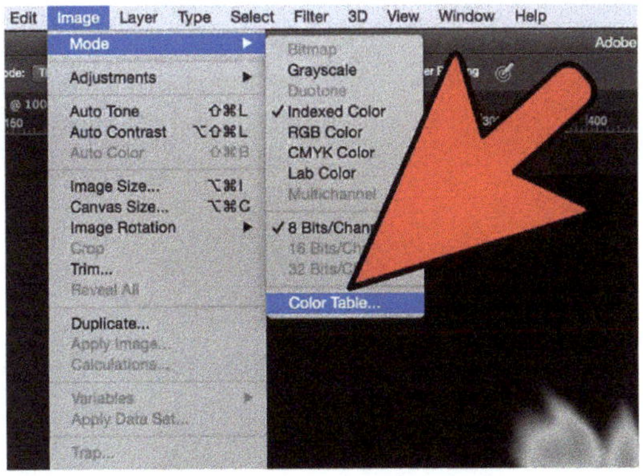

9. Convert to Indexed Color. From the Image menu, select Mode > Indexed Color. Following that, from the same menu, select Color Table.

- From the menu at the top of the Color Table window, select Black Body.

10. Congratulations, you have made fire! Your image should look something like this:

Method 3

Liquid Fire

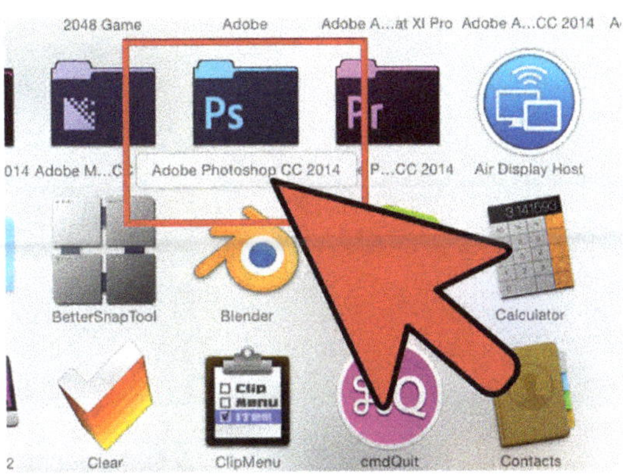

1. Open Adobe Photoshop. Set the foreground color to white, and the background color to black.

A quick way to do this is to press the D key (for Default colors), and the X key (swapping the foreground and background colors).

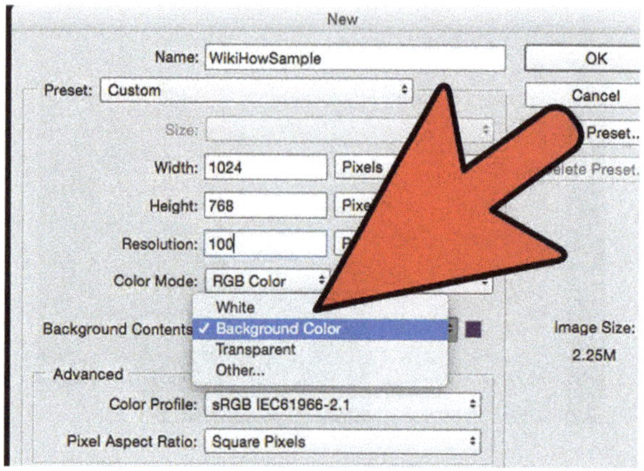

2. Create a new Photoshop image. As with the above method, set the background content to be Background Color.

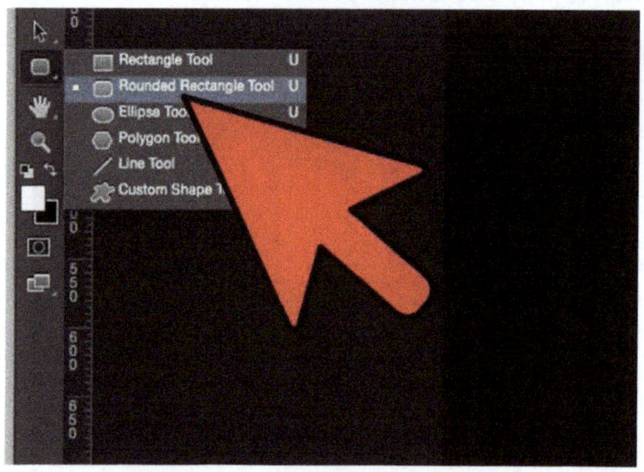

3. Create a Rounded Rectangle by clicking on the shape tool in the task bar on the left hand side. Draw a squarish shape in the middle of the image.

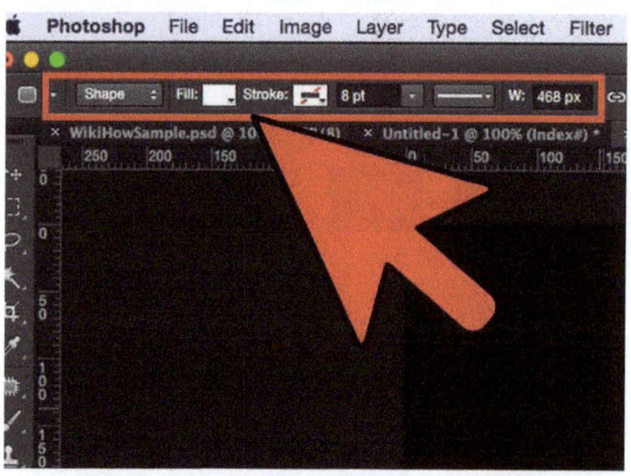

4. Set the attributes of the shape. At the top of the window, select Fill, and choose white. Select the Line attribute, and set it to none, as shown.

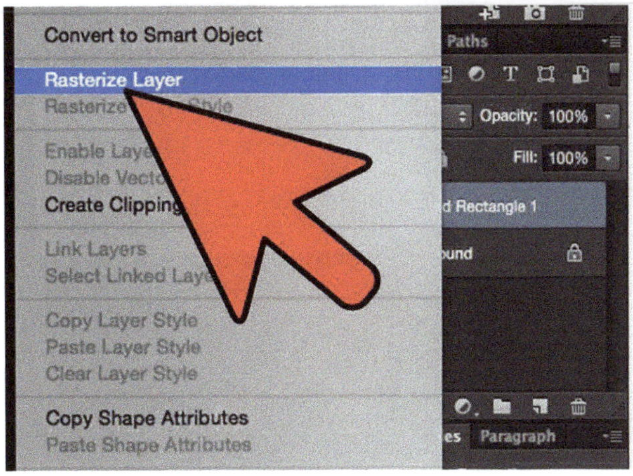

5. Rasterize the layer. Right-click on the name of the new shape layer (Rounded Rectangle 1, by default), and select Rasterize Layer from the contextual menu.

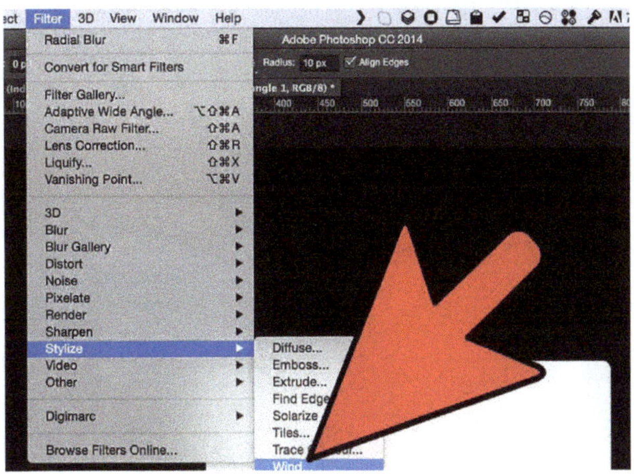

6. Add wind. Ensure the shape layer is still selected. From the Filter menu, select Stylize, and then then Wind.

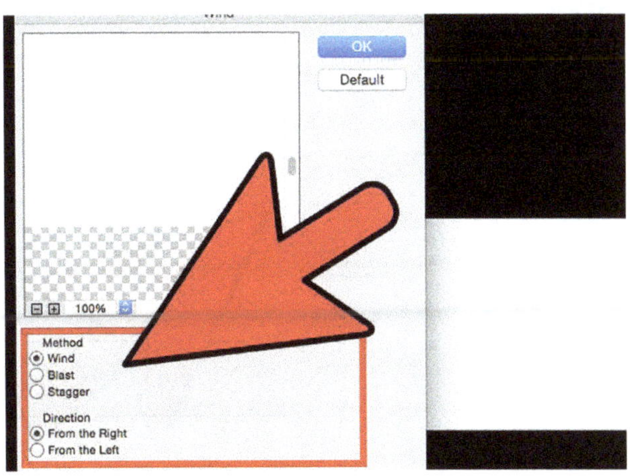

7. Adjust the Wind settings. Choose the following settings in the Wind window: Wind and From the Right, then click OK.

8. Press Command + F (PC: Ctrl + F twice. This adds to the Wind effect. Your rectangle should look something like this:

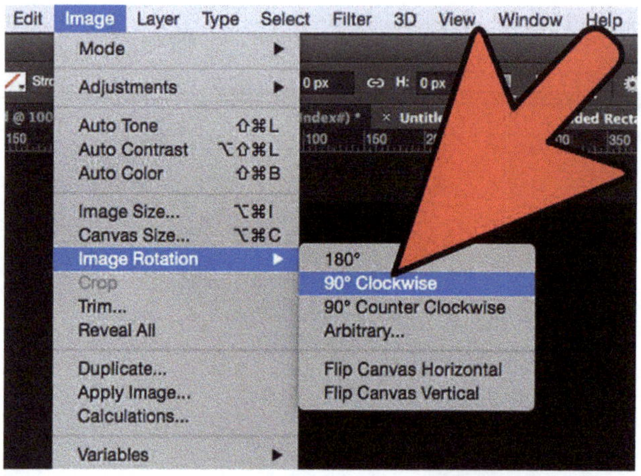

9. Rotate the image. Click on the Image menu, then Image Rotation, then 90° CW.

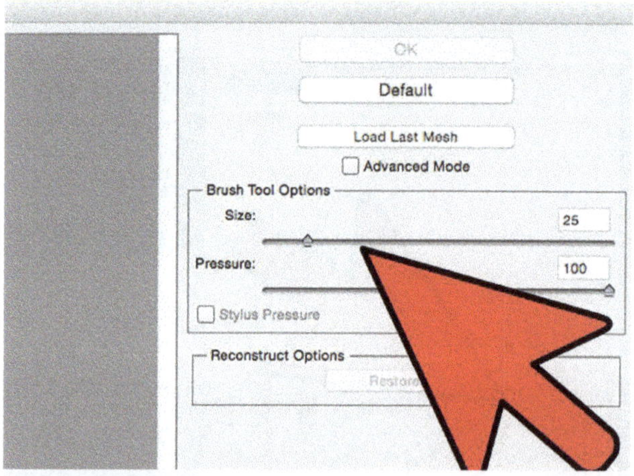

10. From the Filter menu, select Liquify. A window will open. Set the brush size to about 25, initially, then click and drag on the lines made by the wind to distort them into what a flame may look like. Vary the brush size for a more realistic flame look. Once you have done this, click OK.

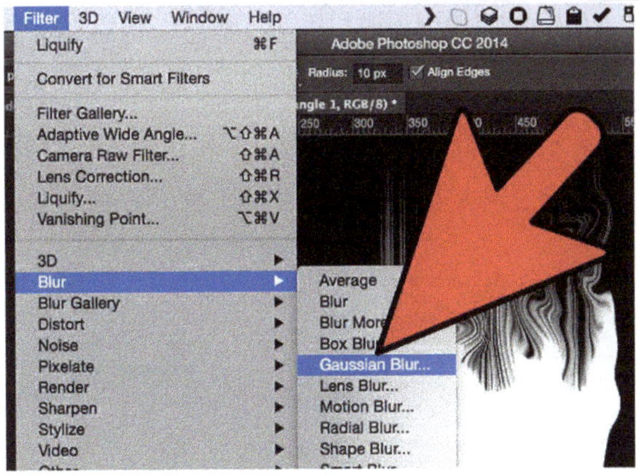

11. Blur the image. Click on Filter, then Blur, then Gaussian Blur, and set the radius to 1 pixel.

- Duplicate the layer twice. You can do this either by dragging the first layer onto the New Layer icon at the bottom of the Layers window, or by pressing Command + J (PC: Ctrl + J) twice.
- Make the top 2 layers invisible by clicking on the eye next to them.

12. Click on the original (bottom) rectangle layer. From the Adjustments window, select the Hue/ Saturation icon.

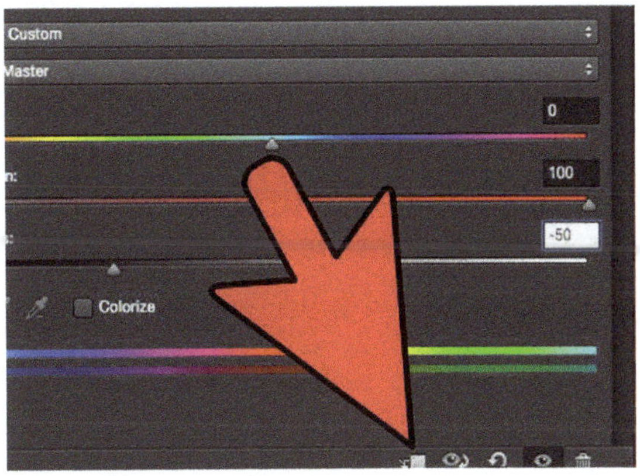

13. Make the Hue/Saturation layer a clipping layer. Click on the clipping layer icon at the bottom

of the Adjustments window. This will limit the effects of the Hue/Saturation layer to only the layer directly below it.

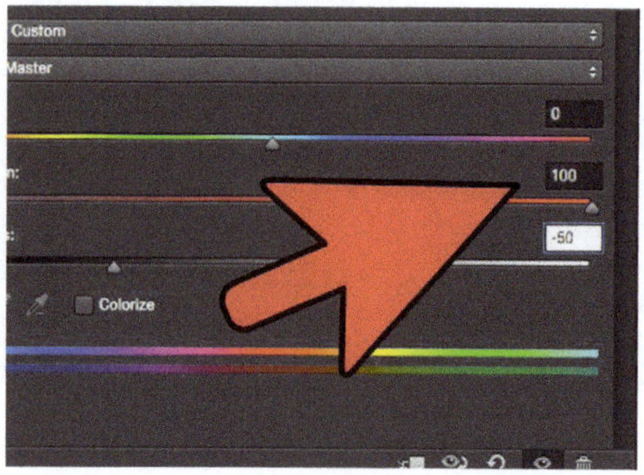

14. Set the Hue/Saturation levels as shown in the above image. Be sure to enable the Colorize checkbox first. Hue is set to 0, Saturation to 100, and Lightness to -50, giving you a rich red color. It should look like this:

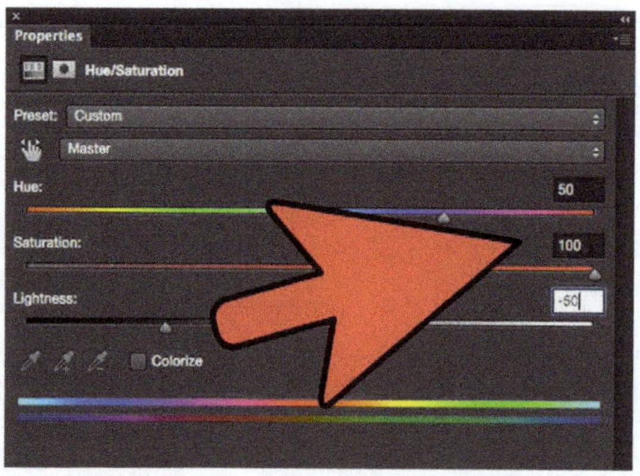

15. Turn the top layer back on. Add another Hue/Saturation adjustment layer as before, and set the clipping as you did with the bottom layer. Change the properties of the top adjustment layer to Hue: 50, Saturation: 100, Lightness: -50. This will make it a yellow color.

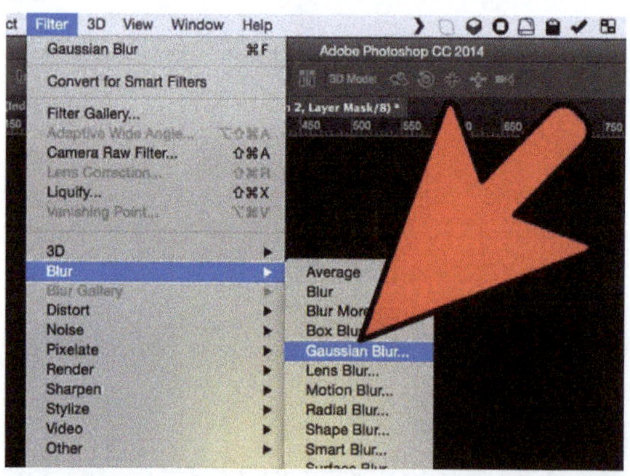

16. Select the remaining white shape (middle layer). Click on Filter, then Blur, then Gaussian Blur. Set the radius to 7 pixels. Your image should look something like this, at this point:

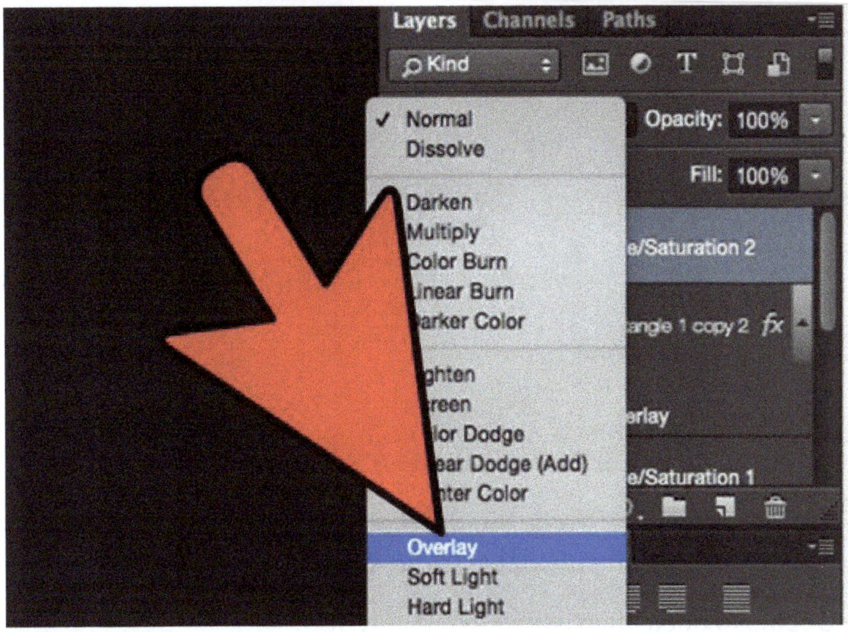

17. Change the overlay method. Select the top Layer and change the layer type by clicking in the drop-down menu that usually reads Normal and select Overlay.

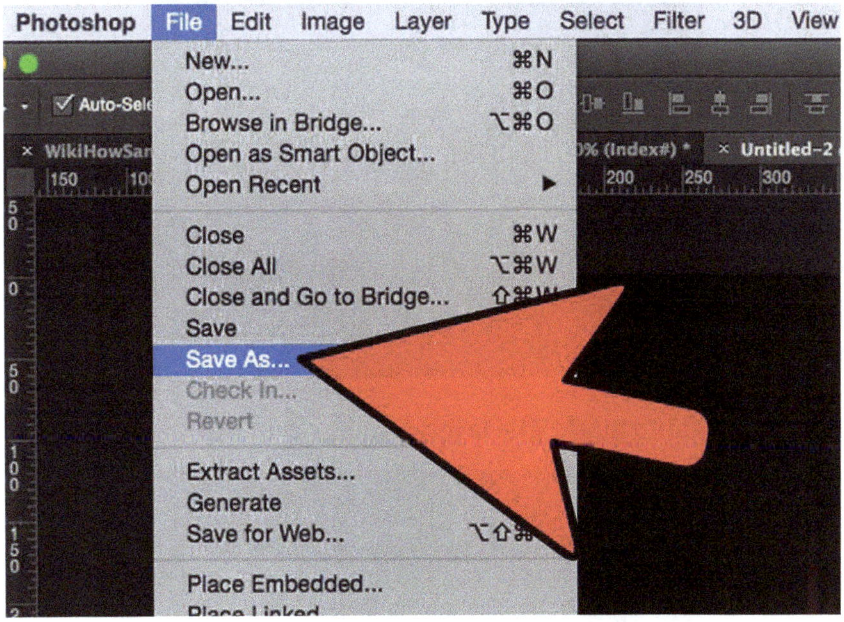

18. Congratulate yourself! The work is done, and your masterpiece is completed.

How to add a Layer Mask in Photoshop

This teaches you how to create a layer mask, which can be used to conceal or reveal parts of other layers in Adobe Photoshop.

Steps

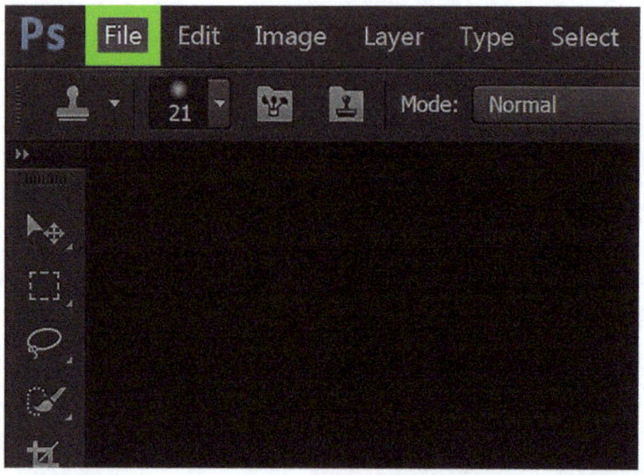

1. Open or create a Photoshop file. To do so, double-click on the blue app icon that contains the letters "Ps," then click on File in the menu bar at the top of the screen, and:

- Click on Open... to open an existing document; or
- Click on New... to create a new document.

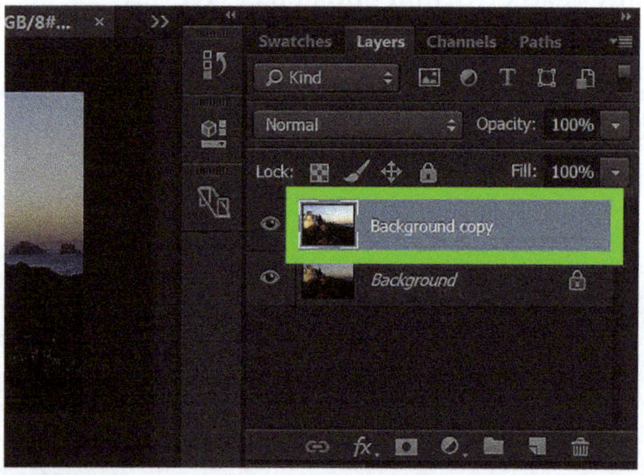

2. Click on the layer you want to mask. The layers window is in the lower-right part of the app.

3. Select the area you wish to remain visible. To do so, use:

- A Marquee Tool to select a larger area that doesn't require fine edges. (The Marquee Tool is the dotted-line icon near the top of the Tool Menu. Long-click on the Marquee Tool to reveal all of the Marquee Tools in a drop-down menu); or
- A Pen Tool to outline the edges of a finer shape, like individual flower petals. (The Pen Tool is the fountain-pen nib icon above the T in the Tool Menu. Long-click on the Pen Tool to reveal all of the Pen Tools in a drop-down menu).

4. Click on the "Add Layer Mask" icon. It's a light gray rectangle that contains a dark gray circle at the bottom of the "Layers" window.

- If you used a Pen Tool to draw the selection, click on the icon one more time, after the label changes to "Add Vector Mask."

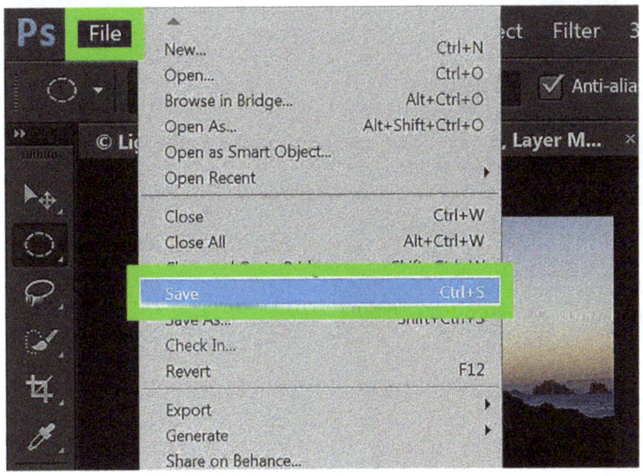

5. Save your changes. To do so, click on File in the menu bar, then Save in the drop-down.

How to create a Silhouette in Photoshop

It doesn't matter what your intended use is, a well-made silhouette can fill that empty space and spice up an image. There are multiple ways to make them, and learning how to make silhouettes is a great way to get used to Photoshop and some basic skills.

Method 1

Creating a Quick Silhouette

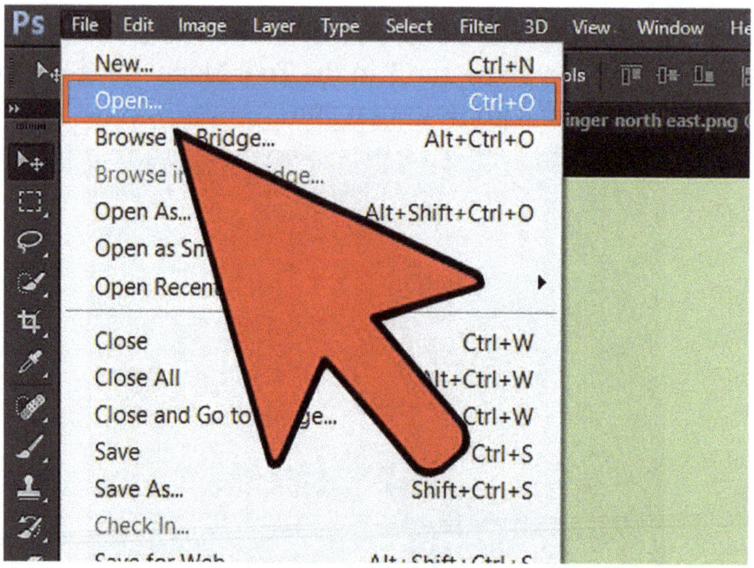

1. Open up an image with simple, easily differentiated background. This method is perfect for simple, easy images where the subject is clearly separated from the background. If the object you're silhouetting is a very different color, has some distance, or is just easy to separate, this method will work perfectly.

- If, after opening the image, you see that there is a padlock on the layer, simply double-click on the layer and hit "Enter" to unlock the layer.

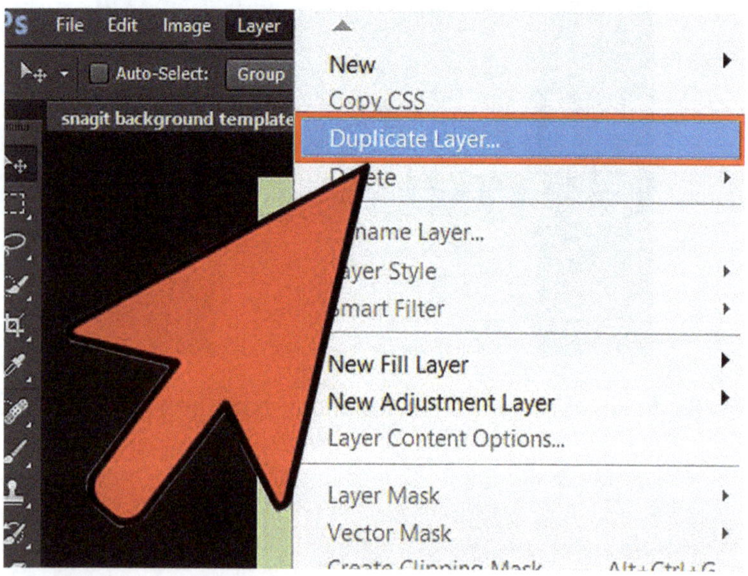

2. Duplicate the layer to ensure you don't ruin your original image. To do so, simply right-click on the layer and select "Duplicate." You can also click on "Layer" → "Duplicate Layer" from the top bar, or press ⌘ Cmd+J or Ctrl+J.

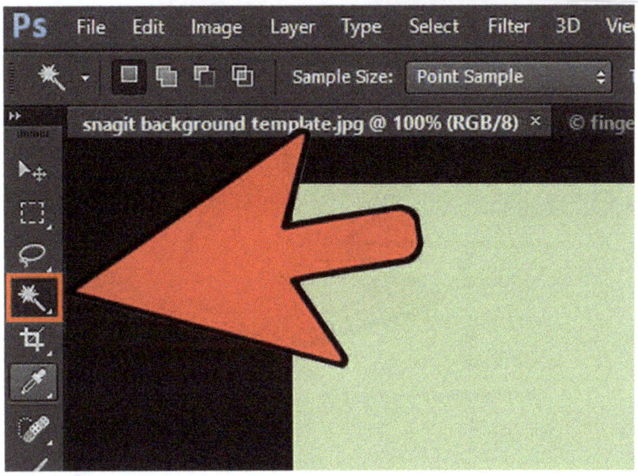

3. Use the Quick Selection (w) tool to rapidly select the object you're making a silhouette. For more precise work you'll need to refine this selection, but for a basic silhouette you should be able to quickly click and drag Quick Selection Tool over the image to select the object. If you can't find the Quick Selection tool, it should be the fourth button down from the toolbar, and you may have to click and hold on the "Magic Wand" to reveal it. For even more control:

- Hold either Alt or ⌥ Opt while clicking to remove parts of your selection.
- Use the two [and] keys to make your selection tool bigger or smaller, making it less or more precise.
- Switch to the Magic Want to quickly select all pixels of similar colors. Ctrl-Click to add selection, alt-click to subtract it.

4. Pull up the "Hue and Saturation" adjustments for your selection. With your selection still on, click on "Image" → "Adjustments" → "Hue and Saturation." You can also get to this menu by:

- Selection "Hue and Saturation" from the Adjustment's panel, usually right above your layers panel.
- Pressing either ⌘ Cmd+U or Ctrl+U.

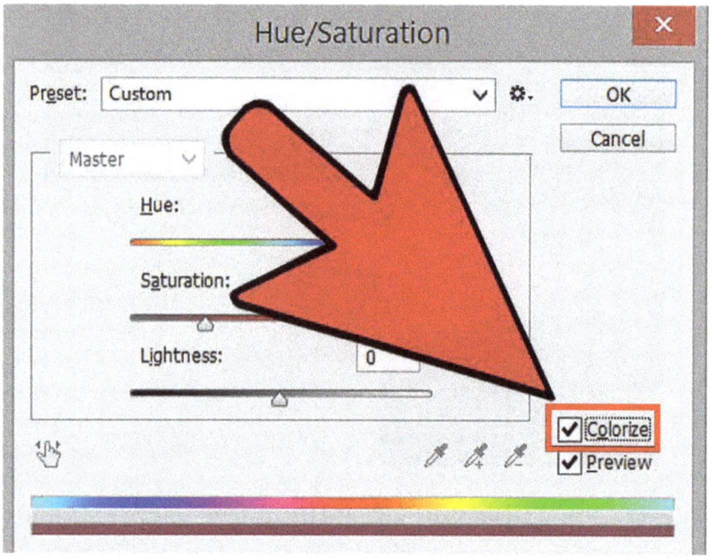

5. Check the "colorize" box in Hue/Saturation then pull all three sliders straight to the left. Take the Hue and Saturation sliders to "0," and the lightness to "-100." The hit "OK." Your image should be silhouetted, or, at least, much darker. If the silhouette is too light the first time, just open the Hue/Saturation options again and do it once more. You can keep lowering lightness until you have your silhouette.

Method 2

Making Vector Silhouettes

1. Use vector silhouettes if you want to adjust, grow, shrink or export your silhouettes without losing quality. Vectors can be easily rescaled without losing image quality. If you're using the silhouette professionally, or just want a more versatile final image, this is the way to go.

- Adobe Illustrator (AI) uses vectors almost exclusively. If using AI, skip the quick route and use this method.

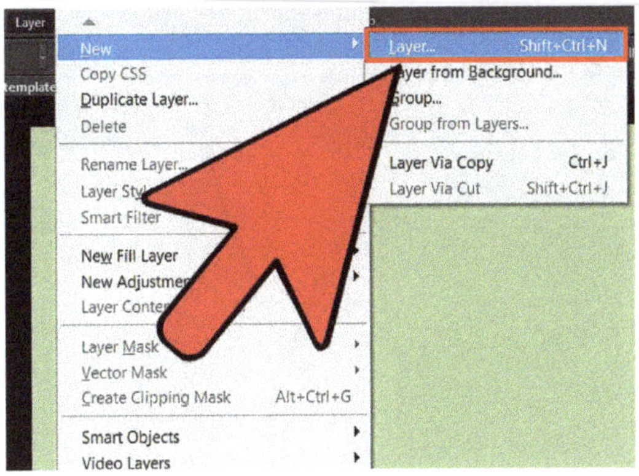

2. Create a new layer above your original image. If you've duplicated the layer already to ensure that you don't ruin the original image, you should be fine. Just make sure you have a second layer to work with above your original image. To create a new layer, press ⌘ Cmd+⇧ Shift+N or Ctrl+⇧ Shift+N

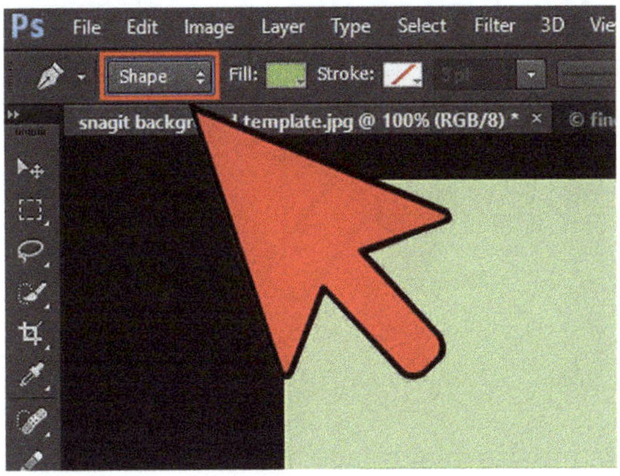

3. Select the image you want silhouetted with the Pen Tool. Choose the Pen Tool (P) from the toolbar. In the menu that appears at the top of Photoshop, find the small drop-down menu that says "Path." It should be to the top right of the screen, but only when the Pen Tool is on. Change this menu to say "Shape."

4. Use the Pen Tool to trace out your entire silhouette. Taking your time, trace out the shape of your silhouette. To make things easier to see, lower the opacity of the new layer you're working on by changing "Opacity" from the top of the layers panel.

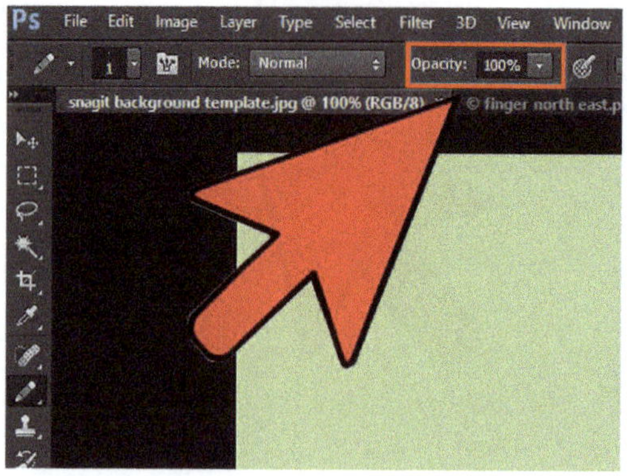

5. Connect the dots back to finish your silhouette. Once you return to the starting point your dots should disappear and the shape will form in front of you. Raise the opacity back up to 100% to see your silhouette.

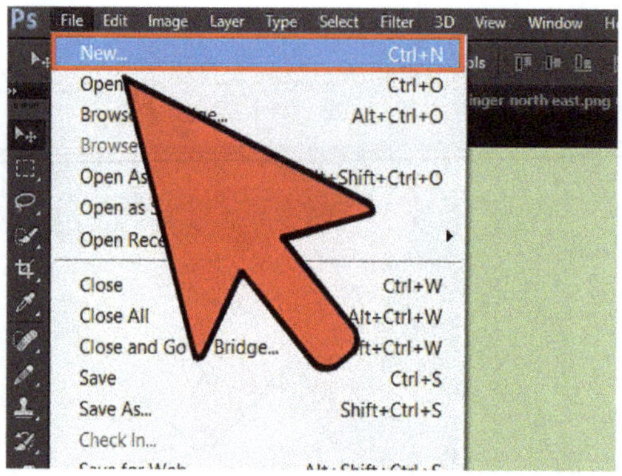

6. Click and drag the silhouette into its own image, to Illustrator, or leave it to finish your silhouette. Once this shape is made, you can do anything with it that you might normally. If you want to isolate it so your image is only the silhouette, either delete the layers below it or click and drag the image to a new Photoshop document.

Method 3

Separating your Image from the Background

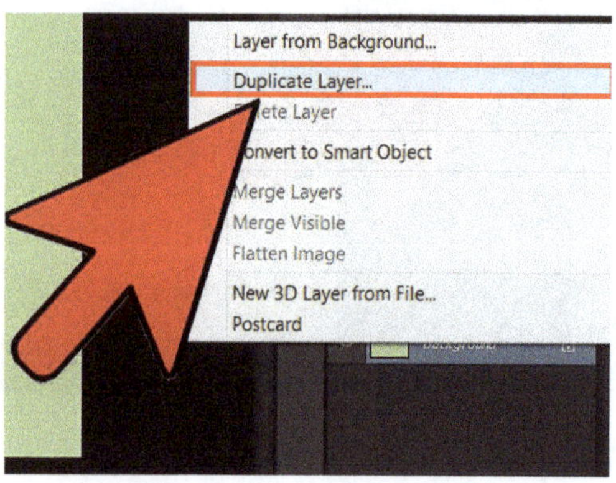

1. Duplicate your original image layer to get a spare copy for your silhouette. To make a professional

quality silhouette, you'll need to take a little time to effectively select the object you're silhouetting. Since some of these techniques require deleting or altering the original image, it is best to just duplicate the layer now and leave the original with it's little padlock, preventing you from ruining it.

- To duplicate a layer, simply right-click it in the layers panel, then select "Duplicate Layer."

2. Use the Pen Tool (P) for the most exact, perfect outlines to make silhouettes from. The Pen tool is, in many ways, Photoshop's most powerful too, though it takes getting used to. Select it from the menu, or press P, then click to create little points around your outline. When you complete the entire selection, you'll have a "Path," or solid line around your entire image. When done, simply right-click on the path and choose "Make Selection."

- If you're working with a very curvy shape, try the "Free Form Pen Tool," found by clicking and holding the Pen Tool in the toolbox.
- The pen tool is perfectly precise, but only if you know how to handle it. Take some time to experiment with it, especially with curves. It will trace the best shape for you, with practice.

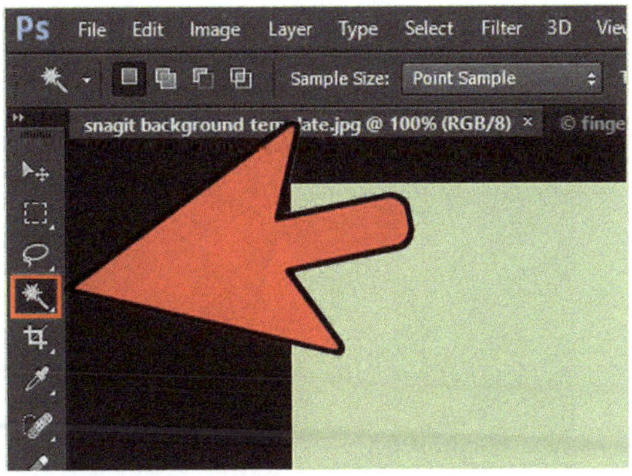

3. Use the Magic Wand (W) tool to separate a simple 1-2 color background. For example, say you've got a woman standing against a mostly blue sky, and you want to silhouette her. Instead of selecting her, you can select the sky behind her, removing it from the layer. Simply use the Magic Wand to select the background, the delete it away to leave just the silhouetted object.

- Change the tolerance at the top bar to make the Wand more or less precise. A higher number

(75-100) selected a wider range of colors while a low tolerance (like 1-10) will only select very similarly colored pixels.

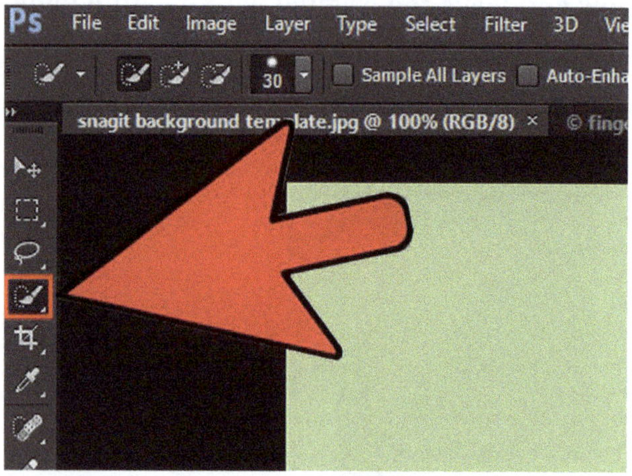

4. Use the remaining selection tools to trace out simple objects. The most intuitive tools for creating selections, these generally require a steady hand and some patience, though they are easy to use. For all of them, simply click and drag around the object with your tool to create a selection. You can add more to a selection by holding Ctrl/Cmd when you click, or subtract from a selection by holding Alt/Opt.

- Quick Selection: Looks like a paintbrush with a circular dotted line around the brush. This object selects everything roughly the same color or clarity, following the edges of shapes.
- Lasso Tools: You have a lot of options here, each of which requires you click the mouse, then manually trace out the object. Clicking again creates an anchor point while completing the circle or shape ends the section.
- Shaped Selections: Looks like a dotted square, but you can click and hold it for more shapes. This simply allows you to easy create geometric shaped selection. When used with Ctrl/Cmd or Alt/Opt, a good way to add or subtract little bits from the selection to refine it.

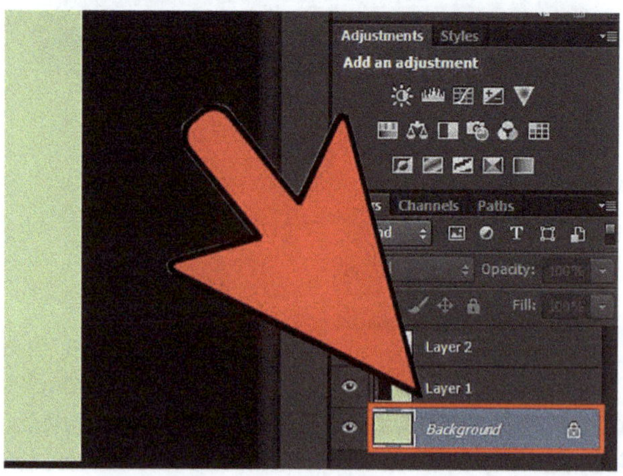

5. Ctrl-Click on a layer from the layers menu to automatically select it. If you have an isolated object you want to silhouette, and it's already in its own dedicated layer, Photoshop will trace it for

you. Simple hold the Ctrl or ⌘ Cmd key and click the little picture of the layer -- your selection edge will appear automatically.

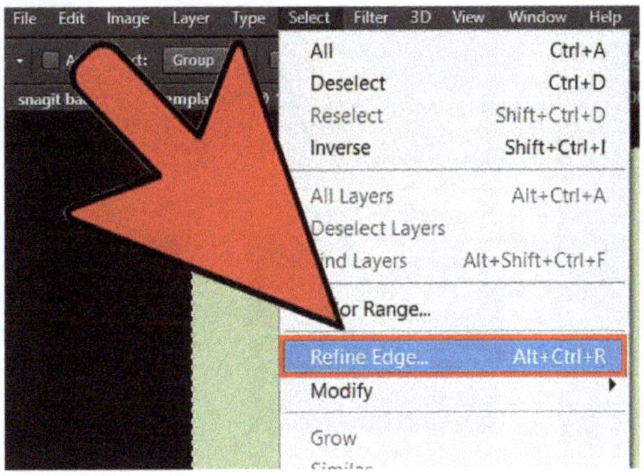

6. Use “Refine Edge” to get the perfect selection. This menu is a powerful tool to make subtle changes to your selection. Open it up through “Selection” → “Refine Edge.” From there, you have a variety of options:

- Radius: Allows you to shrink the edge of the selection.
- Smooth: Rounds and smooths out points and corners.
- Feather: Blurs the edges of everything.
- Contrast: Makes the selection more pointed and sharp -- the inverse of “smoothing.”
- Shift Edge: Grows or shrinks the selection by percentage.

How to create a Magazine Cover in Photoshop

It only takes a few steps to create your own magazine image in Adobe Photoshop. This is very simple to do, but this article assumes you already have a fair amount of knowledge using Photoshop.

Steps

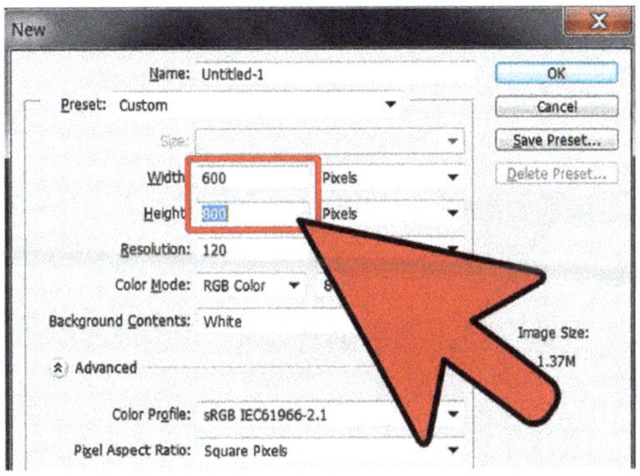

1. Create a new document that is twice the width and about 50% higher than your cover image. Give the new image a gradient for the background. Any colors will do for now.

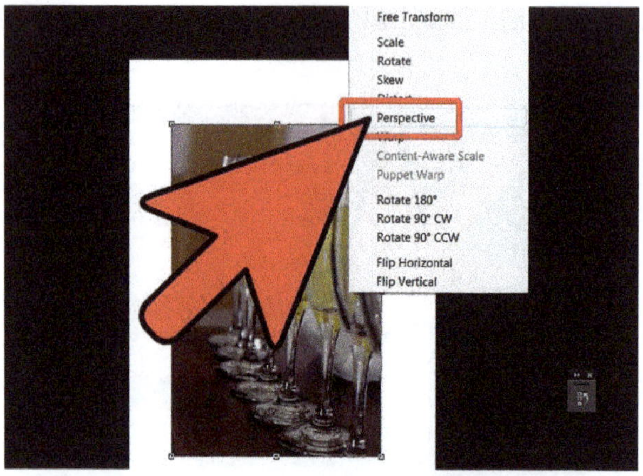

2. Paste in your cover image, name the layer "Cover". Click on Edit>>Transform>>Perspective. Drag the top left handle down just a bit to add the correct perspective to the cover image. It should look something like this:

3. Copy the cover layer by dragging the layer down to the new layer button in the layers palette. Now move this layer behind the cover layer and name it "Back".

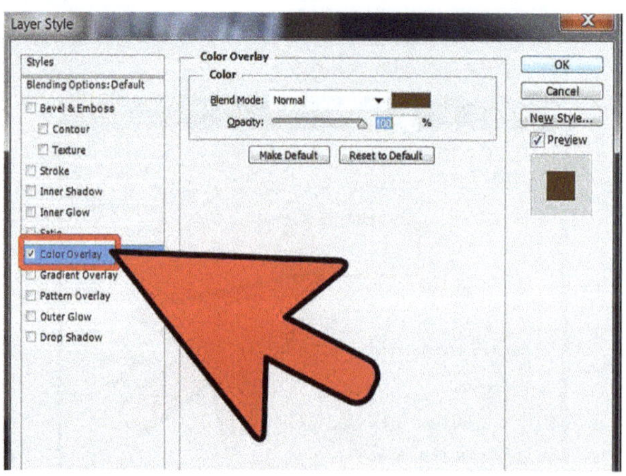

4. Double click the back layer so that the layers style window comes up. Apply a color overlay, using a color that is similar to the cover, but darker.

5. Click on Edit>>Transform>>Perspective. This time drag down the upper right handle. Just a little bit. Your image should now look something like this:

6. Duplicate the back layer by dragging the layer to the new layer button at the bottom of the layers palette. Name this layer "Pages". This layer should be between the cover layer and the back layer.

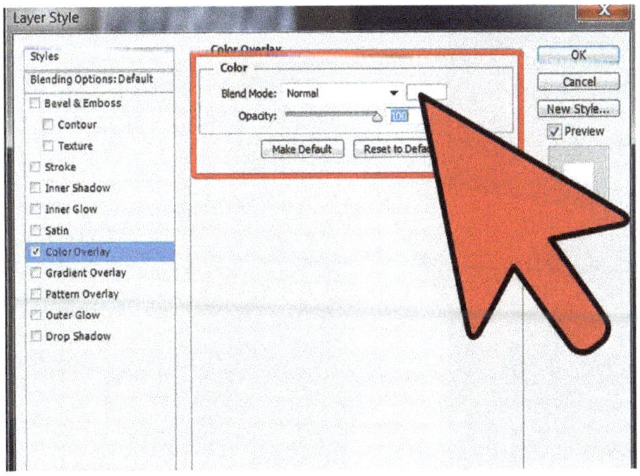

7. Double click the pages layer and apply a white color overlay. Also apply a stroke style. Use black for the color, and 1px for the size. Take the opacity down to about 70%. Click OK.

8. Move this layer down just a bit using the move tool (V). Your image should look something like this:

9. Duplicate the page layer. Observe that magazines have more than one page. Move this layer back just a little bit. Duplicate the layer again, and again move it back just a little.

10. Draw a marquee around the corners that are poking out, using the lasso tool, and delete the extra bits. Your image should look something like this:

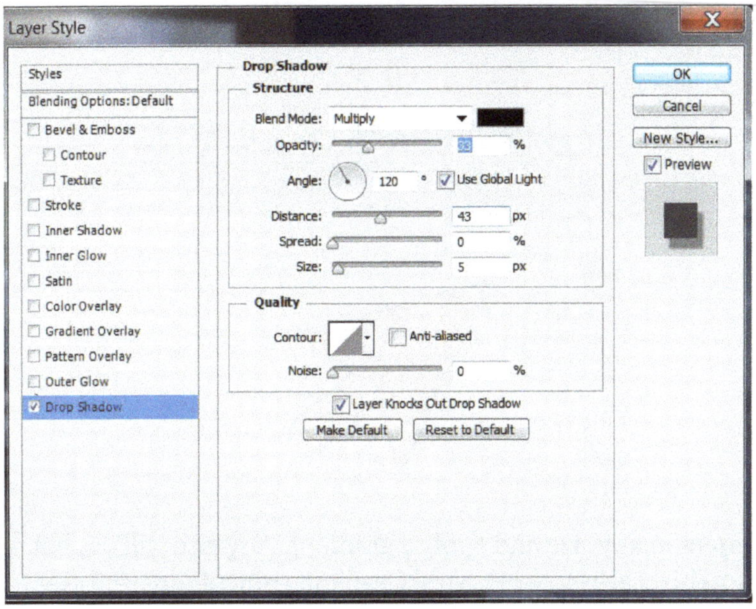

11. Change the background to something you like better, like pure white. You can also add a drop shadow or similar effect. You can crop the image to a more tight size. Use light and dark gradients to add light reflections.

How to create Clouds in Photoshop

Clouds are a prominent aerial feature, both under the daylight sun and in the silvered light of the moon. Adding clouds to your Photoshop illustration can add depth, a sense of majesty, and can even influence the ambiance of a scene. Even if you don't have a steady hand when it comes to drawing these atmospheric puffs, Photoshop tools can help you accomplish this goal in no time.

Method 1

Rendering Clouds with Photoshop

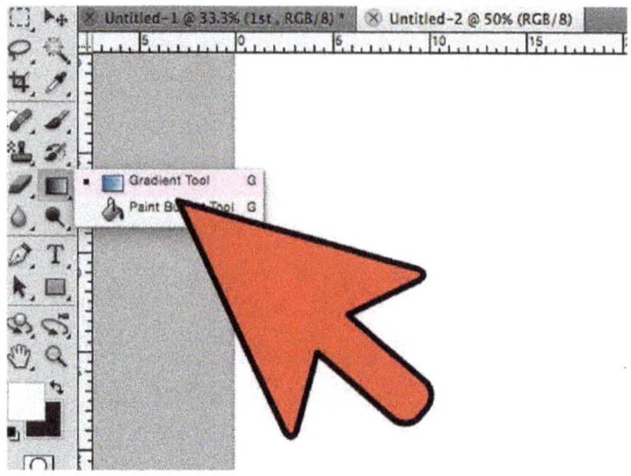

1. Create a new document in any size and apply a gradient. Any size will do, but you likely won't need more than a 1500x1500 pixel area to work with. Gradient controls are represented by an icon shaped like a box with color fading from black to white. Click this and apply a gradient of your choosing.

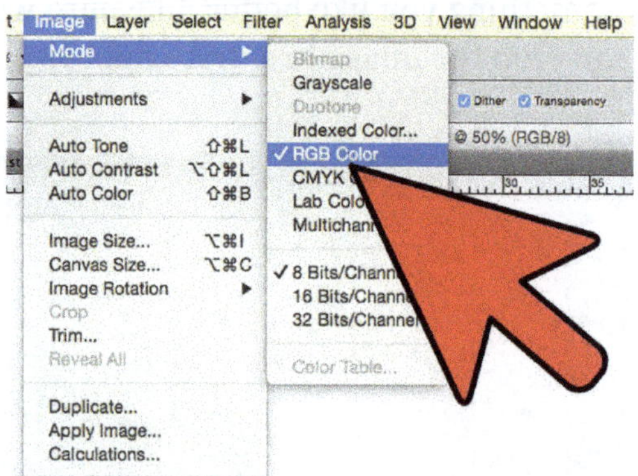

2. Set your resolution and the color mode to RGB. Resolution is a matter of preference, but a closer view will allow for greater precision. To change your color mode to RGB, click on "Image" from your menu bar, and "Modes" from the submenu. Here you should be able to choose your desired color mode.

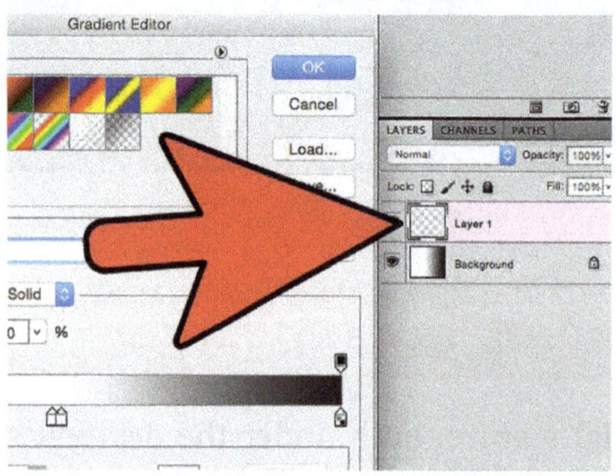

3. Create a new layer. Apply a gradient to your new layer by using your gradient tool again. This time, use the gradient editor and select two variations of blue such as midnight blue and royal blue or dark blue and sky blue to be applied to your new layer.

- New layers can be created or adjusted through the Layers Panel, accessible from the sub-menu under the "Windows" heading on your main menu bar, or through the hotkeys Ctrl+⇧ Shift+N.
- Take care to keep the topmost part of your layer the part with the darker blue.

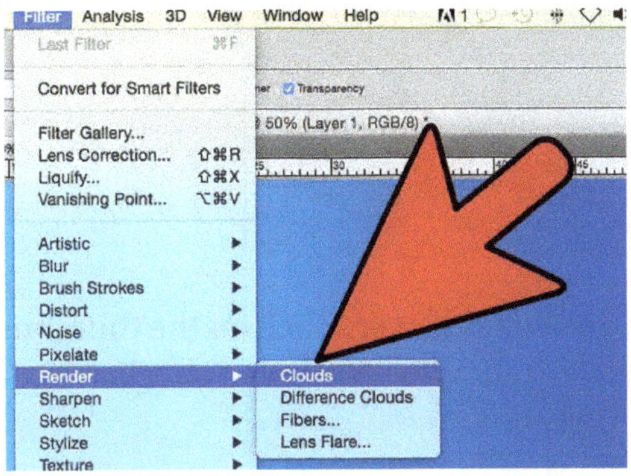

4. Render your clouds. Now that you've got your colors and layers ready, you can have Photoshop render clouds. From the main menu bar, click through: Filter → Render → Clouds. This will create your clouds.

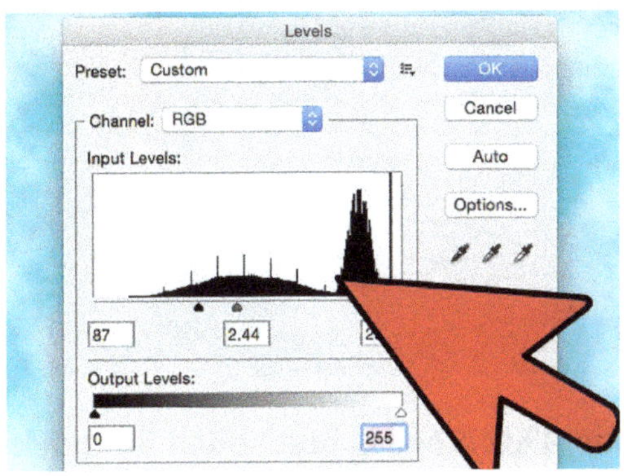

5. Adjust the cloud levels. Type in the shortcut Ctrl+L to make the Levels dialog box to appear. Here you should change the levels of the clouds by adjusting each of the three of the arrows evenly through the middle of the distribution.

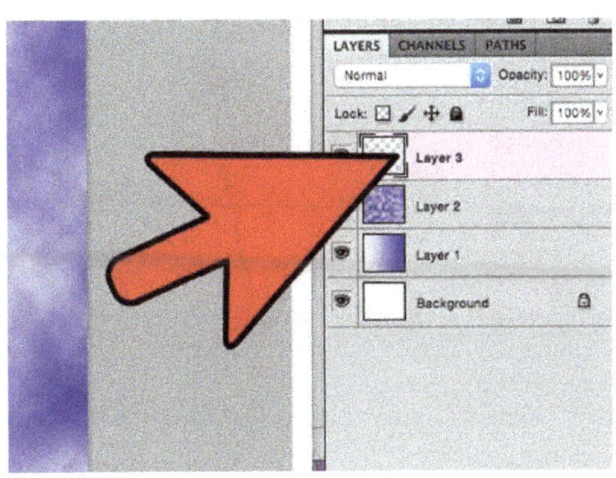

6. Create another new layer. This will be the landing zone for the component parts of your cloud layer. Once you have your blank layer taken care of, return to your cloud layer.

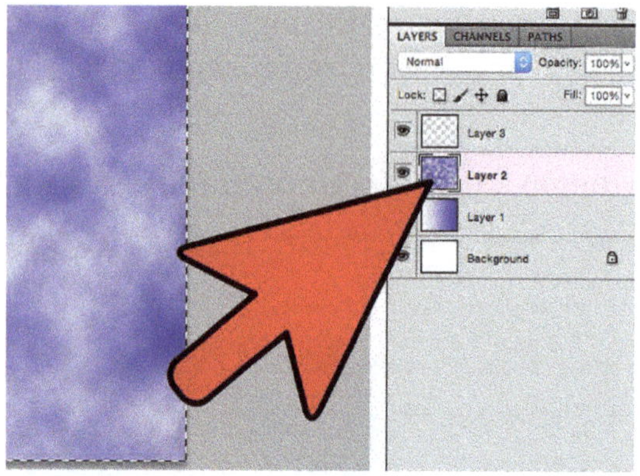

7. Select all the components of your cloud layer. Click on the thumbnail of your cloud layer to select all its parts, or you can use the shortcut Ctrl+A. Then right click and select "copy" to add it to your clipboard, or use the shortcut Ctrl+C.

- Mac users can select all by pressing ⌘ Cmd+A and can quickly copy by pressing ⌘ Cmd+C.

8. Enable the Quick Mask Mode. This mode is best suited for quick editing, and is used to add or subtract from your image to make a "mask," like a digital stencil. Click on the new layer and then type Q on your keyboard to open Quick Mask Mode.

9. Paste the components in your new layer. Speed this process by pressing Ctrl+V to paste in Windows or ⌘ Cmd+V to paste on Mac. After you have added the components of your cloud layer, you can turn off Quick Mask Mode by clicking the layer thumbnail and again pressing Q.

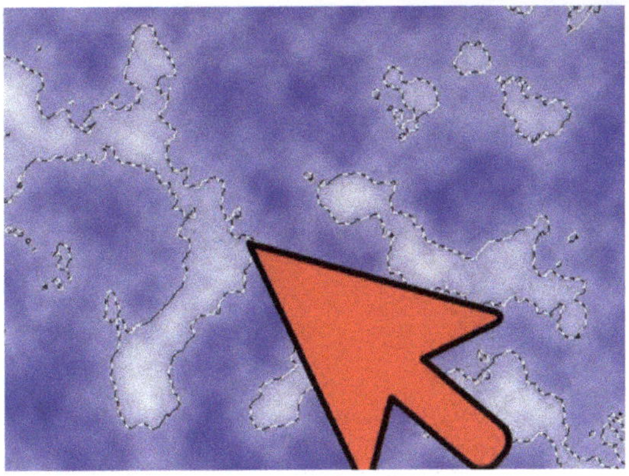

10. Fill in lines created in Quick Mask Mode. Quick Mask Mode acts similarly to a stencil, allowing you to add or subtract to unprotected areas of your image. Now that you've closed Quick Mask Mode, running lines will appear (sometimes referred to as marching ants). Fill these areas with white, or you can use the keyboard shortcut Ctrl+☐ Backspace to automatically fill the selected areas.

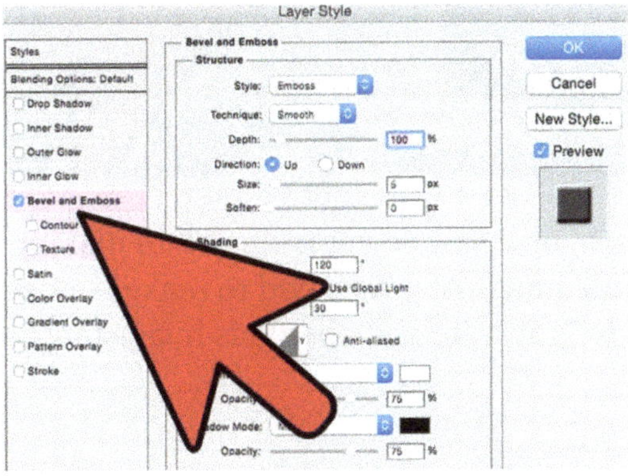

11. Add an emboss effect. This can be applied as a filter to the layer by going to your blending options. On the main menu bar, select the "Filter" option, under which you should find "Emboss." Alter settings with regard to the accompanied illustration for the emboss effect, or you can play with the settings until you find an effect you like.

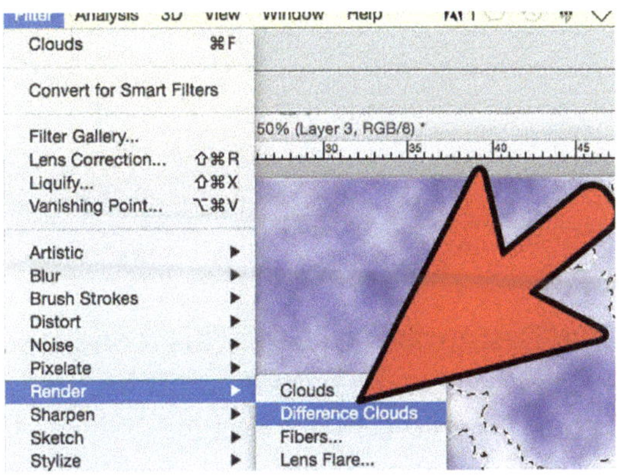

12. Use other filters. One you might want to consider is called "Difference Clouds," which can add a more realistic touch to your clouds. Copy the cloud layer by clicking or pressing Ctrl+J. Apply the

Difference Clouds Filter moving through the "Filter" heading on the main menu bar, to "Render", where you should find "Difference Clouds." Apply the Filter twice using these commands, or simply press Ctrl+F to apply your most recently used filter again.

Method 2

Making a Custom Cloud Brush

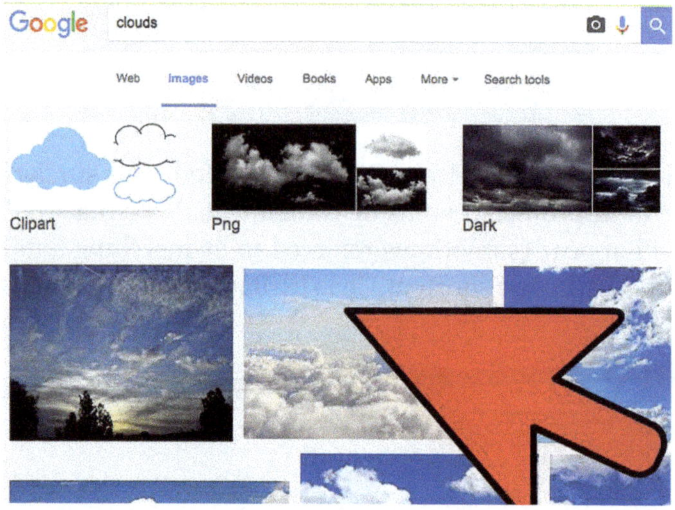

1. Find a clear picture of clouds, or take one yourself. When making your custom brush, you will need to derive a black and white image of your cloud to make your custom brush, so try to find an image that will translate well to grayscale and open this image in Photoshop.

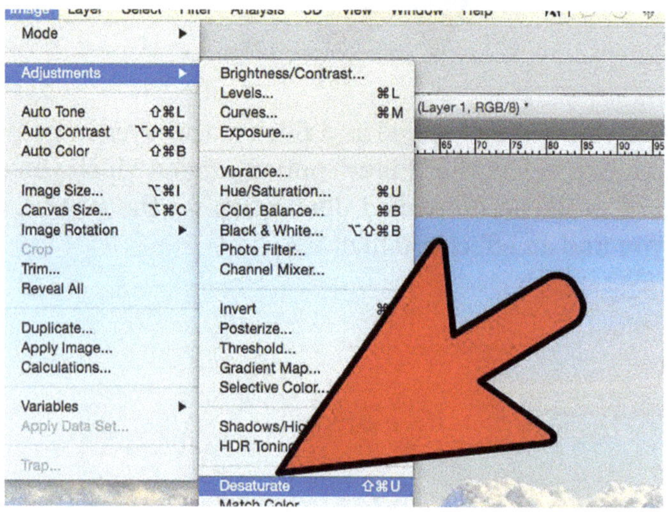

2. Turn black and white with the "Desaturate" feature. This is one of several ways to quickly change your image from color to grayscale, and can be found under the "Image" heading on the menu bar. Under "Image," select "Desaturate" to convert your image.

- Windows users can make use of the hotkeys: Ctrl+⇧ Shift+U
- Mac users can utilize the hotkeys: ⌘ Cmd+⇧ Shift+U

3. Select your brush sample. Using the selection tool, chose a sample from your cloud image that you would like your brush to imitate. Be sure to limit your brush size to a maximum of 2500x2500 pixels, as this is the largest brush size.

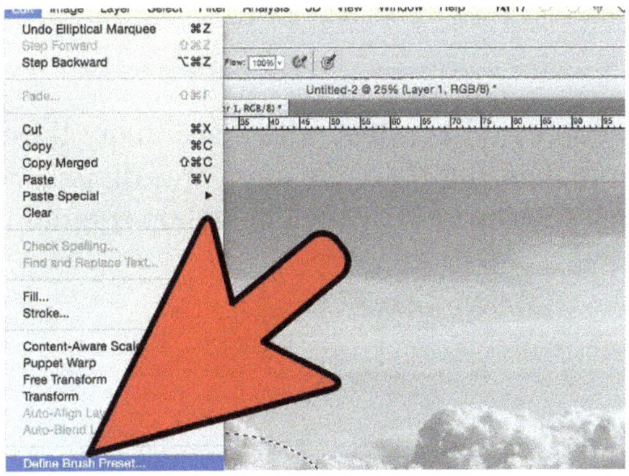

4. Set your brush. Now that you have your brush sample in black and white and selected, click on "Edit" from the top menu bar and then choose "Define Brush Preset." This will prompt a dialogue box asking you to name your new brush.

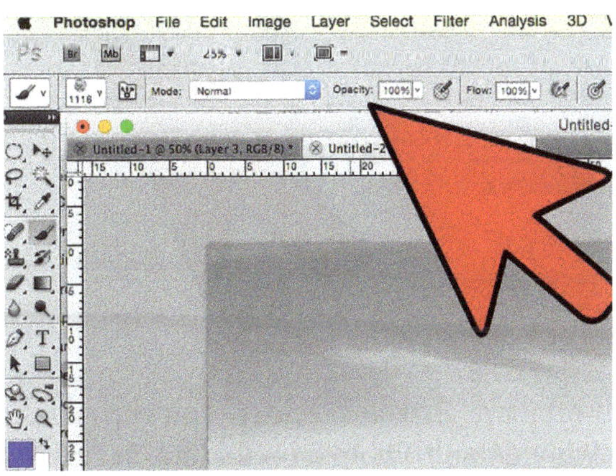

5. Adjust settings as necessary. You can quickly open Brush Settings by pressing the F5 key. Opacity and size can be adjusted in brush settings, and these can give the illusion of variety to even repetitive brush patterns.

Method 3

Using a Pre-made Cloud Brush

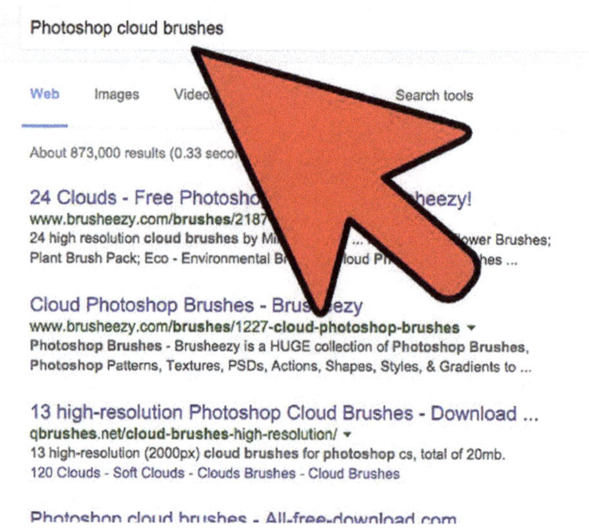

1. Search online for Photoshop cloud brushes. There are many third party developed brushes, some of which may cost you money, but there are many free digital brushes available through artistic communities. Some free sites favored by the Photoshop community are:

- DeviantArt
- BrushKing
- Brusheezy

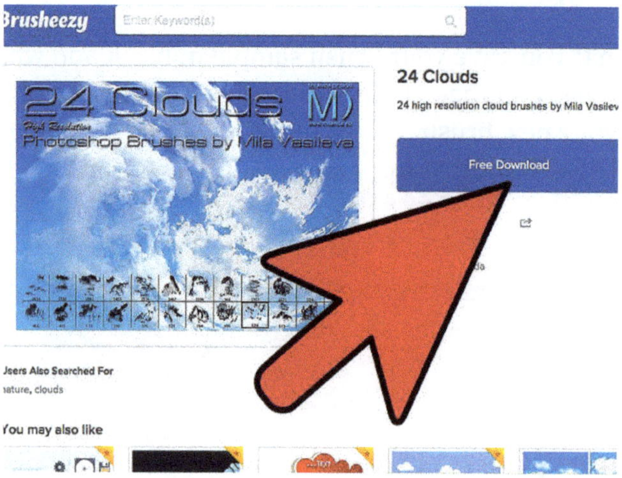

2. Save your digital brush in Adobe's "Brushes" folder. You can save the file directly to this folder by routing through the following default Photoshop folders, saving your brush preset in the final folder: Photoshop → Presets → Brushes.

- Photoshop brushes utilize the file extension ".abr". In your brushes folder, you should find several presets ending in this file extension, and your downloaded digital brush should as well.

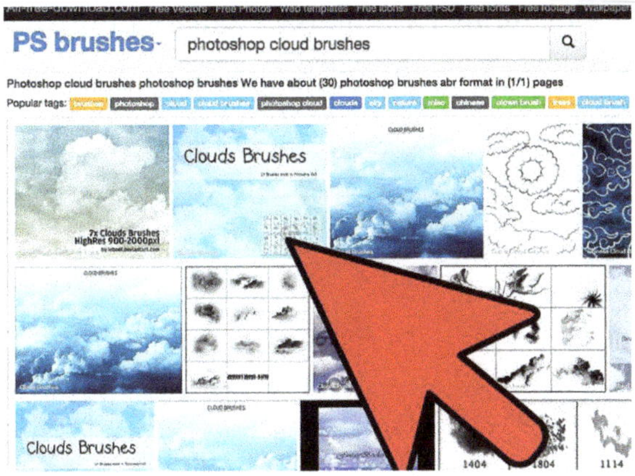

3. Decide on the cloud brush you like best. Think about the kind of clouds you will want in your scene. Each style of cloud brush will have different effect when used as a brush tool, so knowing effect you're looking for can speed this process.

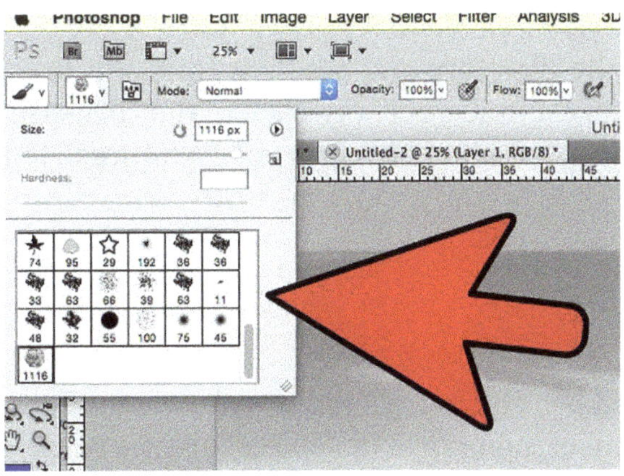

4. Open Photoshop and navigate to the Brush Palette. Click on the Brush Tool to open the Options Palette, which is where you can see the settings for your brush. From the Options Palette you can access brush options and load your new digital paintbrush by clicking the downward pointing triangle to the right of the word "Brush."

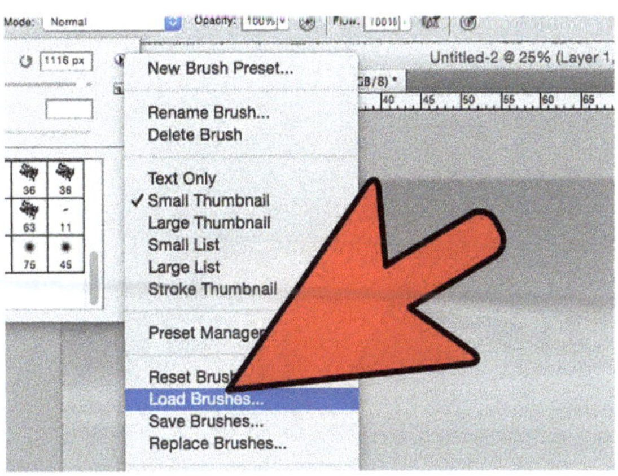

5. Navigate to "Load Brushes" in the Brush Palette. You should see a variety of options in your Brush Palette, most notably a grid of default thicknesses for your brush tool. You can access more

options through a drop-down menu by clicking the triangle in the upper right corner. From the listed options in that menu, choose "Load Brushes".

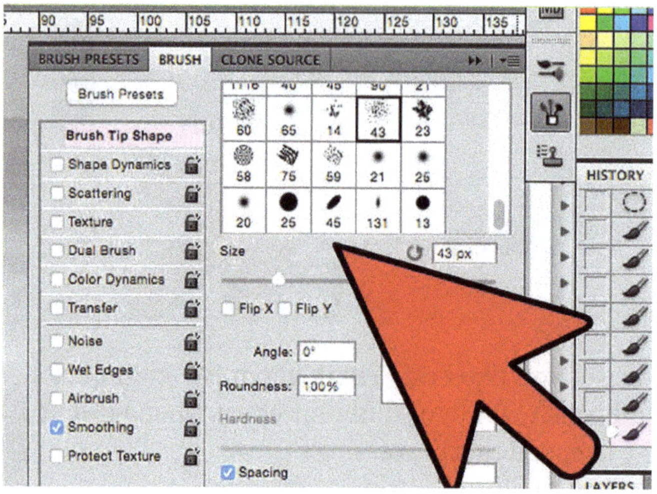

6. Select your brush from the directory and access it from the Brush Palette. Now that you've opened the file directory, you can find your way back to the "Brushes" folder where you've saved your downloaded digital brush. Select and confirm your new brush to load it to your presets.

How to design an ID Card using Adobe Photoshop

Adobe Photoshop is the number one image editing software in the world, used by professionals and amateurs in a wide range of industries. In spite of this, the software can be quite confusing to new users. Read on below the jump to learn how to navigate the Photoshop interface and design your own ID card.

Steps

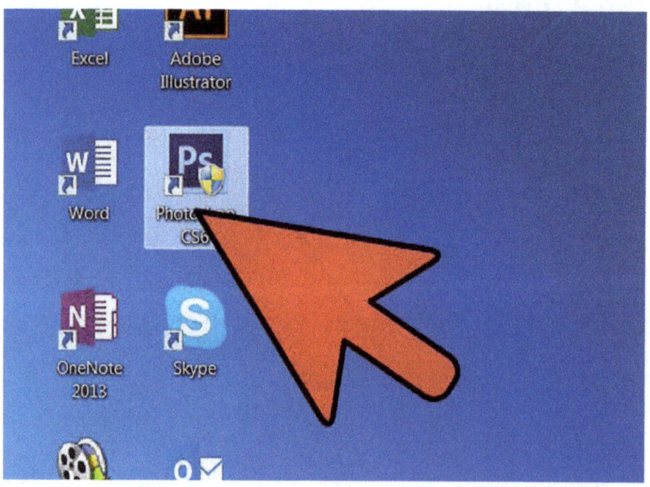

1. In order to complete this guide you will need to obtain the software program Adobe Photoshop.

This software can be quite expensive to purchase, but a full-featured free demo version is available on Adobe's website.

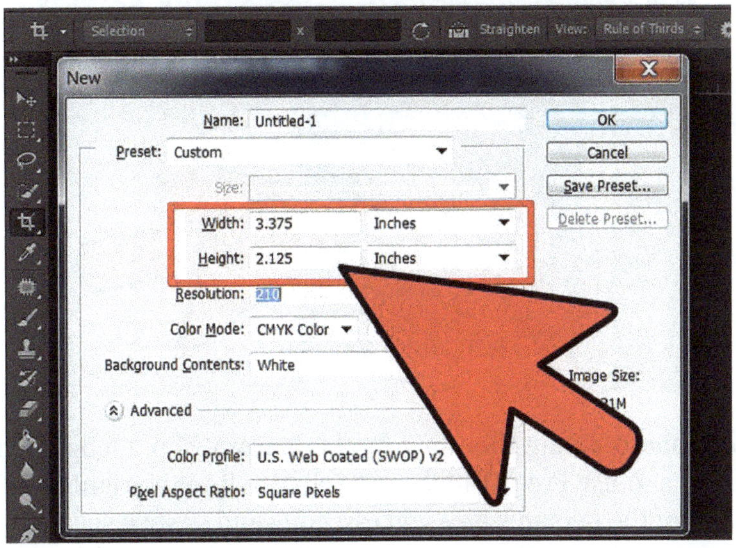

2. Start a new image the size of the ID. ID's are 3.375 inches (8.6 cm) wide by 2.125 inches (5.4 cm) tall. From the File menu click New. Change the units drop down menu from pixels to inches. In the width box type 3.375 and in the height box type 2.125. Depending on the quality of the images you plan to use on your ID, you may want to increase the resolution to 200 to 301 pixels/inch. While increasing the resolution will make the ID appear larger on your screen, its printed size will remain the same.

3. Find your ID background image. Your company/club logo or a stock photo will work. Fill your background layer with the color white. Copy and paste your background image to a new layer above this and decrease the opacity (found in the menu above the layers) until you have the desired look. To change the size of the background image, click the image layer and click the Edit menu (next to the File menu) and select Free Transform (or use the shortcut Control + T). Click and drag the edges to the size you desire.

4. Import the person's photo. Using the same methods from step 2, copy and paste the person's facial image onto the ID and use Free Transform to change it to the right size. If you want your ID to have a "ghost image" of the person's face you can copy and paste a second facial image onto the ID, use Free Transform (Control + T) to make it smaller, and change it's opacity to make it more transparent.

5. Add their personal information and signature. Use the text tool to add the personal information. If you want to add a realistic looking signature you will have to download a signature font online and install it before being able to use it.

How to create a Custom Business Card using Photoshop

Tired of being stuck with run-of-the-mill business card templates? This article shows you how to use simple Photoshop tricks to create your own custom business card that is creative, catchy and ready to print.

Steps

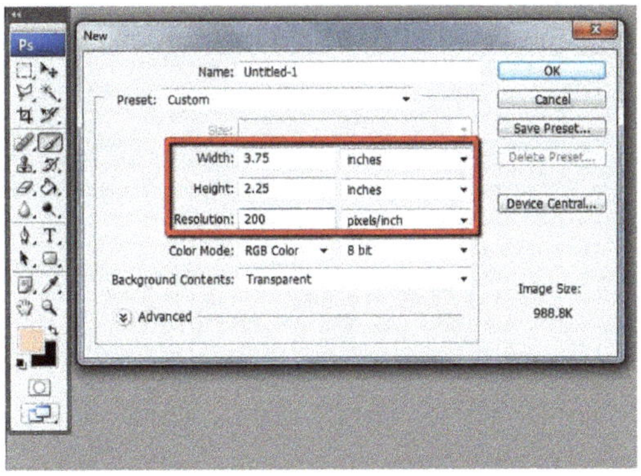

1. Create a template with the right specifications. Open a new image in Photoshop and set the width and height to 3.75 and 2.25 inches respectively. Set the resolution to 200 pixels/inch or more. The final size of your card will be 3.5 x 2 inches but it is customary to include a 1/8th inch 'bleed area' all around, hence the slightly larger image above. The bleed area makes sure that the colours "bleed" out over the edges when the cards are cut, instead of leaving white borders.

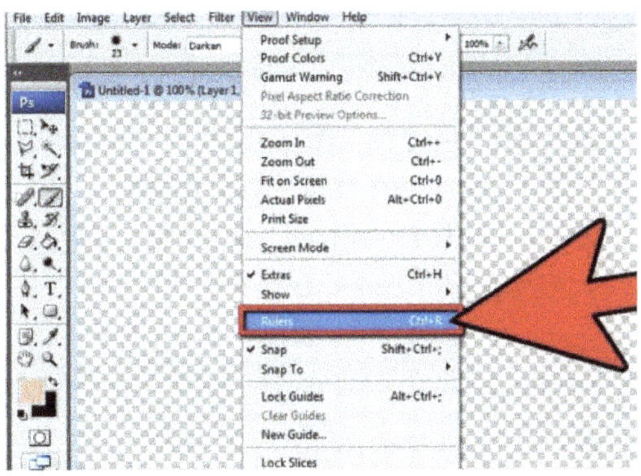

2. Create guidelines for the bleed and safety areas. Turn on rulers (View > Rulers) and right click on the ruler to set the unit to inches. Click on the top ruler and drag down to create two horizontal guide lines, one at 0.125 in and one at 2.125 in. Create two more vertical lines at 0.125 in and 3.625 in. These lines mark the end of the actual business card. You can also create safety guidelines just inside the bleed area to make sure your text does not extend too close to the edges.

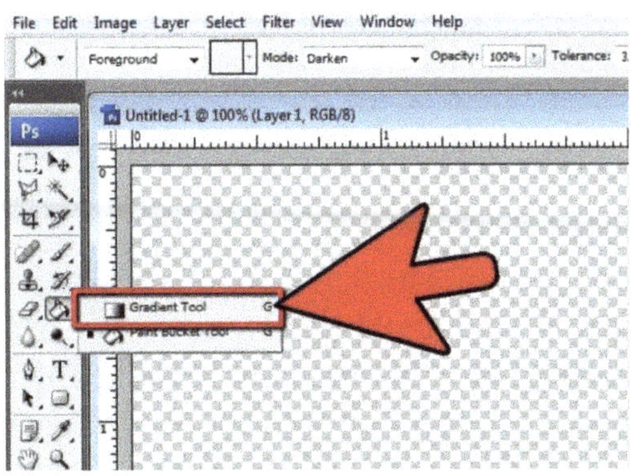

3. Create a background on a new layer. Select the gradient tool and click on the preview on the

top left to edit the colours. Use light or dark colours so that any text or images stand out clearly against the background. When using the gradient tool, draw a line across the entire image to create a gradual transition between colours. You could alternatively draw a shorter line within the image to create a more abrupt transition.

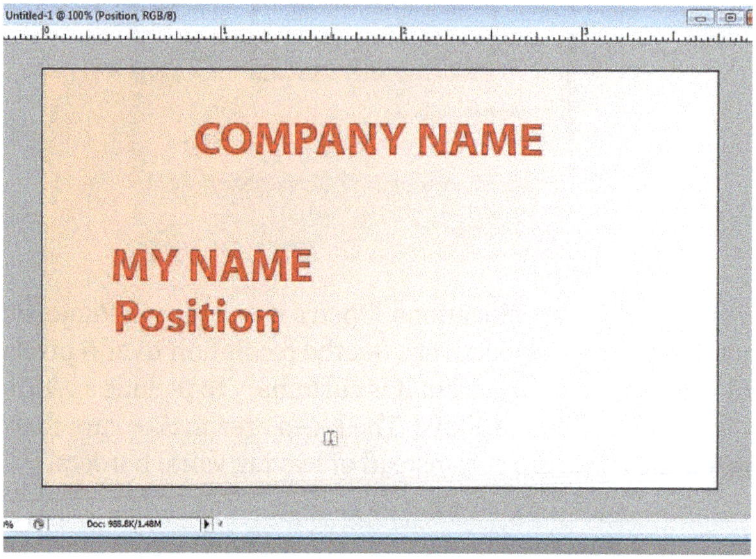

4. Plan the layout of the text. You will need to add, at the very least, your name and designation, your company's name or logo, and your contact information. If you own or work for a small business, you might want to add a tagline below the company's name describing the type of business.

5. Add each part of the text using the text tool in a new layer. Use a larger font size, between 18-20 points, for your name and the name of your company to make them stand out. Experiment with fancy fonts and different styles. The contact information is usually in a smaller font size of 10-12 points. This text must be in a plain, clear font without ambiguous characters (You don't want people wondering if that's a number 1 or lower-case letter l in your email address).

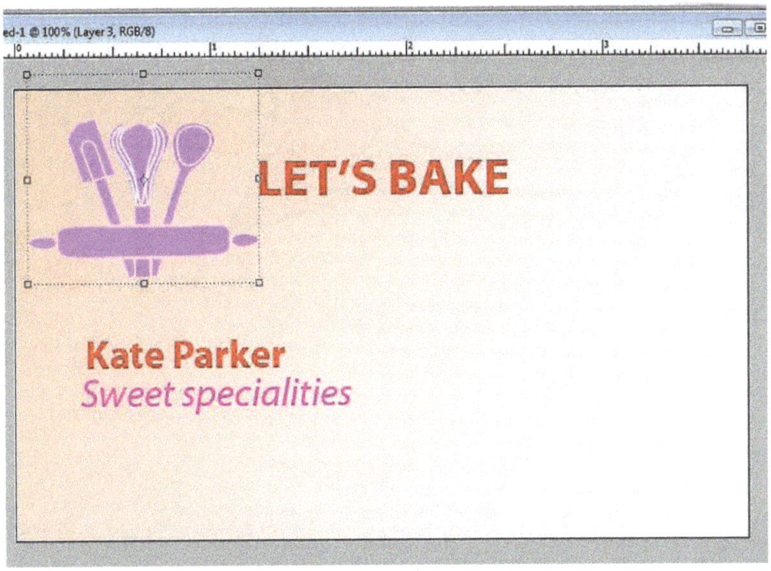

6. Add a company logo in a corner or in place of the company's name (optional). If you have an image of your company's logo, open the image in Photoshop. Use the quick selection tool to select around the border of the logo (reduce the tool size if necessary), avoiding the background. Invert the selected area using Ctrl+Shift+I and use the eraser tool to delete the background around the logo. You can now use any selection tool to copy and paste just the logo onto your card template.

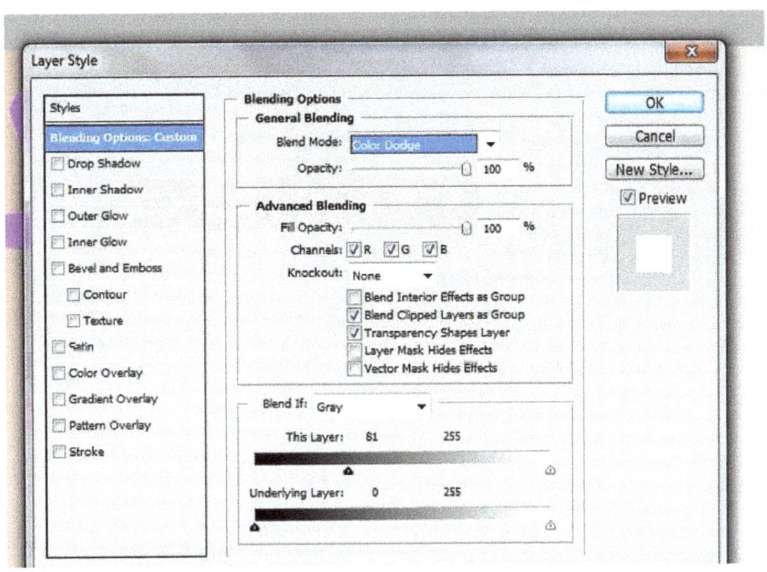

7. Add text effects for a more professional look. Right click on the text layer and open the Blending Options window. Select the Bevel & Emboss option and set the size to 2-3 to give the text a bit of depth. For dark text against a light background, select the outer glow option. With the colour set to a light version of the background, set the spread and size to a small value to create a subtle glow instead of a broad halo. For light text against a dark background, use the Drop Shadow effect instead. Again, set the Spread and Size to a small value and adjust the distance so that the text is subtly outlined.

8. Use brushes to create detail in your background. You can use large abstract brushes with the colour set to match the centre of your background gradient to create a nice subtle contrast. Another way to make brushes blend in is to select Blending Options in the brushes layer, select gradient overlay and modify the gradient with colours similar to your background. You could also use more colourful brushes but lower the brush layer's opacity to make them less flashy. The brush effects must be catchy, but not make the text difficult to read.

9. Add images to reinforce the theme or fill up 'blank' areas. Open an image you own or have permission to use and select a portion using the quick selection tool. Copy and paste it into the card template. You can also create a composite using pieces of many images and brushes on a separate image. Arrange the pieces on separate layers and merge all the layers at the end before copying and pasting the composite onto your template. Paste your image on a new layer in your template and lower the opacity of the layer to 30-40%.

10. Add a border to brighten up your design(optional). Draw a rectangle along the safety guide lines (or slightly outside them) using the rectangle tool. Make sure the path style is selected in the top left corner. Select the brush tool and choose a simple brush style with a size between 5-10 pixels. Select the Paths panel in the layers palette and right click on the Work Path. Click on Stroke Path and select Brush. You can add Blending Options to the border as well.

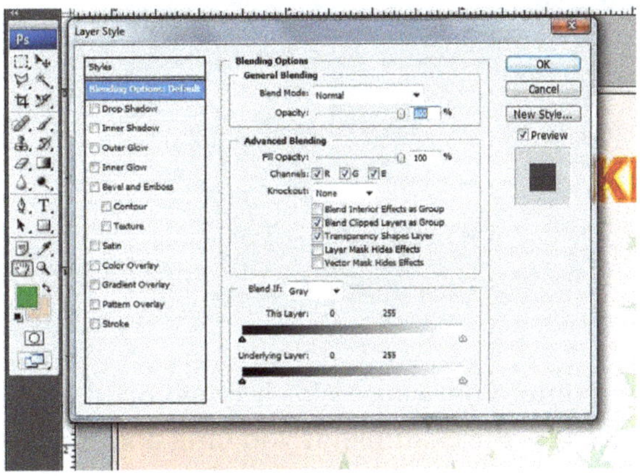

11. Tweak your design. You will probably want to fine-tune your design to move text away from background graphics or remove effects that don't blend with the rest of the template. You may even need to change some font colours if your background has changed considerably.

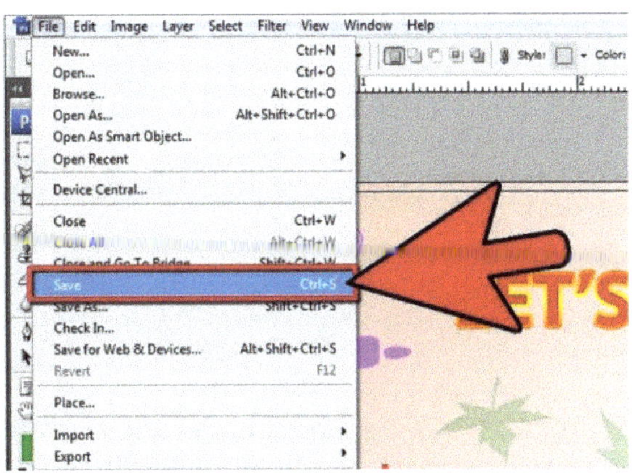

12. Save your file! When you are completely satisfied with your template, save it once as a Photoshop.

psd file (in case you still want to make changes to it) and again as a PDF (or any other format preferred by the printshop). Also make sure to tell the print shop the final size of your business card (3.5 x 2 inches in this case) and that your template includes a bleed area.

How to Design a Blog Background on Photoshop

Have you just created a new blog, and are looking for an exciting background to add some color? Or are you a blogging veteran who wants to spice up their blog with a homemade background? This article can help.

Steps

1. Decide what kind of background you want. Will it be colorful and cheery, or a sleek, modern black? Try to base it off your blog- for example, if you blog about cooking, remind yourself to incorporate some utensils or foods in the final background.

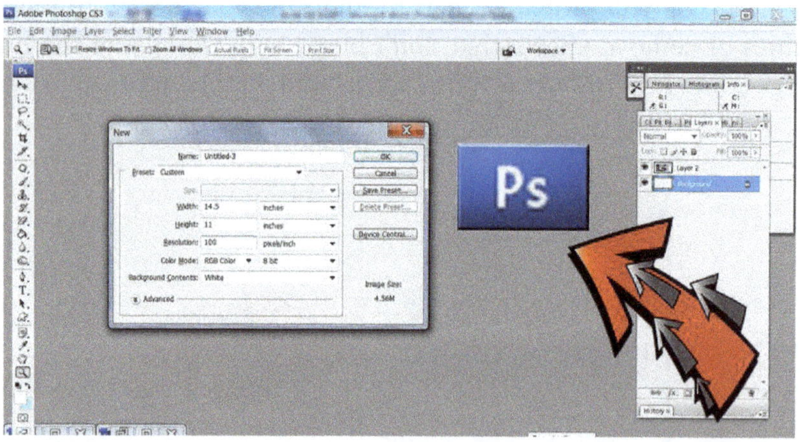

2. Open up your Photoshop program to a new screen. Set the sizes like this: Width, 14.5 inches (36.8 cm); height, 11 inches (27.9 cm); resolution, 100 pixels/inch; color mode, RGB color-8 bit; background color, white. The preset should be custom.

3. Now open up all of the different pictures and patterns that you plan on putting into your background. For example- on a blog about penguins, you could have pictures of penguins, icebergs, and fish over a big blue background. (That's just one idea.) The center part of the background (where text will go) should be 7.5 inches (19.1 cm) wide and be rather light-colored. With that said, stretch and pull the elements to fit your liking.

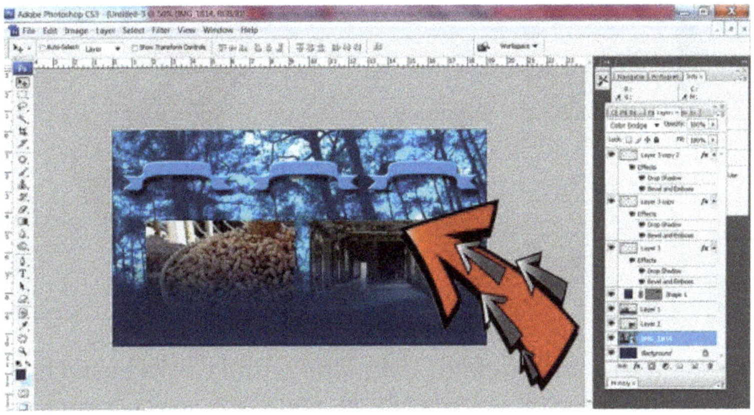

4. Spice it up! Make some things stand out and other things fade in. Add some ribbons, buttons, etc., whatever floats your boat. Use the Photoshop tools to make your background more interesting.

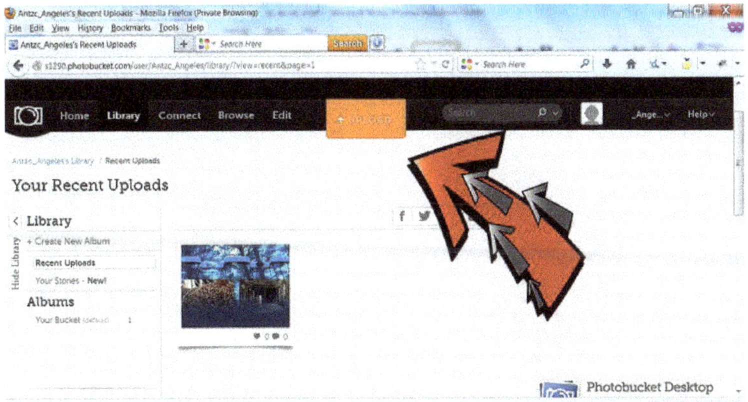

5. Upload the image to Photobucket (www.photobucket.com). When uploading, reduce your image to 1 or 2 megabytes, depending on how large your screen/blog is.

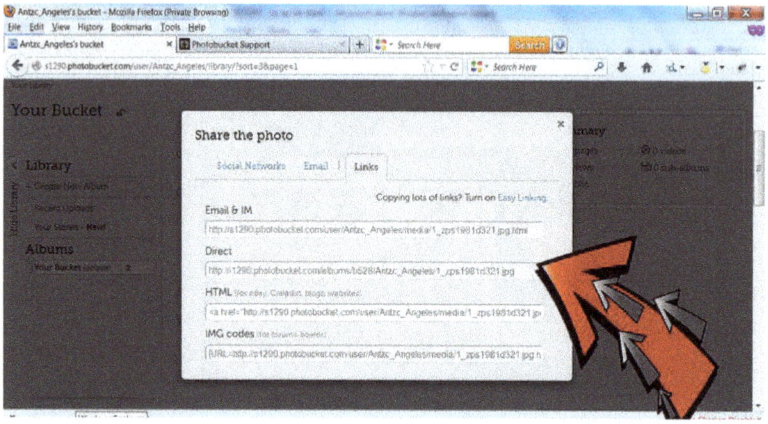

6. Now go to your image and find the “direct link”. Copy it or write it down somewhere, because you will need it later.

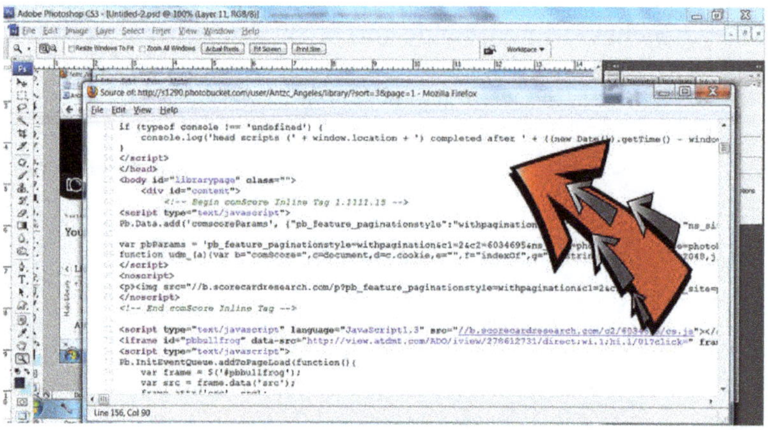

7. Go to your blog and set it to a plain default template- white works best. (If you’re using Blogger, set it to “Minima.”) Now dive into your blog’s HTML code. It’ll seem crazy to the ordinary person, full of weird signs and strange words.

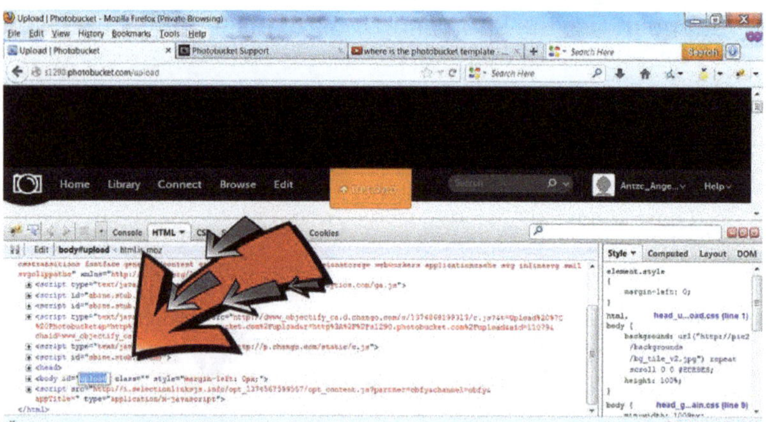

8. Find the place where the HTML reads: “body {#background:$bgcolor;#margin:0; color:$-textcolor; font:x-small Georgia Serif; font-size/* */:/**/small; font-size: /**/small; text-align: center;”.

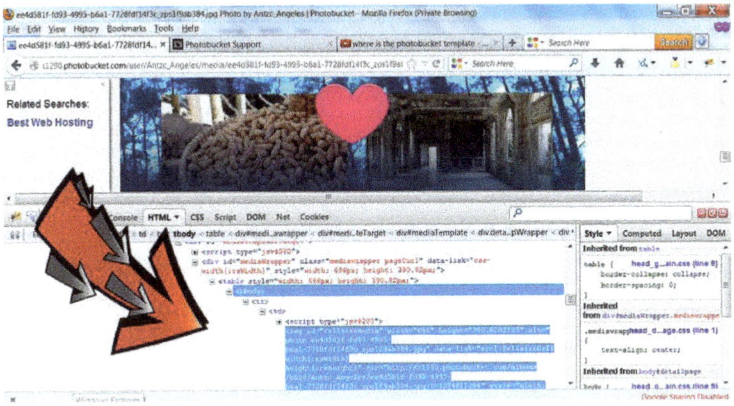

9. Change the HTML to read: body {#background:$bgcolor;background-image:url('/INSERT YOUR DIRECT LINK HERE');background-position: center; background-repeat:no-repeat; background-attachment: fixed;#margin:0; color:$textcolor; font:x-small Georgia Serif; font-size/* */:/**/small; font-size: /**/small; text-align: center;

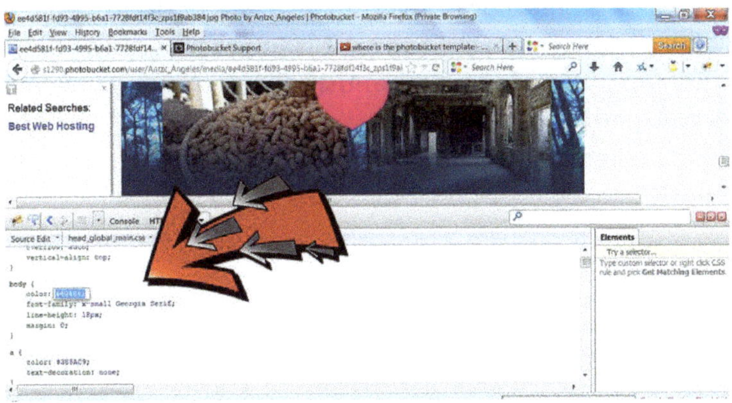

10. Place your direct link where it says "INSERT YOUR DIRECT LINK HERE." Now save your edits and check out your blog. It probably looks FANTASTIC now! Congratulations on successfully creating your very own blog background.

Chapter

4 Basics of InDesign

Adobe InDesign is a software that allows users to use page layout tools to create and design content specific to pages. Newspapers, books, posters, etc. are designed using such software. The chapter strategically encompasses and incorporates the major components and key concepts of InDesign, providing a complete understanding.

How to anchor Objects in InDesign

Anchoring an object, such as a photo or other graphic element, to a specific line or block of text allows the anchored object to flow with the text as it is moved. Knowing how to anchor objects in InDesign, a popular desktop publishing program that allows users to create print documents in a variety of sizes and formats, provides you with the flexibility to move text without having to replace or manually move associated graphics each time the text is moved.

Steps

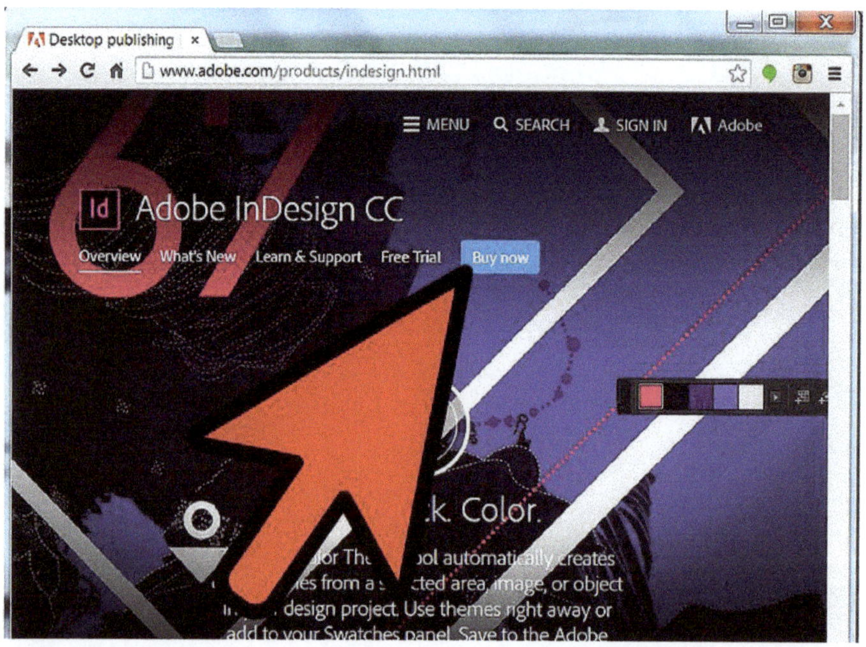

1. Purchase Adobe InDesign if you do not already own it. Follow the on-screen instructions for installing InDesign on your computer and restart your computer if necessary.

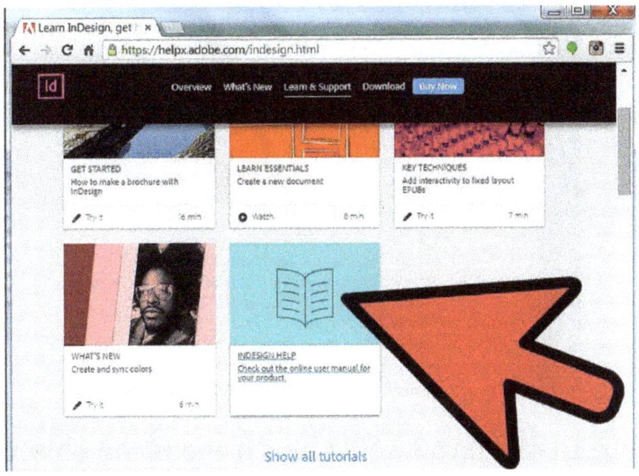

2. Familiarize yourself with the InDesign workspace and the program's available user resources.

3. Open Adobe InDesign.

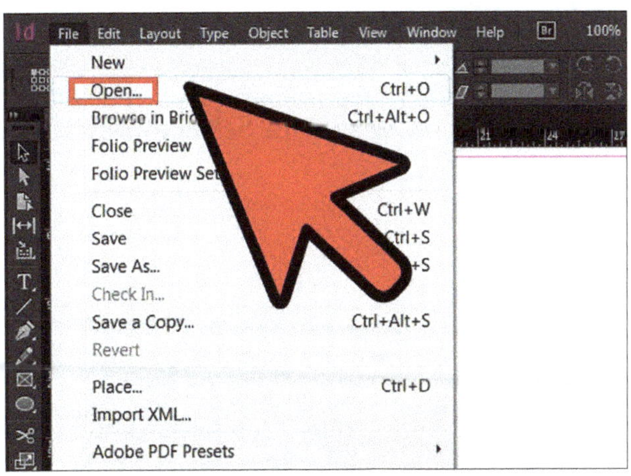

4. Open the InDesign document you want to work in by selecting File>Open from the Control panel at the top of your workspace. If you do not have an existing InDesign document to work in, create a new document by selecting File>New>Document and specifying the settings for your new document.

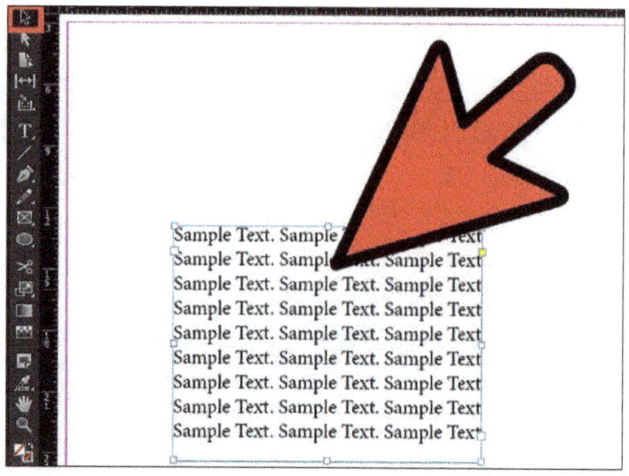

5. Navigate to the text frame to which you would like to anchor an object.

- If your document does not already contain text, you can type text directly into your document by first creating a text frame with your Type tool, which is located in the InDesign Tools palette. With your Type tool still selected, click within the text frame and begin typing your text. If your text already exists in a word processing document, select File>Place, navigate to the file you wish to import and double click the file name. A loaded cursor will appear. Move your mouse to the location where you want your text to appear and click to place the text.

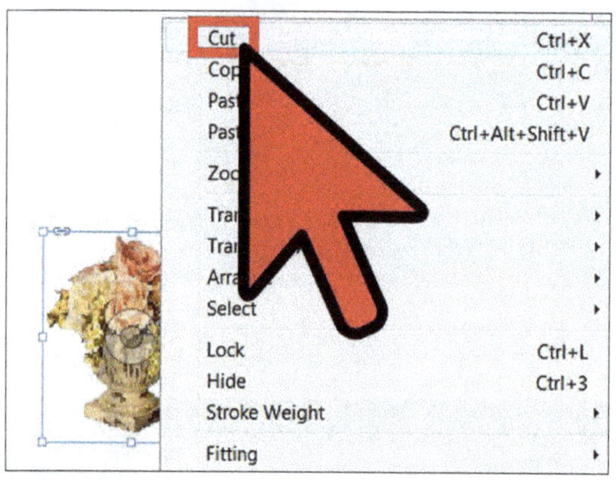

6. Anchor an existing object by clicking on it using the Select tool and selecting Edit>Cut from your Control panel.

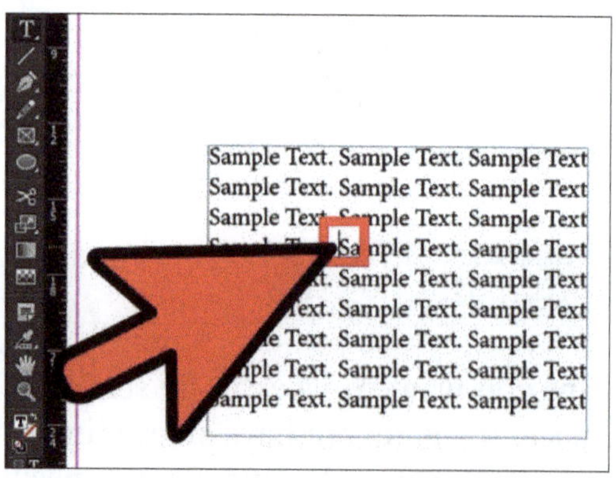

7. Use your Type tool to position an insertion point for your anchored object.

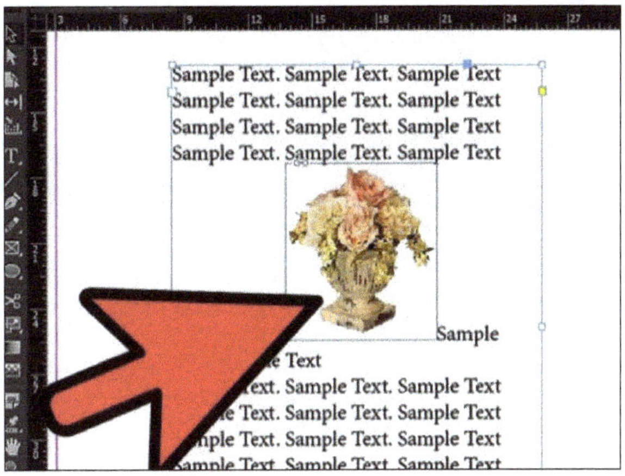

8. Select Edit>Paste from your Control panel to place your object.

Create an Anchored Object from a Placeholder Frame

Use your Type tool to position an insertion point for your anchored object.

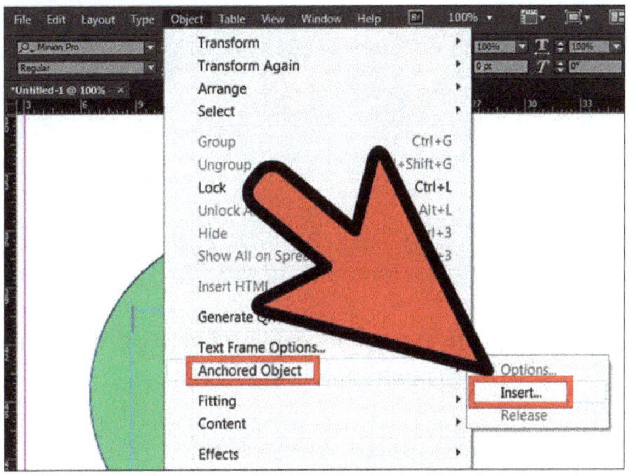

1. Select Object>Anchored Object>Insert from the Control panel.

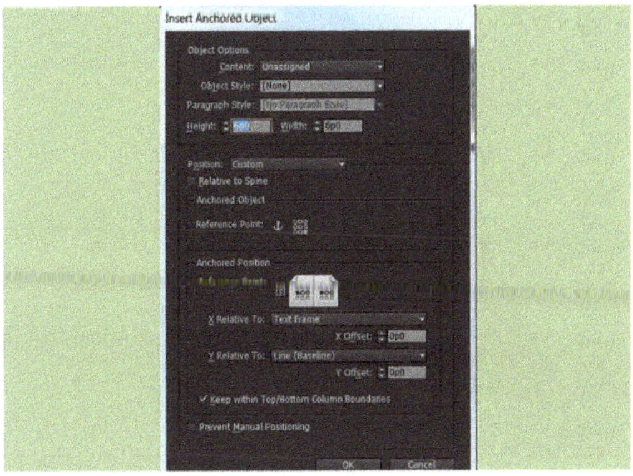

2. Specify options for your anchored object, including content, object style, paragraph style, height and width.

How to add a New Font to InDesign

Adobe InDesign is a desktop publishing software program favored by print designers for its usability, power and flexibility. Adobe InDesign can be used to create a variety of print materials, such as books, posters, flyers, brochures and newspapers and comes with many fonts preinstalled. Because the use of fonts is an effective way of adding visual appeal to your print materials, knowing how to add a new font to InDesign will help you maximize the impact of your print materials.

Steps

1. Purchase and install Adobe InDesign if you do not already own it. You may need to restart your computer after installation.

- If you are new to InDesign, familiarize yourself with the program's workspace before getting started. You may also wish to review available user resources.

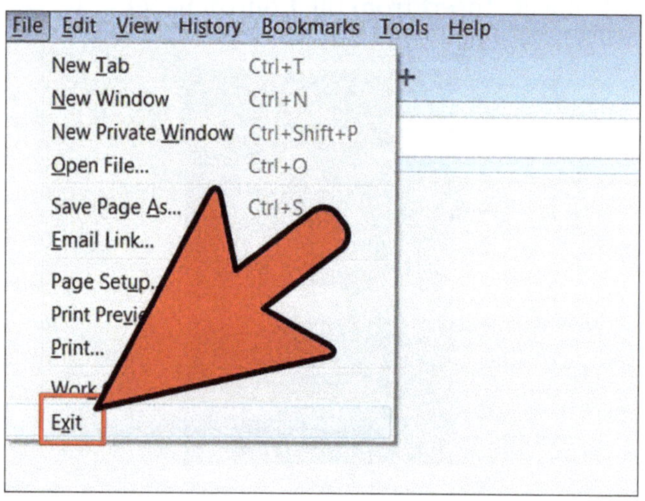

2. Close all applications that you may have open on your computer.

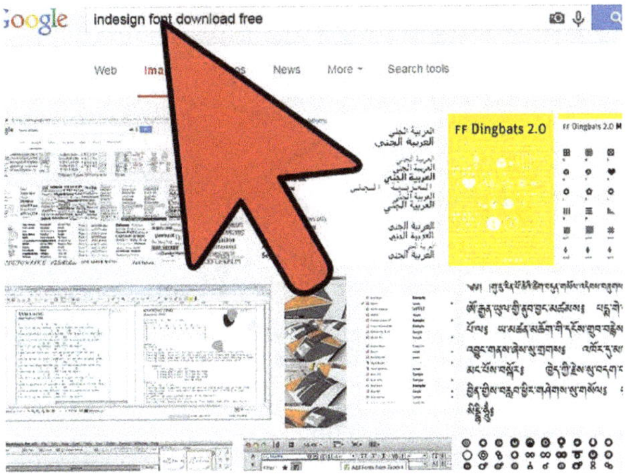

3. Determine the type of font or fonts you wish to use for your project. This will depend on what you are creating as well as your audience.

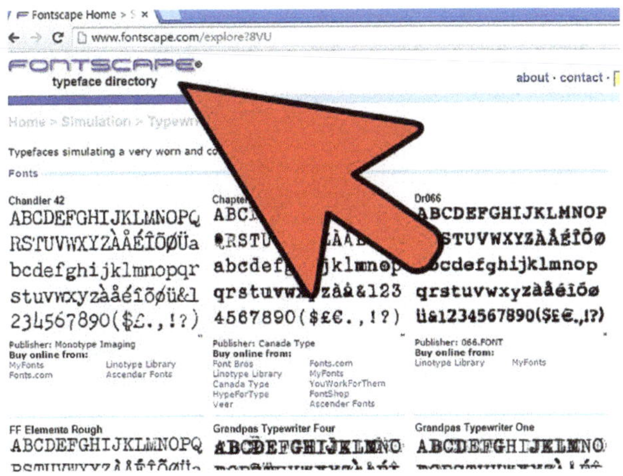

4. Identify the font you wish to install. A number of fonts are available as online downloads, both for purchase and free of charge.

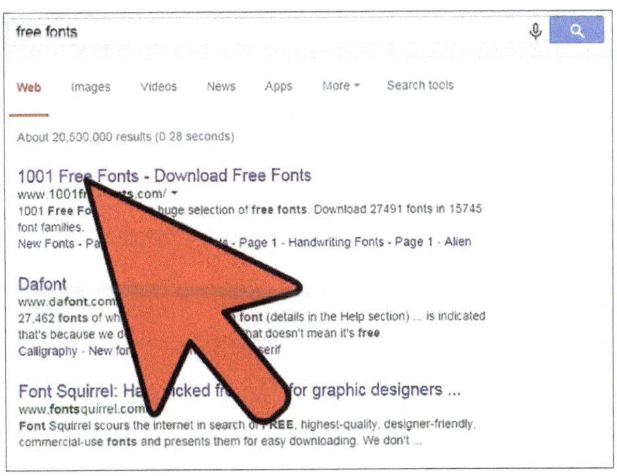

5. Conduct an Internet search for fonts. If you are specifically interested in free fonts, search for free fonts.

6. Identify the font you wish to install and download it to your computer. The font package may consist of multiple files bundled together in a zip folder. If this is the case, you will need to unzip the folder.

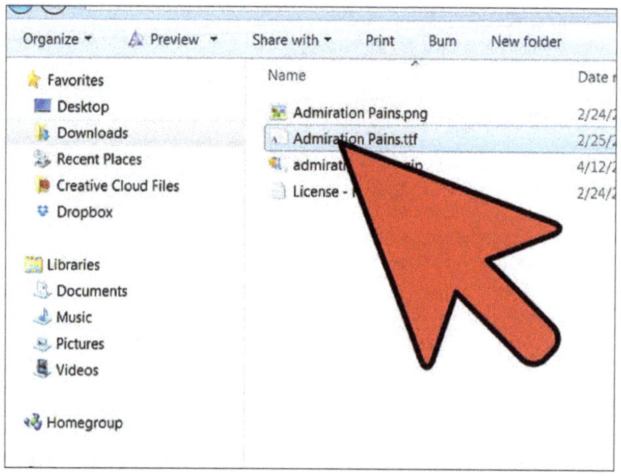

7. Save the font file or files to your computer.

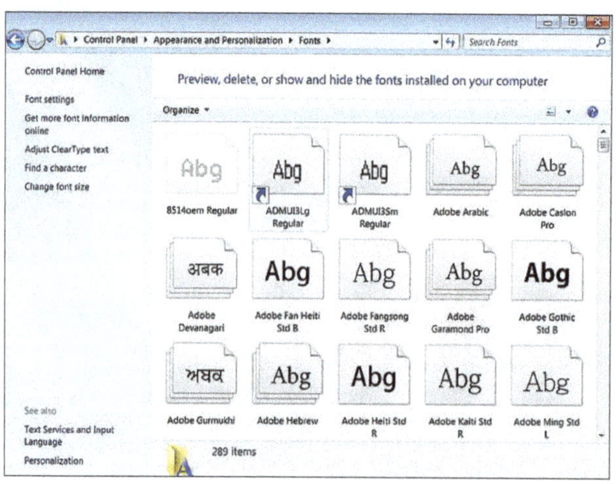

8. Select Start>Control Panel>Appearance and Personalization>Fonts.

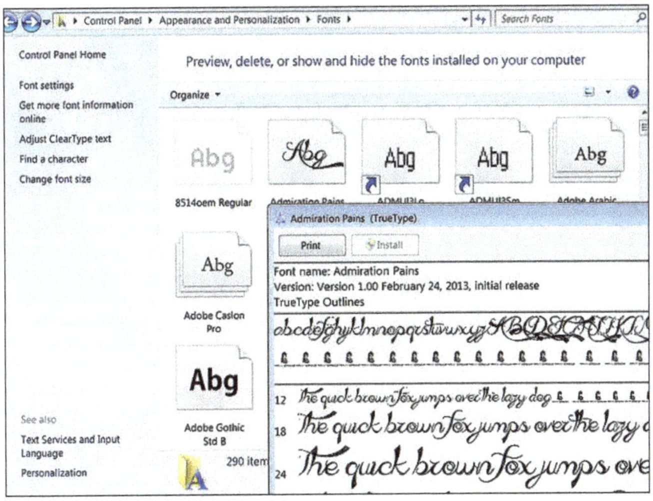

9. Select File>Install New Font. This will open the Add Fonts window.

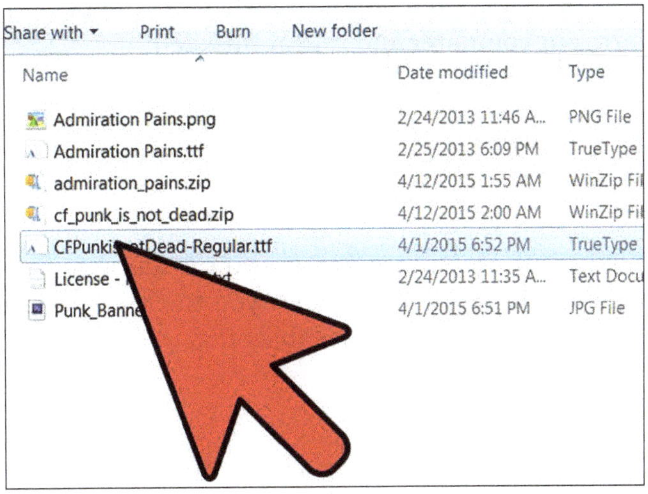

10. Find the font file or files you wish to install.

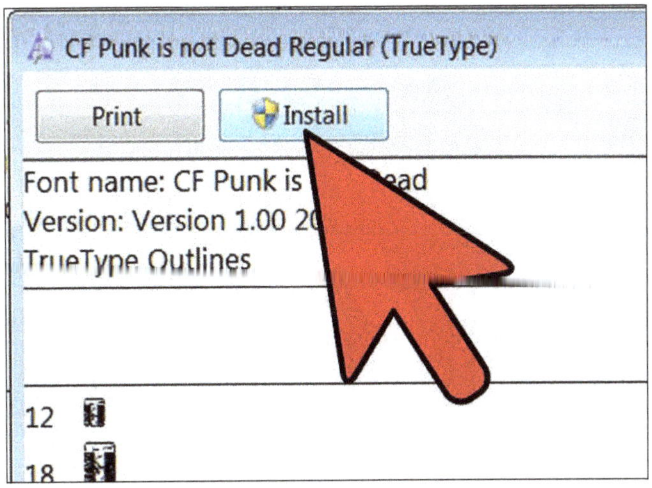

11. Select the font file or files you wish to install and click Install.

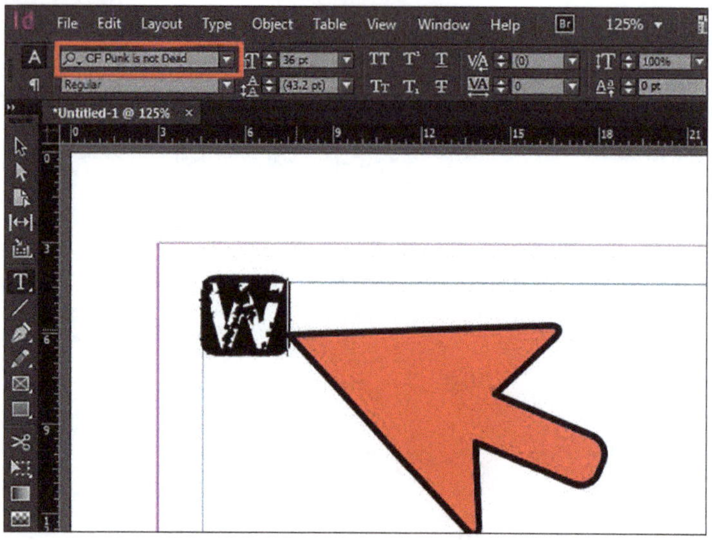

12. Open InDesign and confirm that your newly installed font appears in your list of available fonts. If it does not, restart your computer and repeat this step.

How to add Table in InDesign

Tables are an effective method of presenting information in an organized manner. Using Adobe InDesign, a desktop publishing program that allows you to create print documents in a variety of sizes and formats, you can place and format tables that present your information in a reader-friendly manner.

Steps

1. Purchase Adobe InDesign if you do not already own it. Follow the on-screen instructions for installing InDesign on your computer and restart your computer if necessary.

2. Familiarize yourself with InDesign's workspace and user resources that are available.

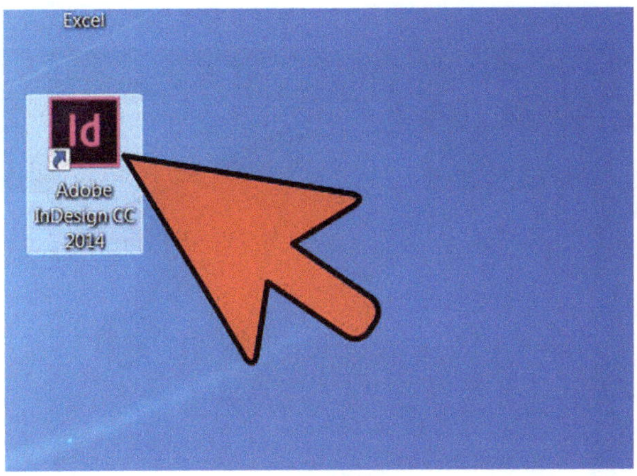

3. Open Adobe InDesign.

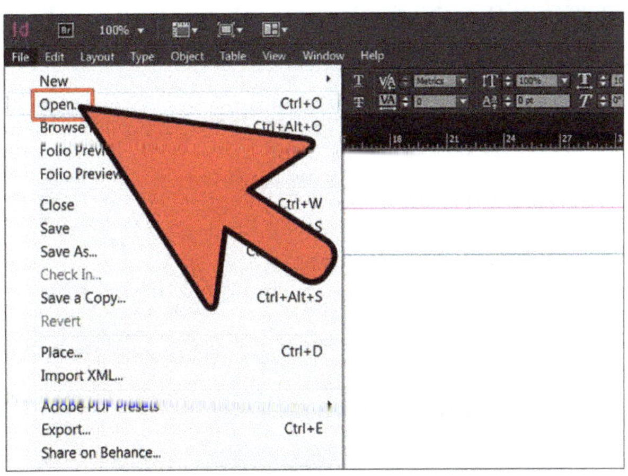

4. Open the InDesign document you want to work in by selecting File>Open from the Control panel at the top of your workspace.

- If you do not have an existing InDesign document to work in, create a new document by selecting File>New>Document and specifying the settings for your new document.

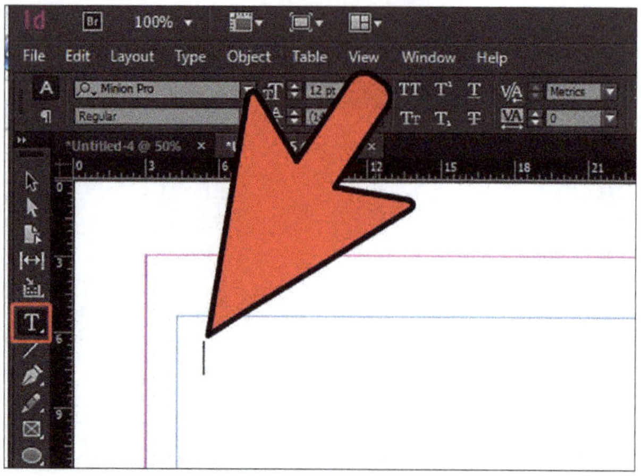

5. Select the Type tool from your Tools palette and click the location where you want to place your table.

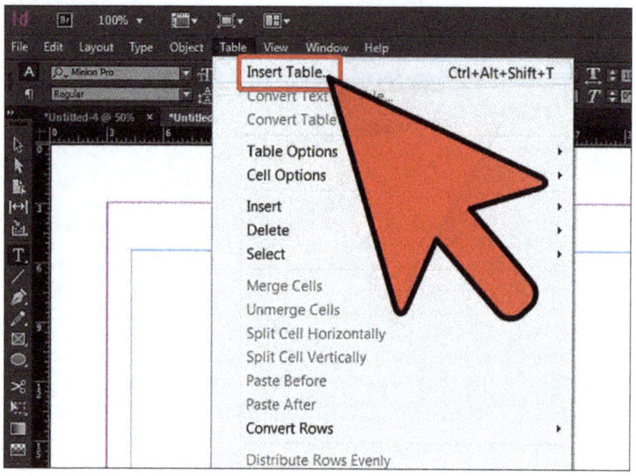

6. Select Table>Insert Table from the Control panel. Enter the number of rows and columns you want your table to contain.

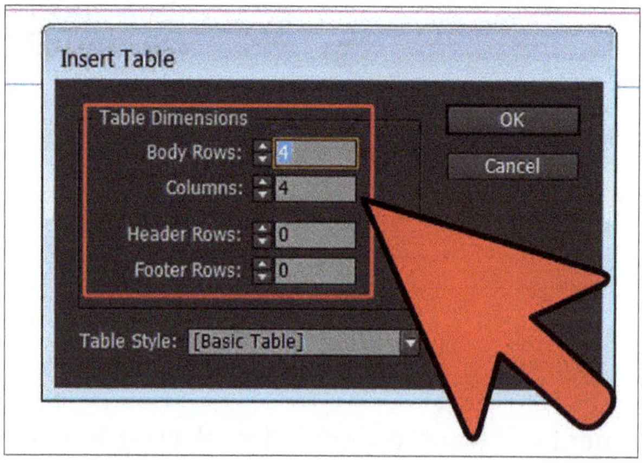

7. Enter the number of header and/or footer rows you want your table to contain. Header and footer rows are rows that repeat at the top of every frame or column. Use them if your table will take up multiple columns or frames.

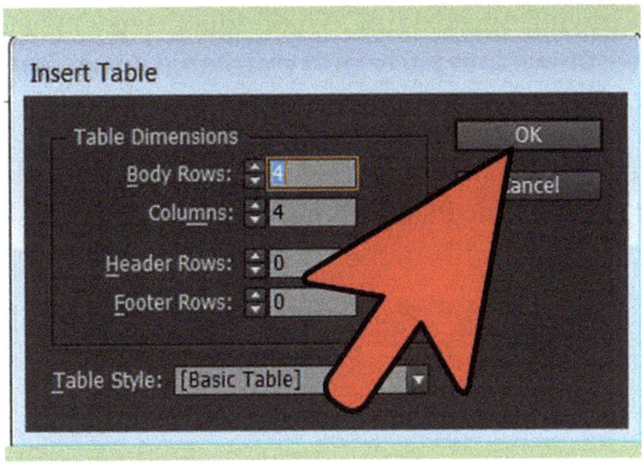

8. Click OK.

Method 1

Adding Text and Graphics to your Table

1. Enter text in your header and/or footer row or rows using your Type tool. Do this by clicking the cell in which you want to enter text.

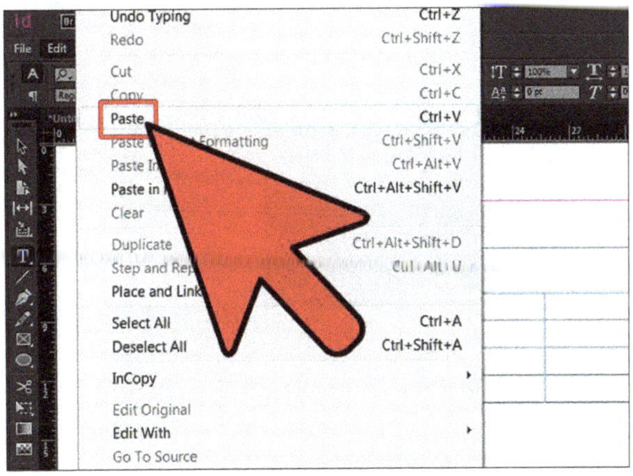

2. Click the cell in which you want to begin entering information and type your text. You can also

import text into a table by copying and pasting. To do this place your cursor where you want your text to appear, copy the text you wish to paste into your table and select Edit>Paste from the Control panel.

- To import text from a file without copying and pasting, place your cursor where you want your text to appear, select File>Place from the Control panel, navigate to the file you wish to import and double click the file name.

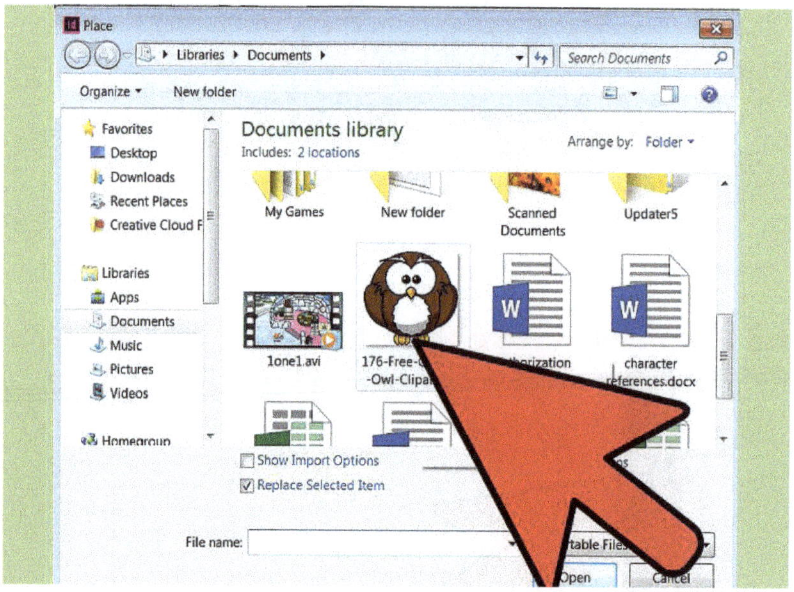

3. Place your cursor where you want your graphic to appear. Select File>Place from the Control panel, navigate to the file you wish to import and double click the file name.

4. Format text within your table by highlighting the text you want to format and adjusting your font and font size using the drop-down menus in the Control panel.

Method 2

Formatting your Table

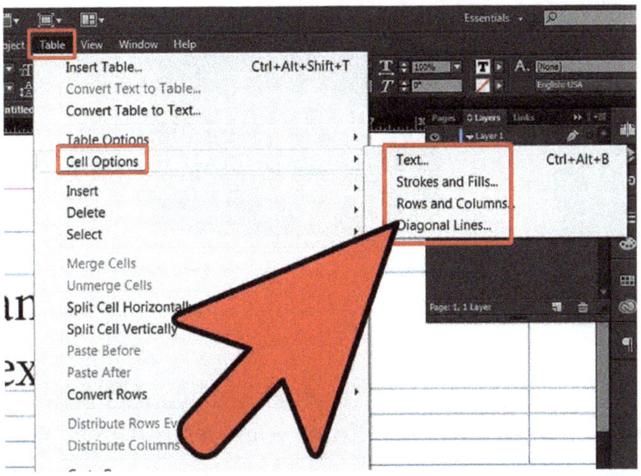

1. Resize columns and rows by selecting the columns and/or rows you want to resize and selecting Table>Cell Options>Rows and Columns and entering the appropriate size.

- You can also do this using the Table panel, which can be accessed via the Window menu located in the Control panel.
- Row and column heights may also be adjusted manually by positioning your cursor over the edge of a row or column and dragging up or down or left or right once the double-arrow icon appears.
- Rows and columns can be distributed evenly throughout a table by clicking Table and selecting either Distribute Rows Evenly or Distribute Columns Evenly.

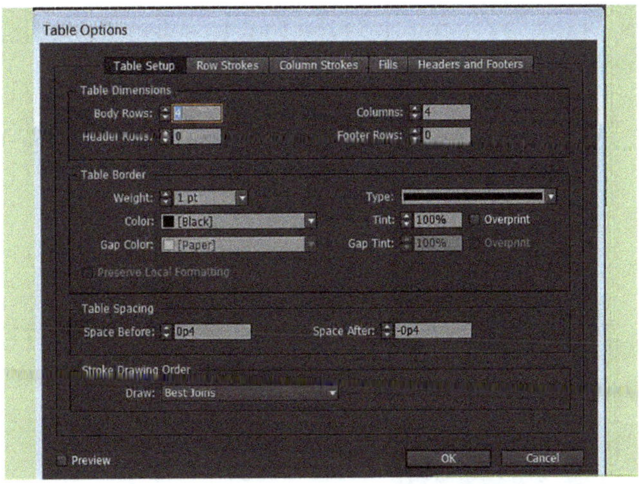

2. Select Table>Table Options>Table Setup.

- In the Table Border menu, enter settings for the weight, type, tint and color of your table's border.

3. Select your Type tool and highlight the cells to which you would like to apply a background color. Select Table>Cell Options>Strokes and Fills. Enter your desired color and tint.

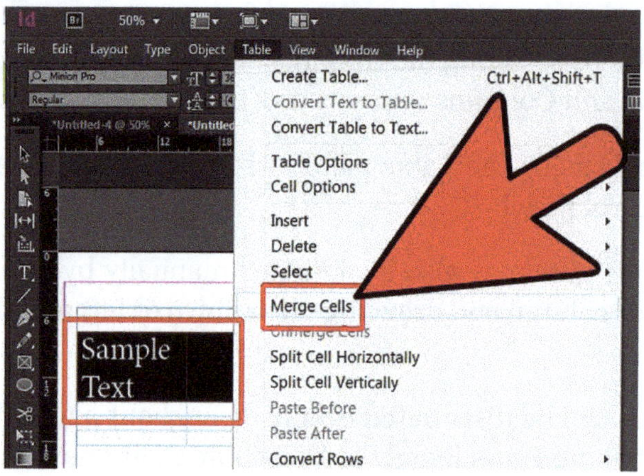

4. Merge cells within your table by using the type tool to select the cells you wish to merge and clicking Table>Merge Cells.

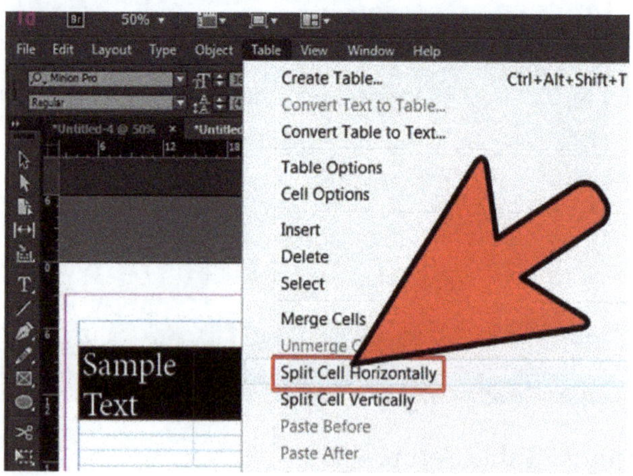

5. Split cells within your table by clicking the cell you wish to split and selecting Table>Split Cell Vertically or Split Cell Horizontally.

How to add Pictures in InDesign

Pictures in print materials enhance the information provided, add visual interest and evoke emotion. Adobe InDesign is a desktop publishing software program that allows users to create a variety of print products. Knowing how to add pictures in InDesign will allow you to create compelling print documents that are also visually appealing.

Steps

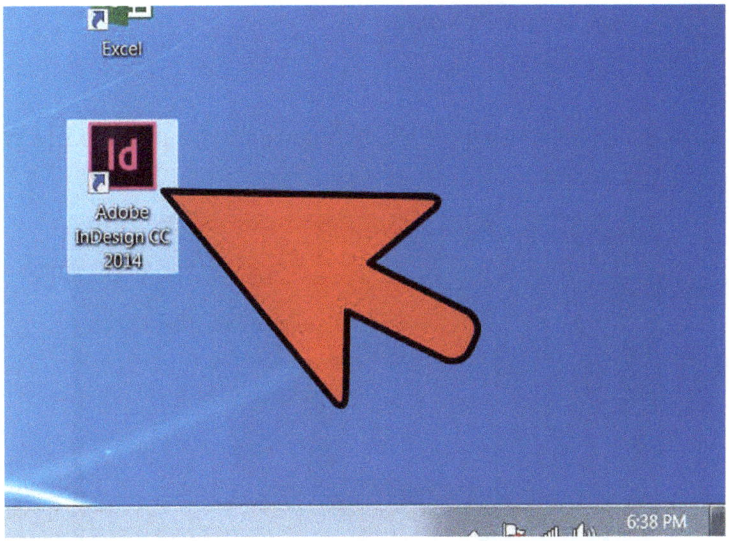

1. Open Adobe InDesign.

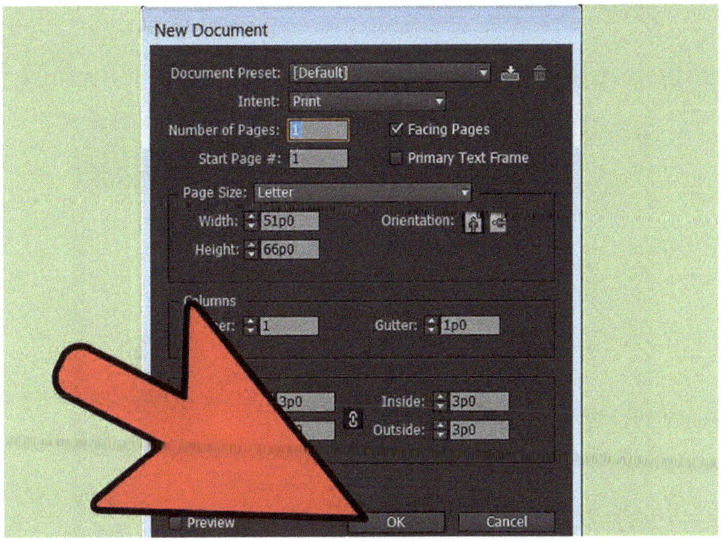

2. Open the InDesign document you will be working from. Do this by selecting File>Open from the Control panel at the top of your workspace. If you do not have an existing InDesign document to work from, create a new document by selecting File>New>Document and specifying the settings for your new document.

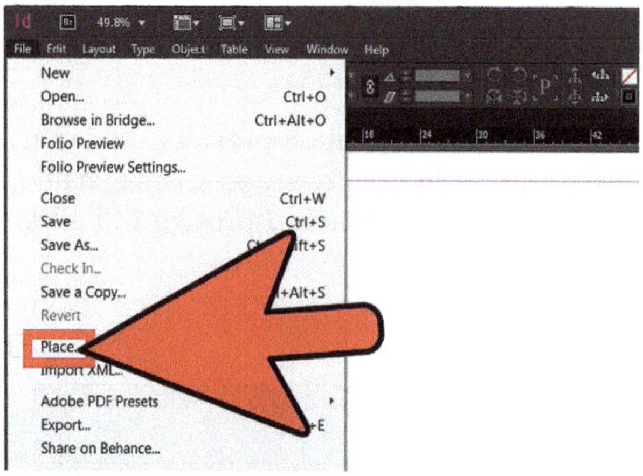

3. Click File>Place in InDesign's Control panel. Navigate to the picture file you would like to import and double click the file name.

4. Drag and place your picture to your desired position and click your mouse.

5. Adjust the size of your picture, if necessary, by selecting the picture using your Select tool and clicking one of the handles (small squares) located on the frame. Drag the handle while simultaneously holding the Control and Shift keys (Or for a mac, Command+Shift). Holding the Shift key will adjust the pictures size proportionally. If you want to crop out a particular portion of your

picture, hold only the Control key as you drag the handle. You may also enter precise values for the pictures height and width in the Height and Width fields located in the Control panel.

6. Repeat these steps for all pictures you wish to add.

How to add Bullets in InDesign

Adobe InDesign was a software publishing application released in 2002. It is useful in creating magazines, posters, newspapers, fliers and books. As well as creating high-resolution images and logos, InDesign also has many text formatting options. The software can be used in 24 languages, and it can handle characters, accents, numbers and bullets with ease. Bullets are an important function for use in flyers, brochures, books and other documents in order to organize text. This article will tell you how to add bullets in InDesign.

Steps

1. Open Adobe InDesign and open your document.

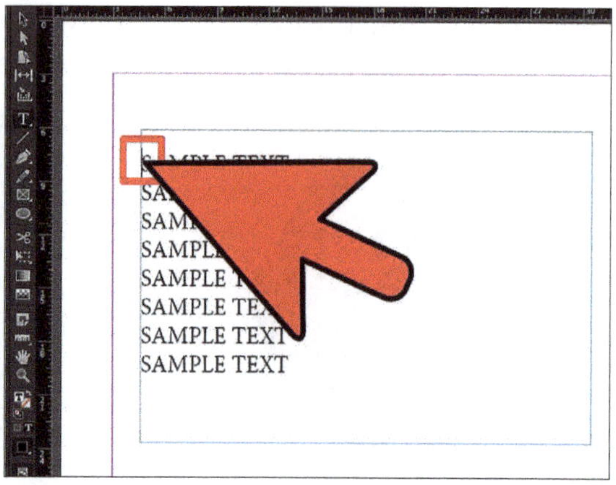

2. Switch to the "Type" tool and click on the text box to activate the text. Select the text where you want the bullets to begin.

- You will most likely want an introduction paragraph to a bulleted list, so be sure not to select that text.

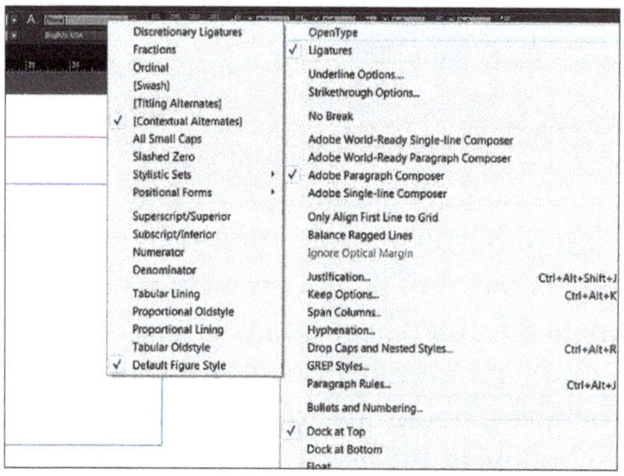

3. Go to the control panel that runs horizontally above your document. Click on the icon on the far right. This will bring up an advanced menu of formatting options and special characters that are currently not on the control panel.

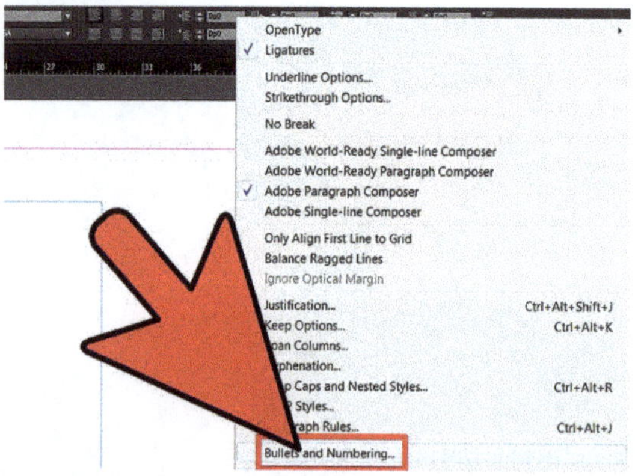

4. Scroll down to the words "Bullets and Numbering" and release your click to open this formatting option.

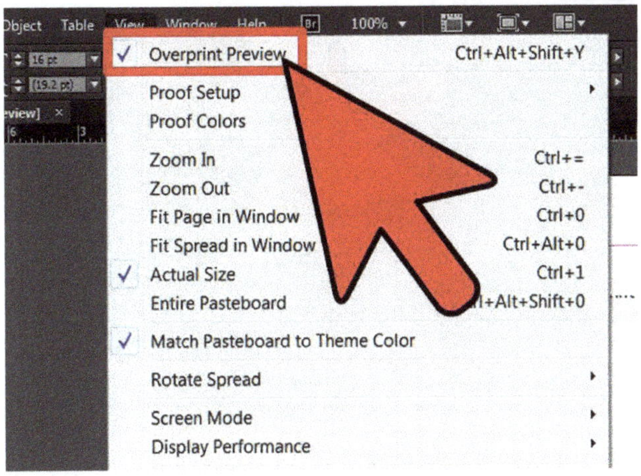

5. Make sure the preview option is turned on in InDesign, then wait for the "Bullets and Numbering" dialogue box to pop up.

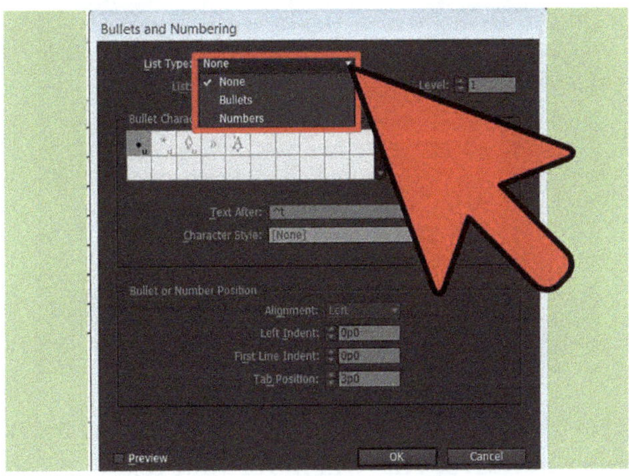

6. Click on "List Type" at the top of the dialogue box. It should be currently set to "None." Click on "Bullets."

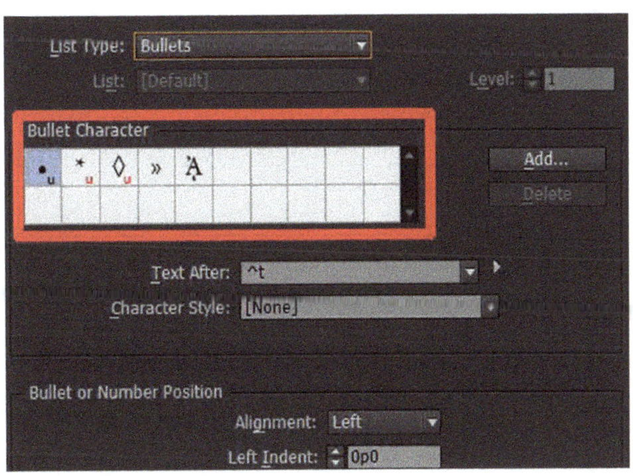

7. Choose the best bullet image to use for your project from the bullet icons. The first option is a round bullet, which is commonly used for bullets in text.

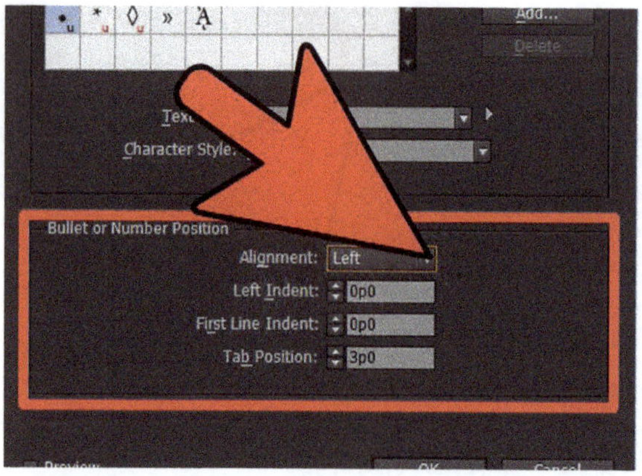

8. Go to the "Left Indent" box and select how far you want your text to be away from the bullet. You may want to choose a low number of picas.

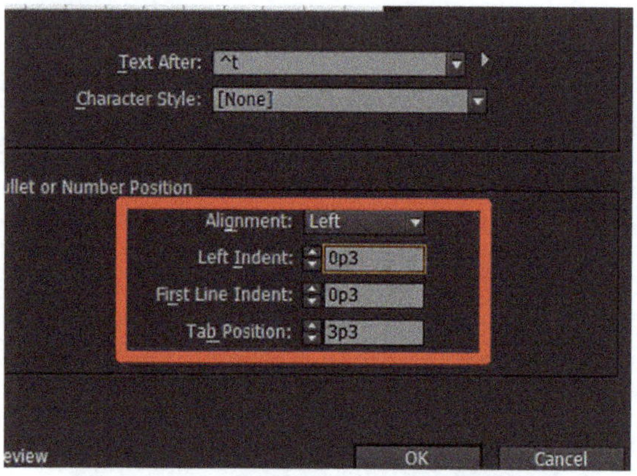

9. Go to the "Right Indent" or "First Line Indent" box and use the same number you used for "Left Indent" but make the number negative. This will move your text close to the bullet and align it in your column or page.

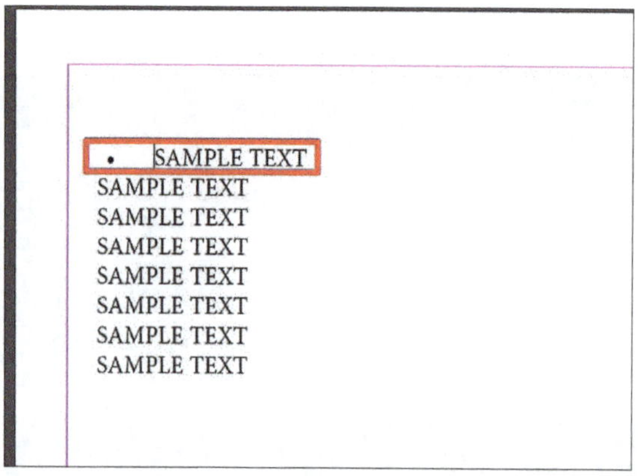

10. Click "OK." InDesign will automatically add bullets to any of the other paragraphs you highlighted.

- If you press "Enter" after any of the bulleted paragraphs, InDesign will automatically place a bullet at the front of the text.

How to wrap Text in Indesign

Text-wrapping is a dynamic design technique that can greatly enhance page layout. Designers use text-wrapping to complement the organic shape of illustrations and other art elements. Follow these steps to effectively wrap text in Indesign.

Steps

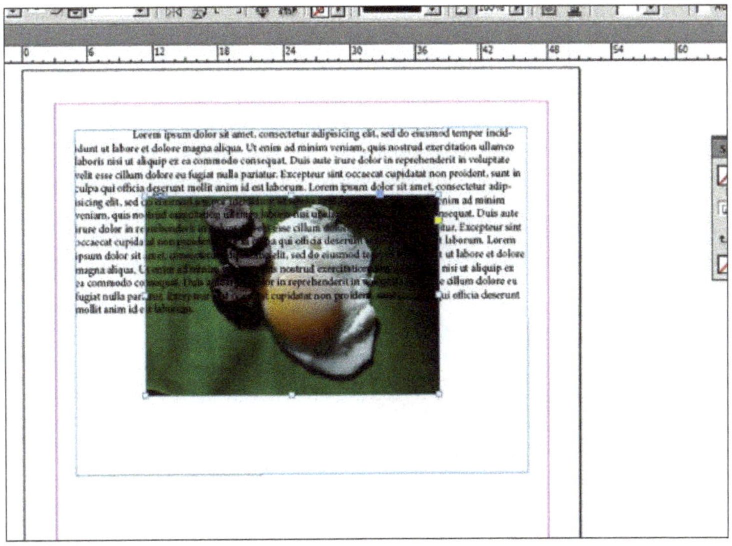

1. Determine around which element the text should wrap. For example, if you want to wrap text around a photo or graphic frame, use the "Selection" tool to click the frame. The element you select will be highlighted with a light-blue border and have handles at its corners.

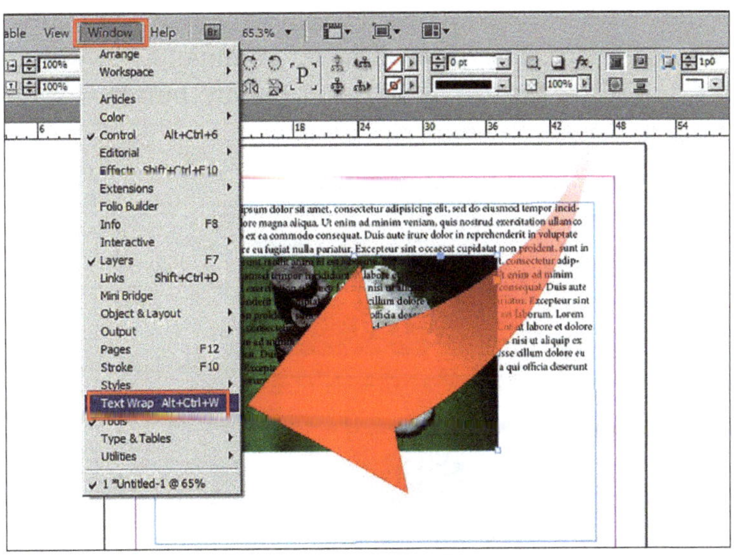

2. Go to the Text Wrap palette. Find the palette by going to "Window," and then select "Text Wrap." You can also use the keyboard command "Ctrl+Alt+W" on a PC or "Command+Option+W" on a Mac.

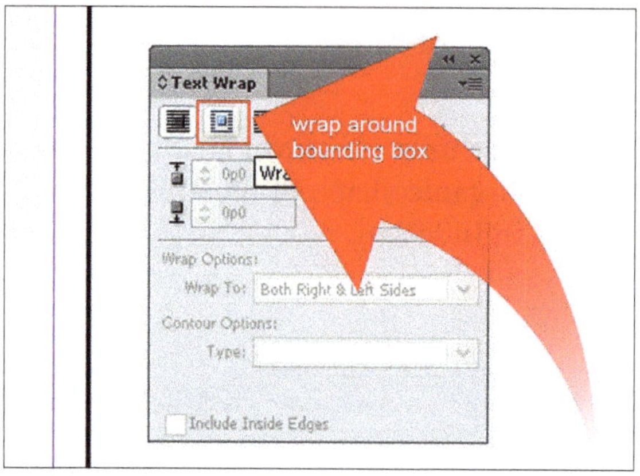

3. Select wrap-around properties. When the palette opens, click "Wrap Around Bounding Box." It is the second icon from the left at the top of the palette. This enables you to wrap text around all sides of the photo or graphic frame. A dialog box will open, prompting you to enter how far off the frame you want the text to run. You can enter different values for each edge of the frame.

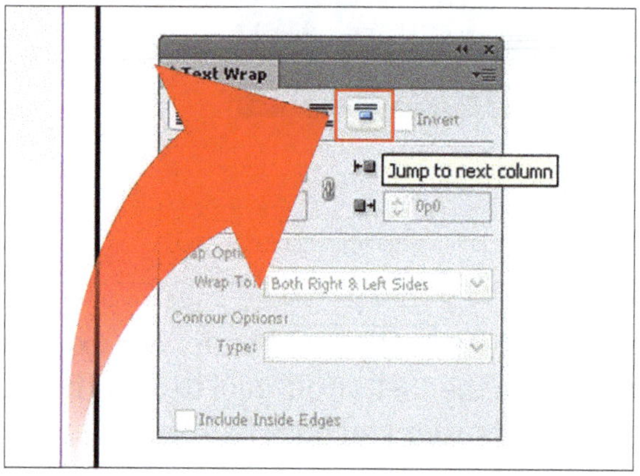

4. Guard against unwanted wraps. The "Jump Object" command prevents undesired text wraps along the sides of the frame. Click the "Jump to Next Column" button to force the text to the next leg of type.

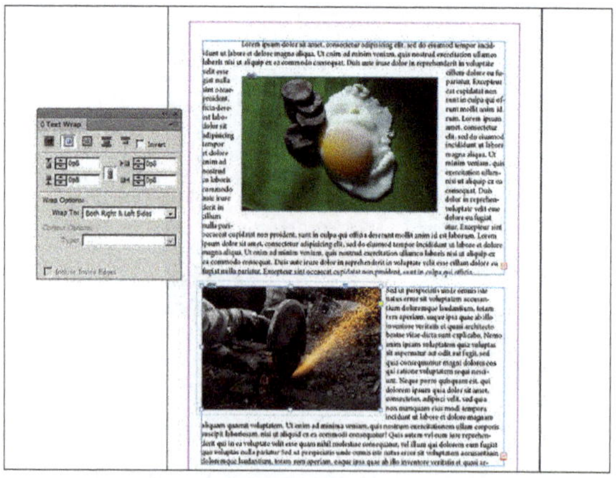

5. Follow the same procedure to wrap body copy around large text. Simply create the display type as a separate item. Select it and utilize the wrap commands as needed.

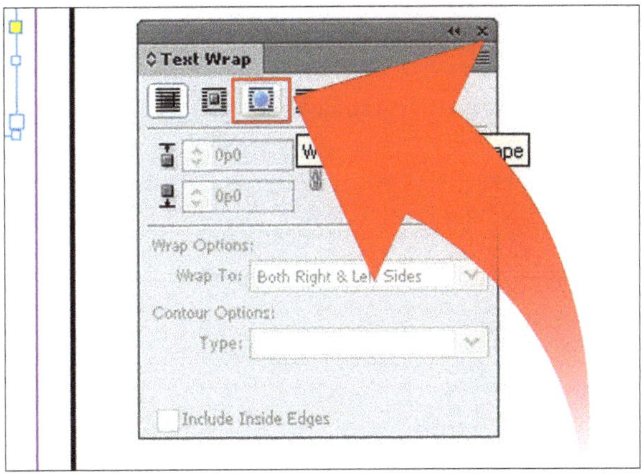

6. Wrap the text around an irregular shape by using the Text Wrap palette. Select an object with an irregular shape. It will be highlighted. Click the “Wrap Around Object Shape” button. It is the third icon from the left in the palette. This function offers a single offset value.

7. Create a clipping path on an object around which you want to wrap type. This is a crucial function to learn if you want to wrap type in Indesign.

- Select an image with a solid background.

- From the main toolbar, click “Object” select “Clipping Path” and then “options”.

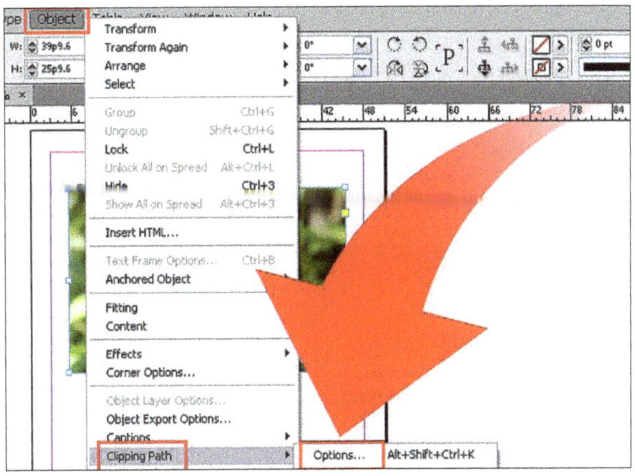

- Use the default settings.

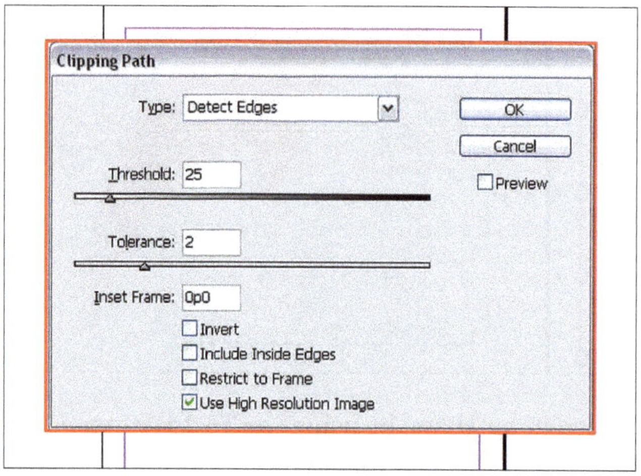

- Drag the Threshold setting to the desired level to help create the path. The higher the setting you choose, the wider the range of pixel removal.

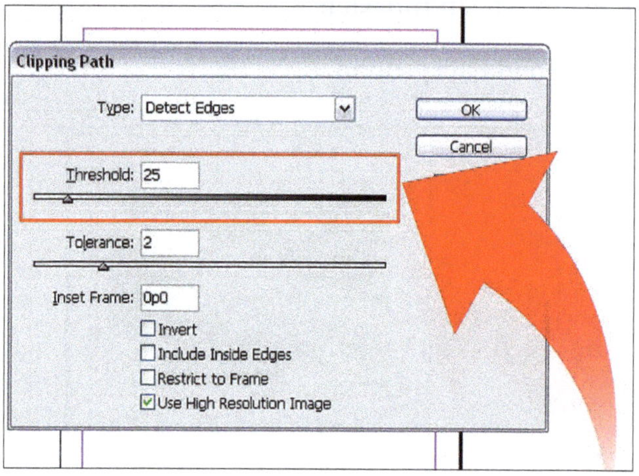

- Manipulate the Tolerance setting to dictate the path's detail. Higher settings make the path less accurate but smoother.

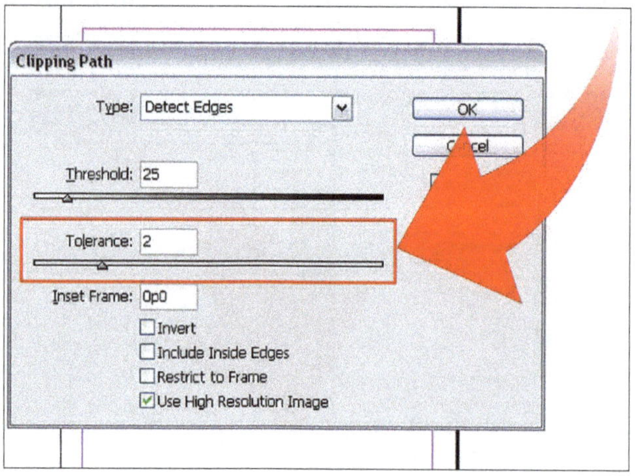

- Enter a value in the "Inset Frame" field. This is a single offset value.

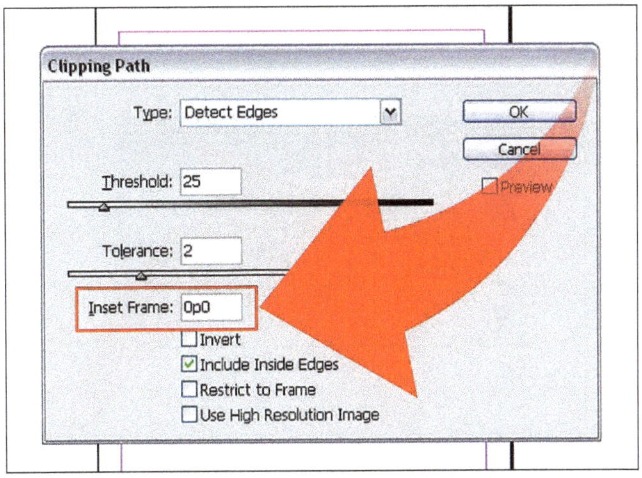

- Choose the "Include Inside Edges" command to make paths inside the image. You might need to adjust the Tolerance setting for the program to select these spaces.

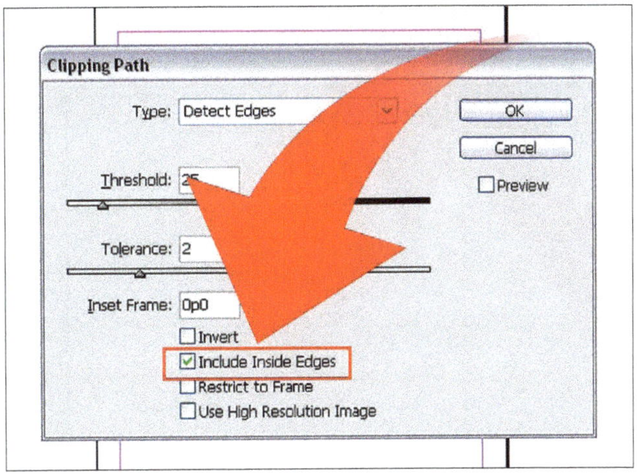

- Save your path, click "ok". Now you're ready to wrap type around this object.

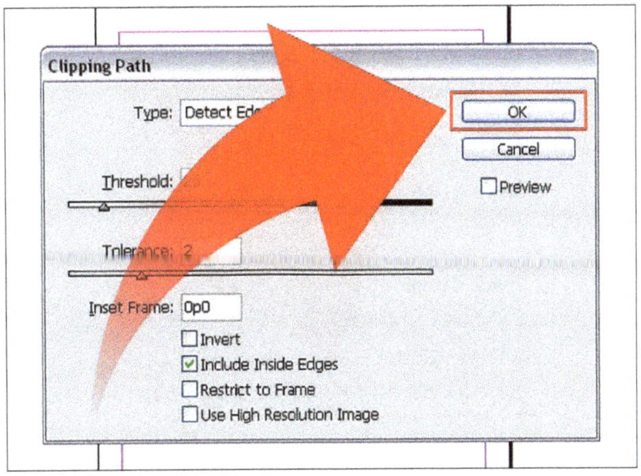

8. Manipulate type to bounce off a clipping path.

- Select the image if the illustration you're using has a clipping path on it. Click the "Wrap Around Object Shape" button.

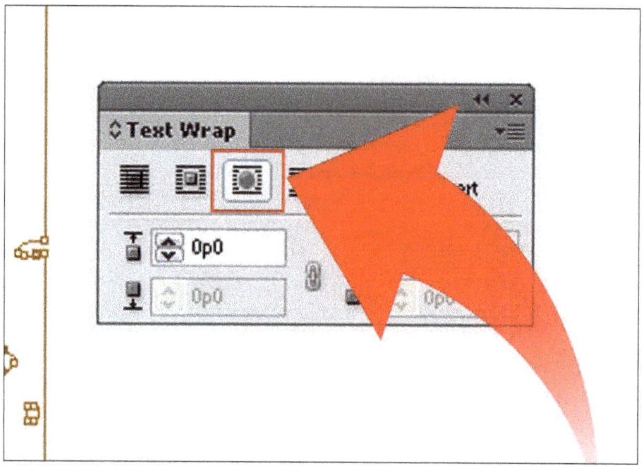

- Select "Show Options" from the palette menu.

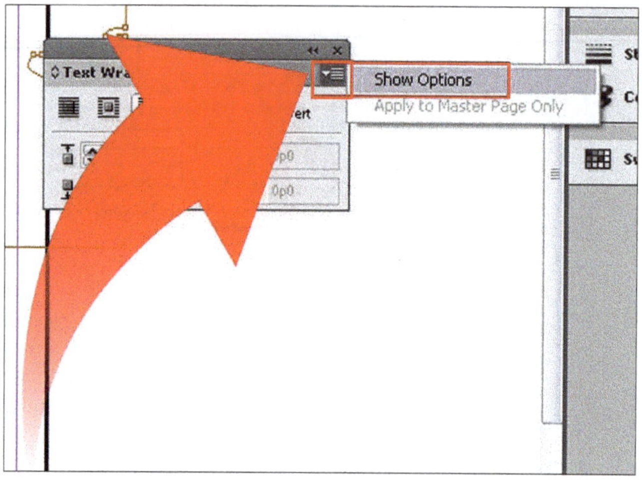

- Choose the "Same As Clipping" option under the "Contour Options" at the bottom of the dialog box.

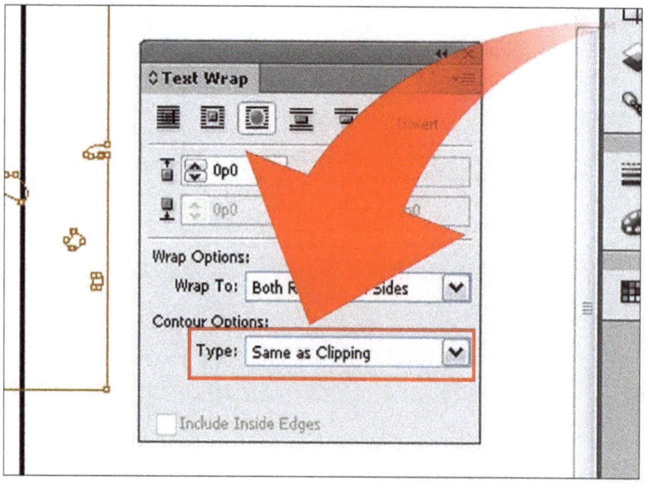

- Enter the value you want the text to bounce off the object.

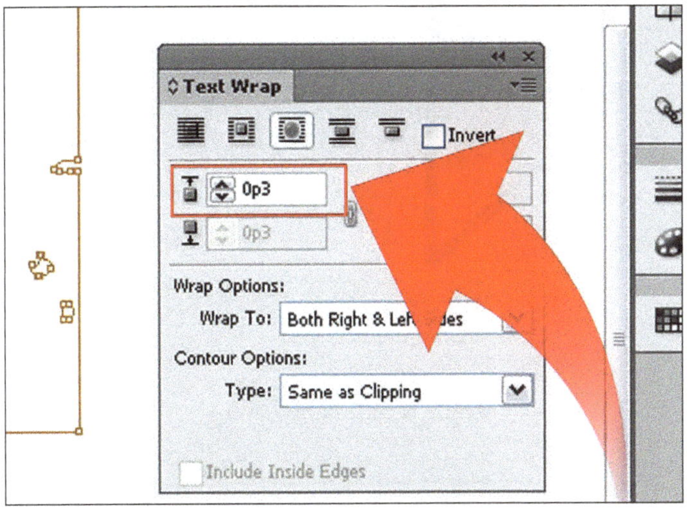

How to create a Background in InDesign

Many print documents benefit from the use of a background to add visual impact or emphasize individual design elements. Backgrounds may be added to a graphic's graphic frame or created by drawing a shape or adjusting the opacity of a photo. Knowing how to create a background in InDesign, a popular desktop publishing program that allows users to create print documents in a variety of sizes and formats, allows to you increase your document's visual appeal.

Method 1

Add a Background to an Image

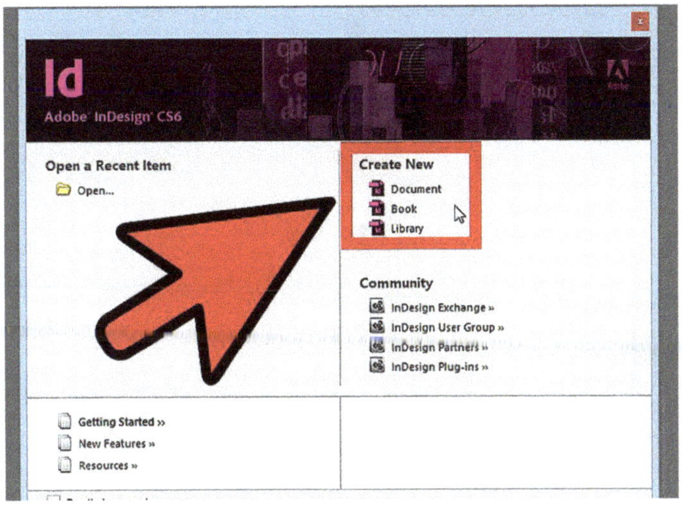

1. Launch InDesign. Create a new document by clicking on the the Document icon in the Create New window, and specifying the settings for your new document.

2. Place an image. From the File menu, select Place. Navigate to the file you would like to import and double click the file name. Move your cursor to the location where you want to place your graphic and click your mouse. This will place the image on your page.

- Adjust the size of your graphic, if necessary, by selecting the picture using the Select tool (V) and dragging a handle while holding the Control + Shift keys (Command + Shift on a Macintosh). This will adjust the graphic's size proportionally.

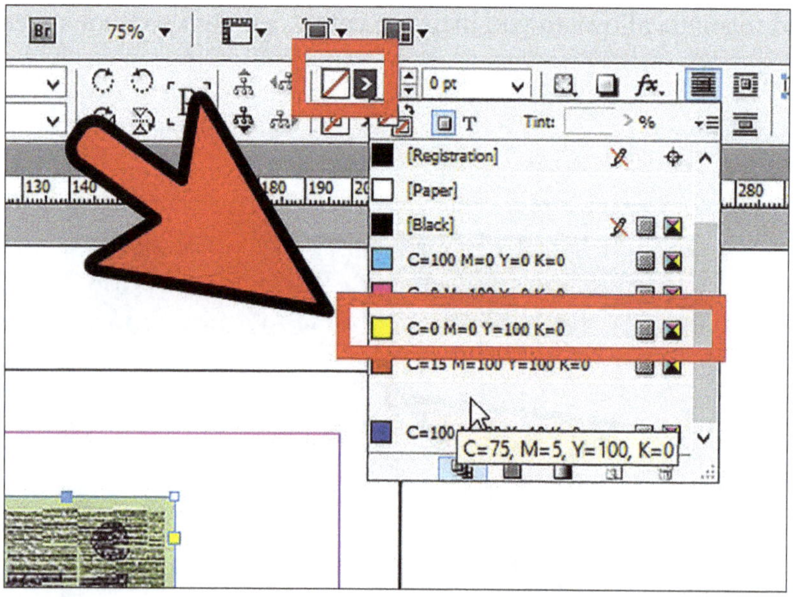

3. Open the Swatches panel. You can access this from a tab group which is located at the right-hand side of your InDesign workspace, or from the toolbar at the top.

- Click the Fill button and select your desired background color. This will apply your selected color behind the graphic and extend it to the edge of the graphic frame.

4. Expand the graphic frame. Pull from a corner of the image while holding the Shift + Alt keys (Shift + Option on a Mac).

- Don't like the color you chose? Select the eyedropper tool (I) and Alt-click (Option-click) a color in the image to find a background color that matches your image perfectly.

Method 2

Creating a Background from an InDesign Object

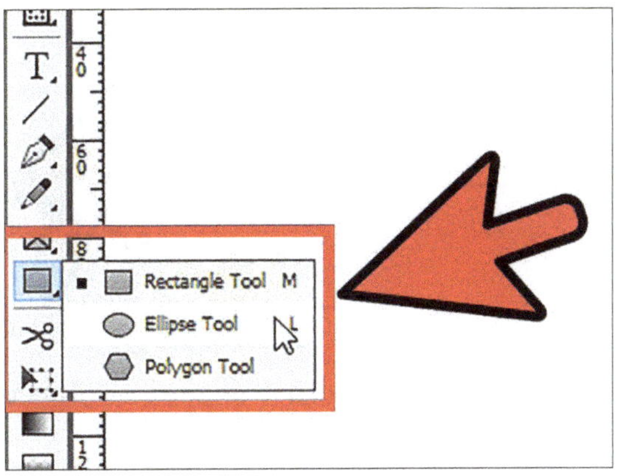

1. Select an object. Choose the Ellipse, Rectangle, or Polygon tool from InDesign's Tools panel.

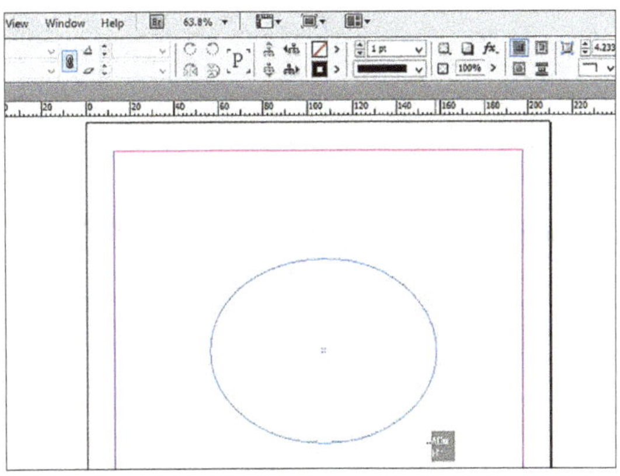

2. Click and drag your mouse to draw your desired background shape. Adjust your background

shape's size by clicking one of your shape's handles with your Select tool and dragging it until your shape is the correct size.

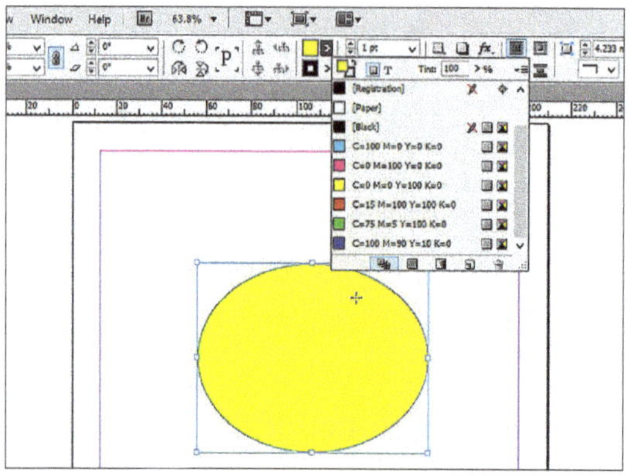

3. Fill the shape. Make sure the object is selected, then open InDesign's Swatches panel and select the Fill button. Choose the color you want to apply from the Swatches panel. Your shape will be filled with that color or gradient.

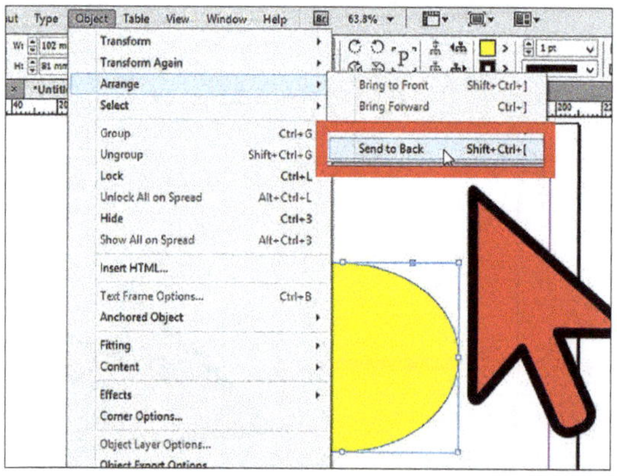

4. Adjust placement of the object. If there are other shapes or objects on the page, click on your background object with your Select tool.

- From the Object menu, chose Arrange > Send to Back This will ensure that your background object stays behind all other objects on your page.

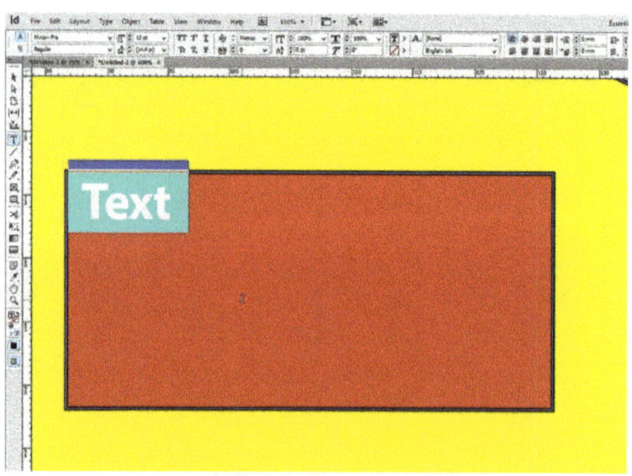

5. Place your desired objects over your background shape.

Method 3

Creating a Background by Adjusting the Opacity of a Photo

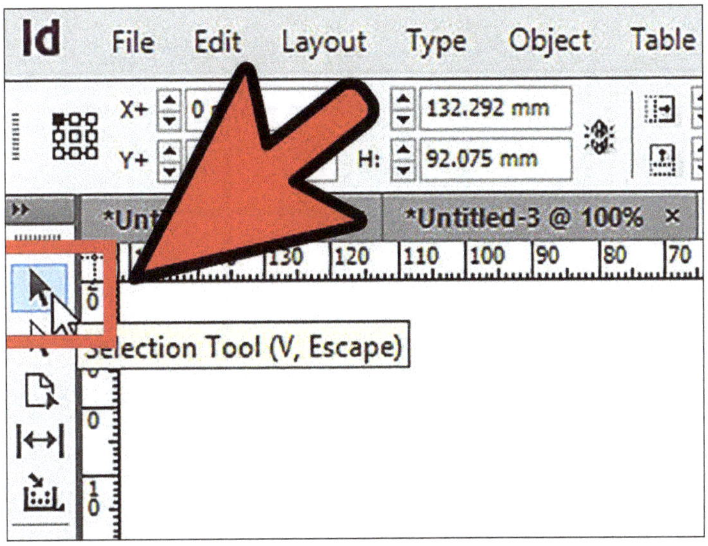

1. Choose the Selection tool (V). Click on the photo you would like to use as a background. (If your document does not have an image, follow the procedure outlined in *Add a Background to an Image,* above.

2. Click the FX button. This is located at the top in the toolbar. From the resulting menu, choose Transparency.

- Adjust your blending mode and transparency as desired. Enable the Preview checkbox on the bottom left to see your changes in real time.
- When you're done, click OK.
- From the Object menu, select Arrange > Send to Back to place your background photo behind all other objects on your page.

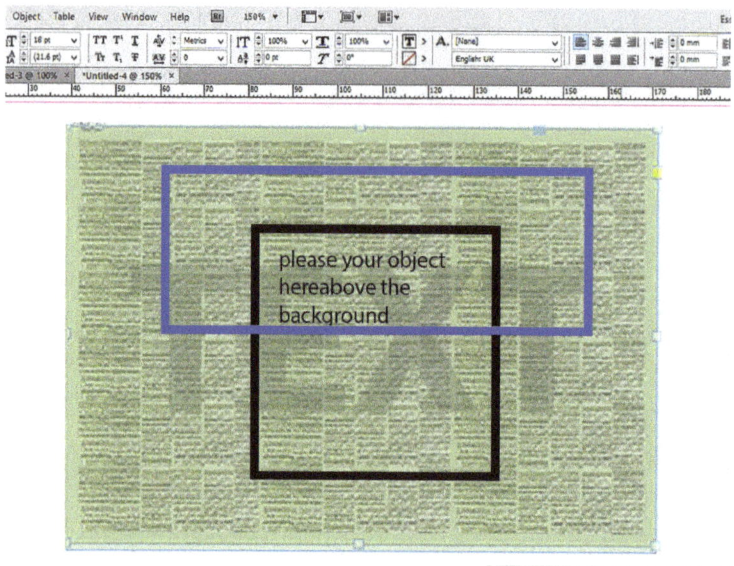

3. Place your desired objects over your background image.

How to create a Brochure using InDesign

Adobe InDesign is a software product that allows you to create desktop publishing projects quickly and easily. You can make brochures and other documents by using the included templates and adjusting them to your needs. Here's how you can use InDesign to create a brochure.

Steps

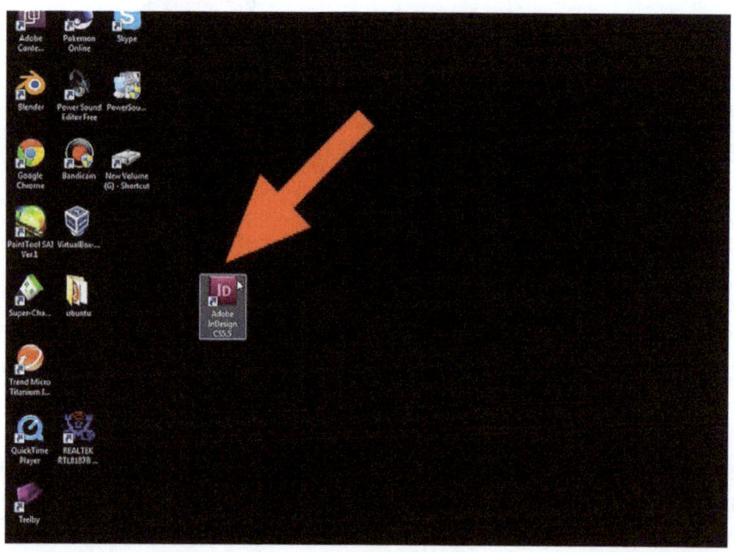

1. Double-clicking on the InDesign icon on your desktop.

- It may also be in the list of installed programs under your Start Menu or Mac Dock.

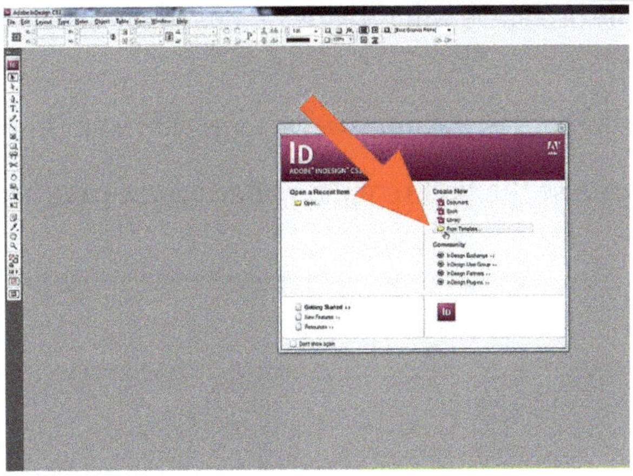

2. Choose "From Template" under the "Create New" command.

- A separate window will launch with several types of document templates.

3. Double-click the "Brochures" folder.

4. Select the size and shape you need to create a brochure.

- Don't worry about the layout or color themes at this stage. You will change those to your preference at a later stage in the process.

- Clicking each sample brochure will provide details of the specific layout at the right side of the window.
- Choose a template that offers the number of pages you want in your brochure.
- For this example, choose the first template offering a 2-page brochure by double-clicking the icon.

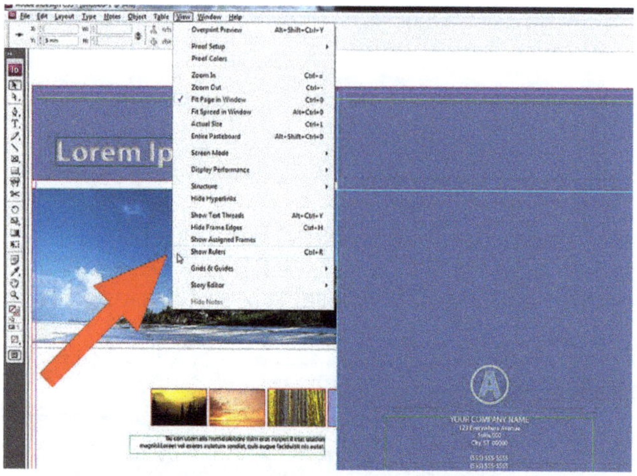

5. Add rulers to the top and side of your brochure, if not already shown, by clicking the "View Options" button in the uppermost toolbar.

- You can also use "View Options" to add guides and frame edges for ease in manipulating the layout.

6. Note the layout of the brochure.

- The first 8 x 11-inch sheet is split down the middle into 2 brochure pages. These will be the fourth and first pages of your brochure, respectively.
- Scroll down to see the next sheet, which will be split into pages 2 and 3 from left to right.
- Scroll back up to work on the first sheet.

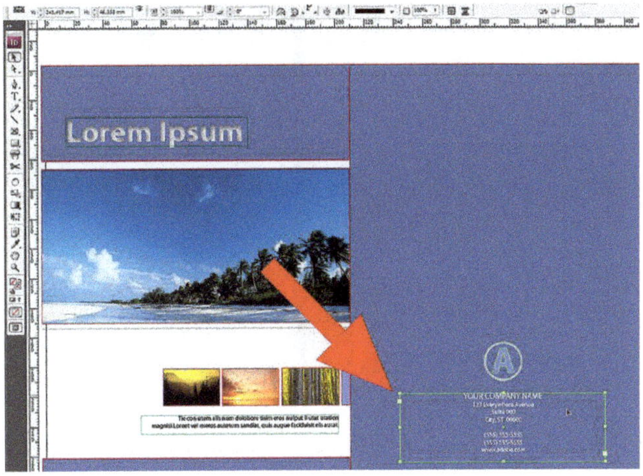

7. Double-click inside the green-edged text box to change the title and description of your brochure.

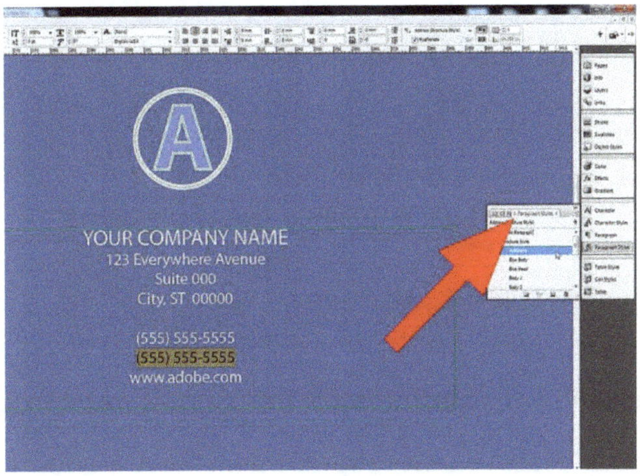

8. Change the text font and size by using the "Paragraph Styles" option in the right pane or by making your own selections in the toolbar at the top of the window.

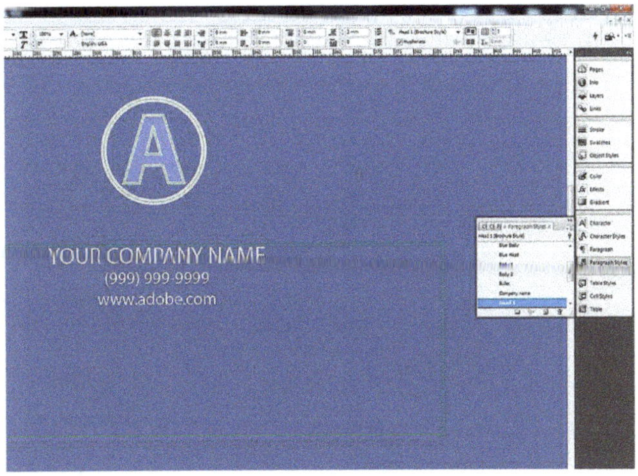

9. Click anywhere outside the text box to accept your changes.

10. Click the photograph on the first page of the brochure and then press "Delete" to remove it.

 - You may need press the "V" key first. This changes to the Selection Tool.

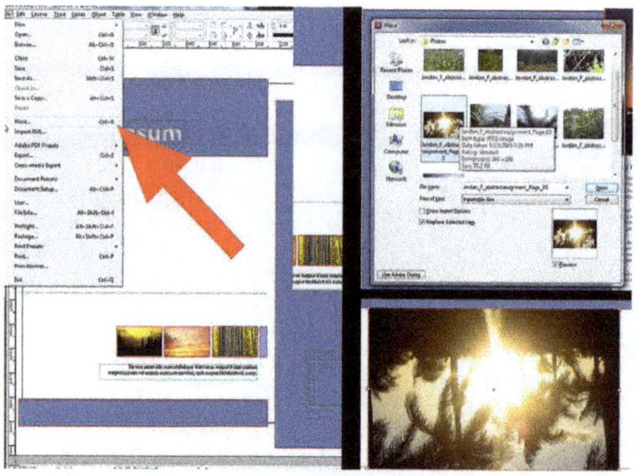

11. Place your own photograph or image file on the first page of your brochure.

 - Click "File" and then "Place" on the drop-down menu. A window will launch.
 - Browse to and select the image file you want to place on your brochure.
 - Use your mouse to draw a rectangle where your image will fit.
 - Once placed, you can resize your image by clicking on a corner and dragging the image.

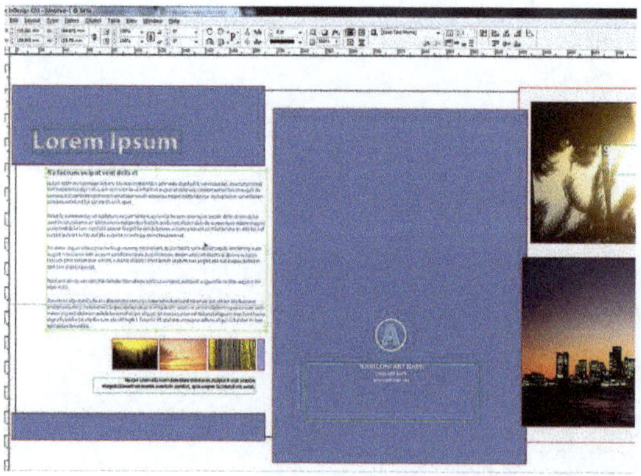

12. Change the other text boxes and images on the first sheet of your brochure.

13. Repeat the process on the second sheet below, keeping in mind that these brochure pages will face each another on the inside.

14. Make any desired changes to colors, fonts and text sizes.

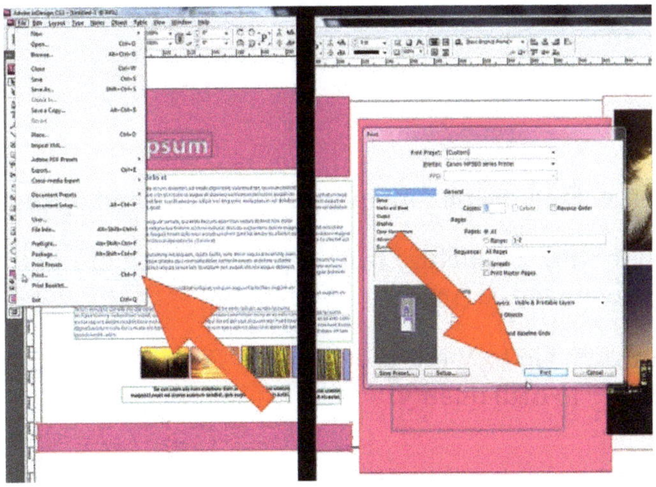

15. Print the first sheet of your brochure.

- Click "File" and then "Print" from the drop-down menu.
- Change the page range to "1" and click "Print."

16. Remove the printed sheet, turn it over and reinsert it into your printer.

17. Print page 2 of your file.

18. Fold the brochure in half lengthwise.

- The right half of the first sheet should be page 1.
- Pages 2 and 3 will be inside the brochure.
- Page 4 will be the left side of the first sheet.

How to make a Flyer in Adobe Indesign

This article explains how to create an effective flyer in Adobe InDesign. These tips will help you make any kind of flyer for your business, class, concert, etc.

Part 1

Starting Off

1. Open the InDesign application. Start a new Document.

2. Click on File on the top left corner. Scroll over to New it will open up three options, select Document.

- You can also open new Document by pressing Ctrl-N for (Windows) and Command-N for (Mac).

3. Choose the margins on this new window that pops up. Also select how many pages and if it will be printed or not.

Part 2

Placing the Background Picture

1. Go to File and then Place. Find the picture in your hard drive and open it.

2. Drag the pointer that is with the picture from top left to bottom right to cover full screen. Or press Ctrl-D (windows) Command-D (mac).

3. Change the picture quality. Go to View, then Display Performance, then High Quality Performance to change the picture to high quality.

Part 3

Adding Information on the Flyer

1. Add the heading. Click on Text (T) on the left panel. Choose where to place the text and then change the Font and Font style at the top.

2. Add other information and lock it. Draw a box by choosing Box on left panel.

3. Fill the box with Black color to contrast it with background.

4. Use the Text (T) tool from left panel to add other information.

5. Select Object from the top bar and click on Lock to lock the text to avoid any accidental changes.

6. Change the font and the color of the text. Make it something that can be easily read. You can change all of these settings at the top.

- Select the color of the text with Eyedropper. Click on the Eyedropper on the left panel.

- Drag it on almost half of the flyer and it will pick up all the colors.
- Choose the color that is appealing to you.

7. Add a QR code. Go to Object and click on Generate QR Code.

8. Add your Website URL for the QR code. Type the website URL in the box and click OK. Place the QR code wherever you would like.

9. Save the InDesign file. Go to File and click on Save As... to save the document as InDesign File. You can name it whatever you would like. Select the destination to save the file.

Part 4

Exporting and Printing the Flyer

1. Click on File and then Export in order to print you must export to PDF first.

2. Change the format to Adobe PDF (print) by using the drop down menu. Then click Save.

3. Select High Quality Print on the next popup menu and click Export.

4. Open the PDF file and print your flyer.

How to create a Newsletter in InDesign

This teaches you how to create a newsletter using Adobe's InDesign publishing app.

Part 1

Setting up a Newsletter

1. Create a new file in Adobe InDesign. To do so, double-click on the pink app with the letters "Id," click on File in the menu bar, click on New, and click on Document.... A dialog box will open.

2. Select a publishing type. To do so, click on the "Intent:" drop-down menu and choose from:

- Print to create a printed newsletter;
- Web to create a newsletter that will be published on a website; or
- Digital Publishing to create a newsletter that will be electronically delivered to a device.

3. Select a size for the pages of your newsletter. Use the "Page Size:" drop-down to do so.

- Use this drop-down to select the target screen-size for digitally-published newsletters.
- Many print newsletters have standard, letter-sized pages.

4. Set the length of your newsletter in the "Number of Pages:" field.

- If you're creating a print newsletter that you intend to fold, and it's not already checked, check "Facing Pages."

5. Set the number of columns on each page. To do so, click on the small arrows next to the "Number:" field in the "Columns" section to increase or decrease the number.

- The value in the "Gutter:" field is the amount space between columns.
- Newsletters appear neater and more legible if the text is broken into columns.
- Two or three columns are common on a letter-sized newsletter.

6. Click on OK.

Part 2

Creating a Masthead

1. Click on the Type Tool. It's the T in the tool menu on the left side of the window.

2. Click and drag to create a text field. Start in the upper-left corner of the left column, drag the pointer to the upper-right corner of the right column, then drag downward until the text field is the size of the masthead you'd like.

3. Release the click.

4. Click in the text field.

5. Type the name of the newsletter. Add any additional information that you'd like, such as date, volume, or issue number.

6. Make adjustments to the text. To do so, highlight the text you want to adjust with the cursor and use the tools at the top of the window:

- Use the drop-down menus on the left side of the toolbar to change the font and/or text style.
- Click in the field with the big and small "T"s, next to the font name, to adjust the size of the text.

- Use the alignment buttons (eight icons made up of horizontal lines) on the right side of the toolbar to: Center the text; align it to the left side of the text box; align it to the right side; or justify the text so it's distributed across the text box and aligned to both sides.

Part 3

Adding Body Text

1. Click on the Type Tool. It's the T in the tool menu on the left side of the window.

2. Click and drag to create a text field. Start in the upper-left of a column, below the masthead, drag the pointer to the lower-right corner of the column so that the text box is the same length and width of the column.

   - The masthead will typically only be on the front page.

3. Release the click.

4. Click in the text field.

5. Type or paste the text of the article in the text box.

6. Make adjustments to the text. To do so, highlight the text with the cursor and use the tools at the top of the window:

   - Use the drop-down menus on the left side of the toolbar to change the font and/or text style.
     - Headlines above articles are often bold or italic and sometimes use a different font from the main text of an article.
   - Click in the field with the big and small "T"s, next to the font name, to adjust the size of the text.
     - Body text is usually 10- or 12-point type. Headlines are typically larger.
   - Use the alignment buttons (eight icons made up of horizontal lines) on the right side of the toolbar to align the text.
     - Body text in columns is usually aligned left or justified.
     - Headlines are typically aligned left, centered, or justified.

Part 4

Adding Images

1. Click on the Selection Tool. It's the black pointer at the top of the tool menu on the left side of the screen.

2. Click on File in the menu bar, then Place.

3. Select the image you want to add and click on Open.

4. Click on and drag the image to position it in the newsletter.

- To change the size of the image, click on Object in the menu bar, then click on Transform and Scale.... Enter the percentage by which you'd like to shrink or enlarge the image and click on OK.

5. Wrap text around the image. To align newsletter text around the image, click on the image and click on a "text wrap" button (four icons of horizontal lines around an object) toward the right side of the toolbar at the top of the window.

- To wrap text around a rectangular image, click on the button that has a square in the middle, which is surrounded, but not overlapped, by horizontal lines.
- To wrap text around an irregularly-shaped image, click on the button that has a circle in the middle, which is surrounded, but not overlapped, by horizontal lines.
- To have the text stop above and continue below the image, without wrapping along the sides, click on the button with a rectangle in the center and horizontal lines above and below it.

Chapter 5

Animation: An Introduction

Macromedia Flash is one of the software that is used to create multimedia and animated images. Animation may be in 2D or 3D. Animation process is best understood in confluence with the major topics listed in the following chapter.

How to make a Simple Animation in Macromedia Flash

This article gives you the basics of creating a simple animation in Macromedia Flash.

Steps

1. Open Macromedia Flash 10

2. Choose frame 1 on the timeline which is located above the canvas.

3. Draw whatever you want to in your first frame (eg: a stick figure).

4. Choose the next frame depending upon the length of your animation. The larger the difference between the frames, the longer the animation.

5. Right click on the frame and click “Insert KEYFrame”.

6. Right click anywhere between the first and the last frame and select "Create Motion Tween". Now the same picture you drew in the first frame will appear in the last frame you made.

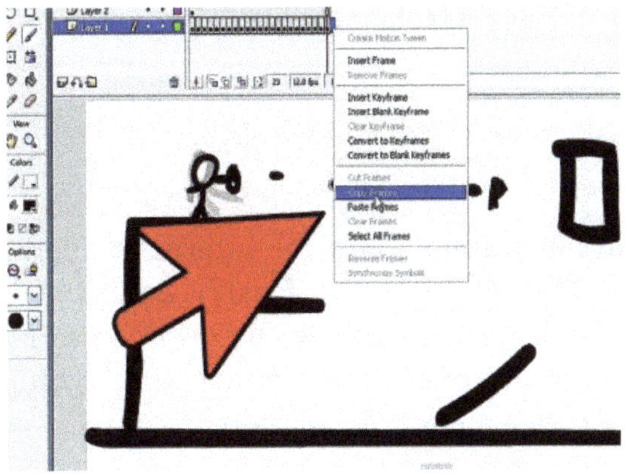

7. Edit this picture in any way. You can change its size, position or other effects such as alpha, tint, etc. They appear when you right click on the object and click "Properties".

8. Press

Ctrl

↵ Enter

to view the animation.

9. Play around and experiment. There is a lot more to flash animation than just this.

How to create a Flash Animation

Flash is the premier medium for Animation on the Internet, and even on other formats such as Television. Creating a simple Flash Animation in Flash is actually fairly simple to accomplish, as Flash provides a lot of useful Tools that simplify the entire process. If you've got an idea for a Flash Animation or a Cartoon, you can probably have a rough sketch going in just a couple hours. See Step #1 below to learn how to create a Flash Animation.

Part 1

Making a Frame-by-Frame Flash Animation

1. Understand the basics of frame-by-frame animation. This is considered the "traditional" method of animation, in that each frame has the same picture but slightly altered. When the frames are played together, the images appear to move. This is the same basic technique used by traditional hand-animators, and is more time-consuming than tweening.

- By default, Flash will produce animations at 24 frames per second (FPS). That means one second of animation will have 24 frames, but not every frame has to be different. You can adjust this if you'd like, and many Flash animations use 12 FPS, but 24 will produce much "smoother"-looking animation.

2. Install Flash Professional. There are a variety of Flash animation programs available, but the most powerful is Adobe's Flash Professional CC. You can install the trial for free, or you can use another product if subscribing to Adobe's Creative Cloud doesn't appeal to you. The rest of this article will refer to Flash Professional or any other editing program as "Flash".

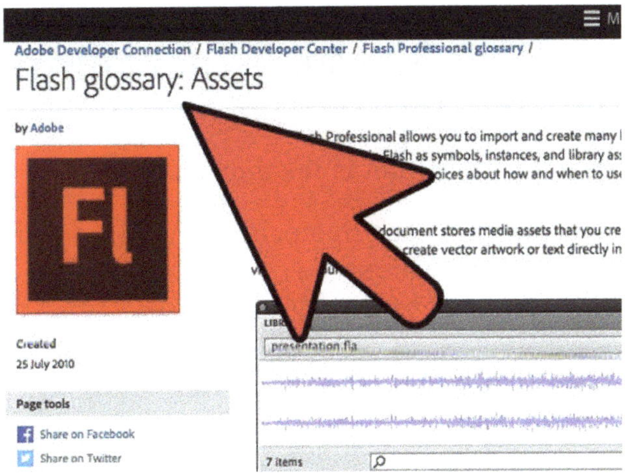

3. Create your assets. Because frame-by-frame animation requires multiple images with slight differences, you will need to create all of these assets by hand. You can create them all before you begin, or make them as you go. You can use the Flash program to draw directly in your project, or you can draw your assets in your favorite image creation program.

- If you want your images to scale without sacrificing quality, you will want to create them as vectors instead of rasters. Vector images will redraw themselves whenever they are scaled, which means there won't be any pixelation or aliasing. Raster images are the traditional images you're probably used to (photos, Paint images, etc.). These do not scale well, and can look quite ugly if you want to make them larger.

4. Create your first frame. When you first start Flash, you will have a blank layer and an empty Timeline. As you add frames, your timeline will be populated automatically. You can interact with layers much in the same way that you would in Photoshop.

- Before adding your image, create a basic background for your movie. Rename Layer 1 to "Background" and then lock the layer. Create a second layer and name it whatever you'd like. This will be the layer that you create your animation on.
- Add your drawing to the canvas in the first frame. You can either import your drawing from your computer, or you can use Flash's drawing tools to create a drawing directly in the program.
- Your first frame will be a *keyframe*. Keyframes are frames that have an image, and form the backbone of your animation. You will be creating a new keyframe each time the picture changes.
- Keyframes are denoted by a black dot in the timeline.
- You don't need a new image in each frame. In general having a keyframe every four-five frames will produce a good animation.

5. Turn your drawing into a *symbol*. By turning your drawing into a symbol, you can easily add it multiple times in a frame. This is especially useful if you need to quickly create multiple objects, such as a school of fish.

- Select your entire drawing. Right-click on the selection and select "Convert to Symbol". This will add the image to your Library where you can quickly access it in the future.

- Delete the drawing. Don't worry! You will be adding it back to the scene by simply dragging the object from your Library. You can add multiple instances of the same drawing to your scene with ease.

6. Add some blank frames. Once you have your first frame ready, you can add your blank frames that will exist between the first keyframe and the second keyframe. Press F5 four or five times to add blank frames after your first keyframe.

7. Create your second keyframe. Once you've added a few blank frames, you're ready to create your second keyframe. There are essentially two different ways you can do this: you can copy your existing keyframe and make small adjustments, or you can create a blank keyframe and insert a new image. If you are using art created in another program, you'll want the second method. If you created your art using Flash's design tools, use the first method.

- To create a keyframe using the contents of the previous keyframe, press F6. To create a blank keyframe, right-click on the last frame in your timeline and select "Insert Blank Keyframe". Anything in your scene will be removed.

- Once you've created your second keyframe, you will need to make adjustments to the image to give the effect of motion. If you're using Flash's design tools, you can use the

Transform tool to select aspects of your drawing and move them slightly, such as the arm of a stick-person.

- If you're inserting new art for each keyframe, you will want to ensure that it is placed in the same location or in the next logical location on the screen. This will ensure that the art doesn't jump around between frames.

8. Repeat the process. Now that you've created two keyframes, it's time to iterate. You will be repeating essentially the same process until you are finished with your animation. Add a few blank frames between each keyframe, and ensure that your movements look fluid.

- Make small, incremental changes. Your animation will look much smoother if you make very small changes to the keyframe. For example, if you want a stick person waving an arm, your second keyframe should not be the other end of the wave. Instead, use a few keyframes to transition from the beginning of the wave to the end. This will produce a much smoother animation.

Part 2

Making a Point-to-Point Animation (Tweening)

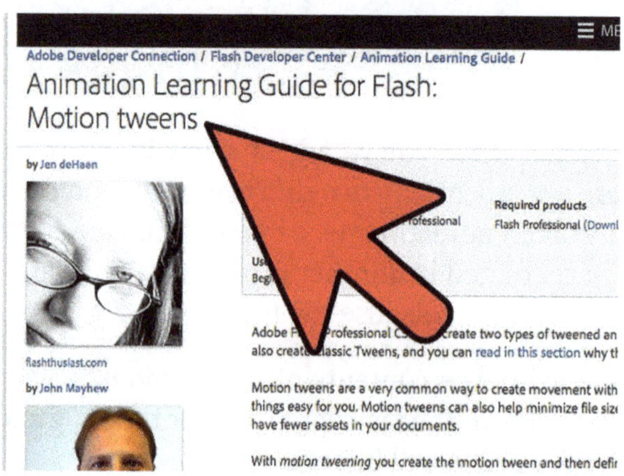

1. Understand the basics of *tweening*. Flash contains a function called tweening, which allows you to essentially set start- and end-points for your object. Flash will then move and transform the

object based on your settings between these two points, creating the illusion of animation. You will not need to create images for every keyframe like you would with frame-by-frame animation.

- Tweening is especially useful for creating "morphing" effects, where one object becomes another one over the course of the animation.
- Frame-by-frame animation and tweening can be used in conjunction in the same movie.
- You can only have one object undergoing a motion tween at a time. This means that if you want multiple objects to animate at once, they will all need to be on separate layers.

2. Create your first object. Unlike frame-by-frame animation, you will not need to create multiple objects to animate using the tween function. Instead, you will be creating one object, and then changing its properties during the tweening process.

- Before adding your image, create a basic background for your movie. Rename Layer 1 to "Background" and then lock the layer. Create a second layer and name it whatever you'd like. This will be the layer that you create your animation on.
- It is highly-recommended that you use Flash's built-in design tools or import your image from a vector-drawing program. Vectors can scale easily without distortion, while traditional raster images will not scale and transform well.

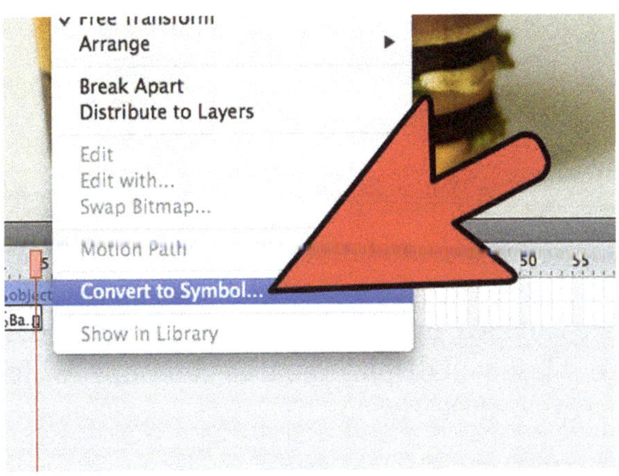

3. Convert your object to a symbol. In order to tween your object, you will need to convert it into

a symbol. This is the format for objects that Flash uses in order to manipulate them. If you try to tween an object that has not been made into a symbol, you will be prompted to do so first.

- Right-click on your object and select "Convert to Symbol" The object will be added to your Library, which makes it easy to clone objects.

4. Create your first motion tween. A motion tween moves the object from one location to another Right-click the symbol in your scene and select "Create Motion Tween". 24 frames will be added to your timeline, as this is the default length of a tween. Remember, by default Flash will animate at 24 frames per second, meaning that this motion tween will take one second to complete.

- When you create the motion tween, you are automatically moved to the last frame of the tween.

5. Create the trajectory. Once you have created the tween, you can move the object to the location that you want it to end up at. Flash will display the trajectory line, which is dotted to show the location of the object for each frame of the tween.

- When you first create the trajectory, it will be a straight line from the starting point to the ending point.

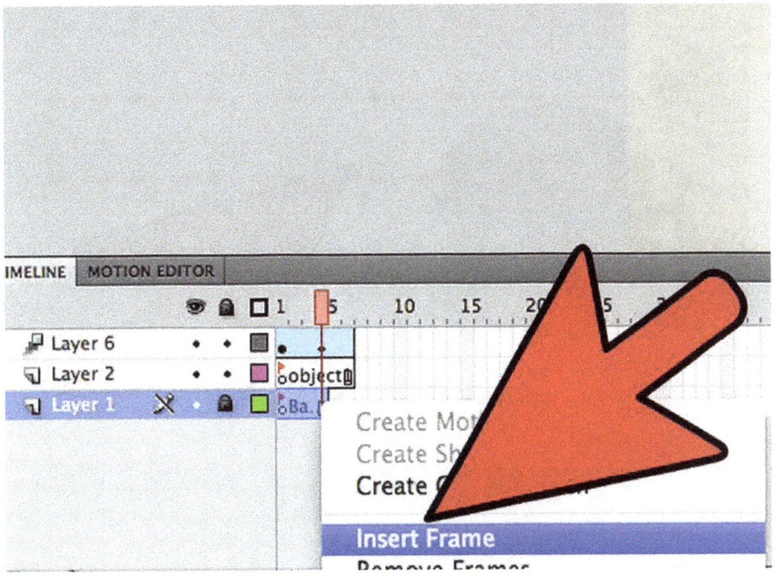

6. Extend your background frames. If you ran your animation right now, your object would move along the trajectory, but your background would disappear after one frame. To fix this, you will need to extend your background across all the frames of the animation.

- Select your background layer in the timeline. Click the last frame on your timeline, which should also be the frame your motion tween ends on. Press F5 to insert frames up to this point, which will keep your background displayed during the entirety of the tween.

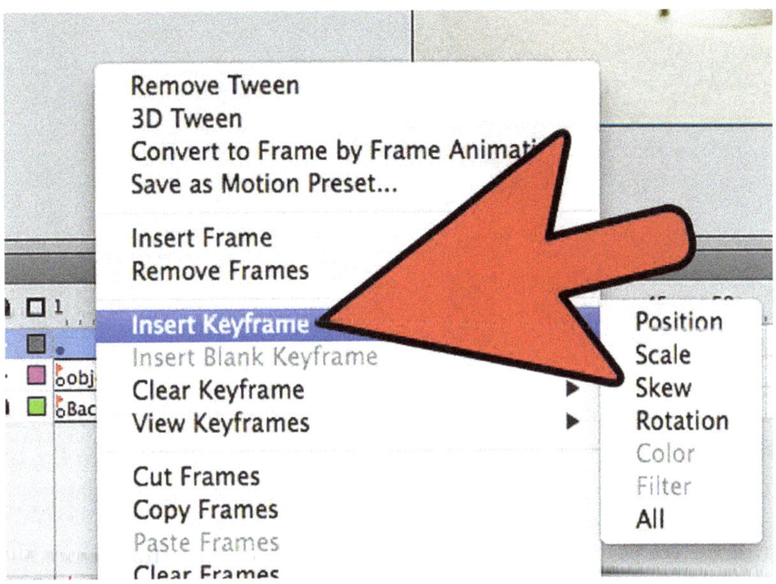

7. Add keyframes. Adding keyframes to your trajectory will allow you to transform your object during the motion tween. You can only make changes to an object if it is keyframed. To add keyframes to your trajectory, first select the frame in the timeline that you want to turn into a keyframe. Then, click and drag the object into the position you want it to be at during that frame. Your trajectory will adjust automatically, and a keyframe will be added to the timeline. Keyframes are denoted by diamond icons in the timeline.

8. Adjust your tween trajectory. To change the path of your object, you can click and drag each of the frame position markers on the path to a new location. Avoid putting to much variation in the path, or the object will move in an erratic fashion (unless this is your goal!).

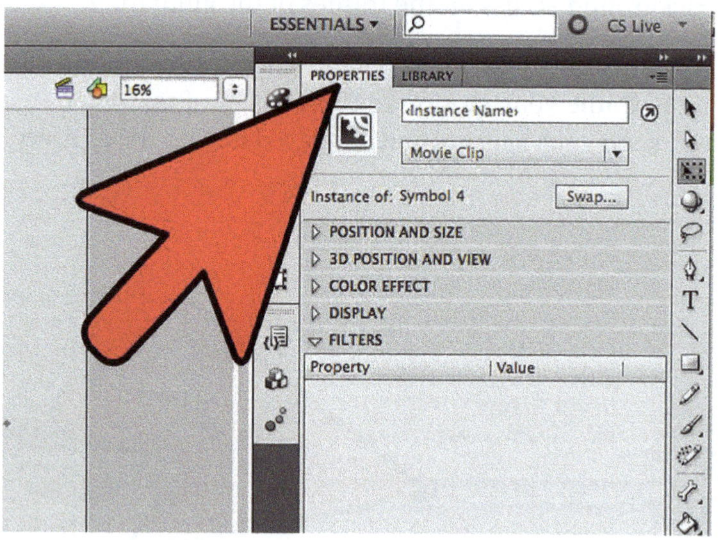

9. Transform your object. Once you have your keyframes and trajectory established, you can transform your object so that it changes as it moves through the motion tween trajectory. You can change the shape, color, rotation, size, and any other property of the object.

- Select the frame that you want the transformation to occur in.
- Open the object's Properties panel. You can press Ctrl+F3 if the panel is not currently visible.
- Change any values in the Properties window to affect the object. For example, you can change the hue or color, add filters, or change the scale.
- You can also use the Free Transform tool to freely change the shape however you'd like.

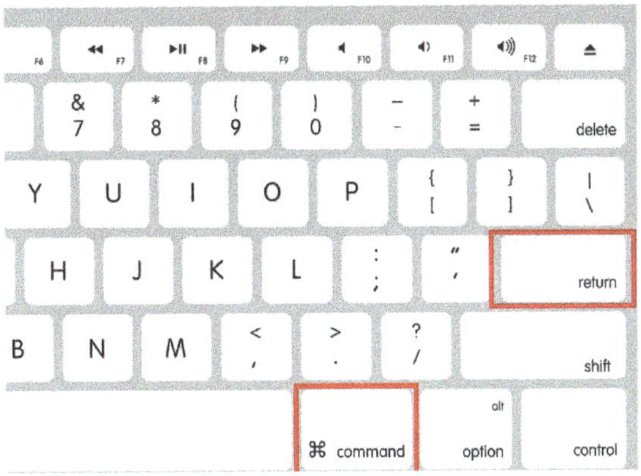

10. Make finishing touches to your tween. Test your motion tween by pressing Ctrl+☐ Enter. Ensure that the transformations look good and that the animation is moving at the correct speed. If your animation is moving too fast, you can either lower the FPS of the scene or increase the tween span.

- By default, the FPS is 24, so try lowering it to 12. To do so, click outside the scene and then change the FPS in the Properties panel. Changing it to 12 will double the length of your animation, but may make it more "jerky".
- To change your tween span, select the layer that contains the tween and use the slider to pull it out. If you want the tween to be twice as long, extend it to 48 frames. Make sure to insert blank frames in your background layer so that the background doesn't disappear halfway through the animation. To extend the background, select the layer, click the last frame of the animation in the timeline, and then press F5

Part 3

Adding Sound and Music

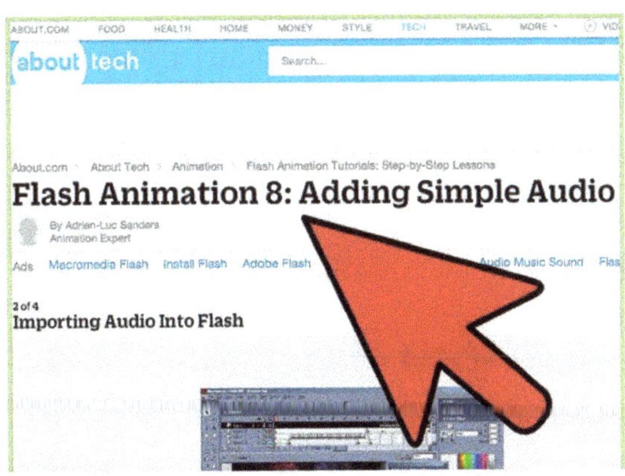

1. Record or find your sound effects and music. You can add sound effects to actions that occur in your animation to help make it stand out and give it some personality. Music makes your animation more immersive, and can make a good animation into an incredible one. Flash supports a variety of file formats, including AAC, MP3, WAV, and AU. Choose the on that gives you the best quality for the lowest file size.

- MP3 will typically give you perfectly acceptable sound quality while keeping the file size to a minimum. Avoid WAV files if possible, as these are often quite large.

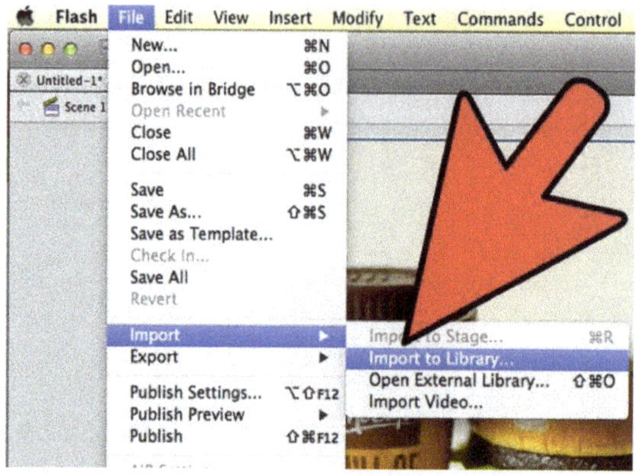

2. Import the sound files to your Library. Before you can add sounds to your project, they need to be added to Flash's Library. This will allow you to quickly add them to your project later. Click File → Import → Import to Library. Browse for the sound file on your computer. Make sure that the sound file has an easy to remember name, so you can quickly find it from the menu later.

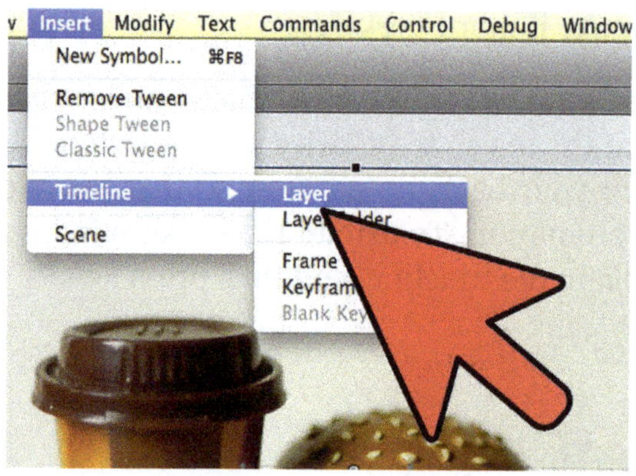

3. Create a new layer for each sound file. This is not strictly necessary, as you can add sound to existing layers, but putting each file on its own layer will give you much more control over fading in and out, when to start and stop, and it is easier to move sounds around.

4. Create a keyframe where the sound will start. On the sound's layer, select the frame in the

animation that you want the sound to start at. Press F7 to insert a blank keyframe. For example, if you want to include a music file that plays for the duration of the animation, select the first frame on the music file's layer. If you are adding dialog for a character, select the frame where the character begins talking.

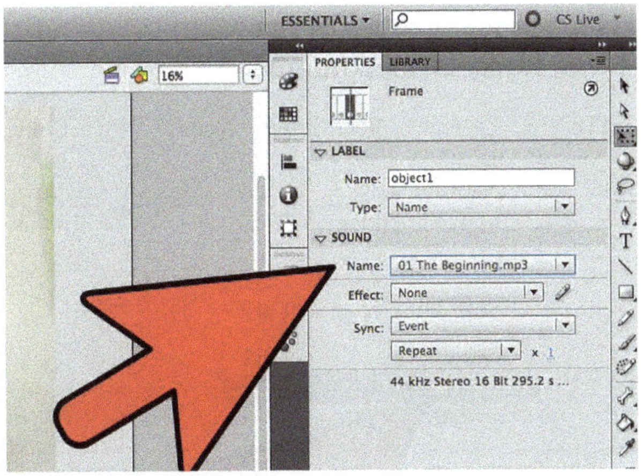

5. Add the sound or music file. In the Properties frame, you will see a Sound section. You may need to expand it to see the options. Click the "Name" menu and select the file you want from your Library.

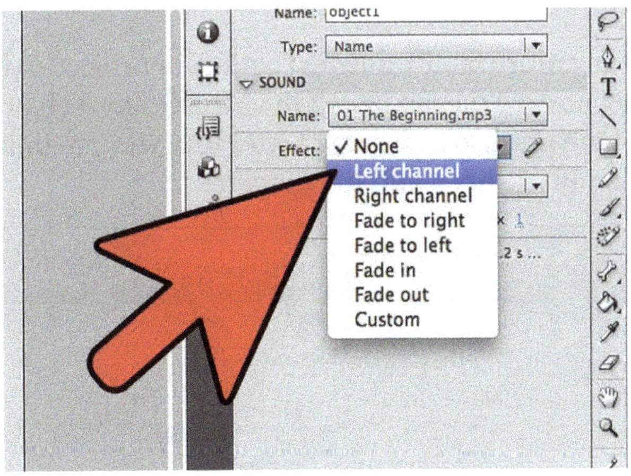

6. Configure the sound file. Once you've selected a file, you can configure how it will play. What you select will be based on what you need the sound to accomplish in the animation. You can change the Effect, the Sync, and the Repeat settings of each sound using the menu underneath the Name menu in the Properties frame.

- Effect - This lets add effects to the sound, such as fading in and out or adding echo. You can select from preset settings in the drop-down menu, or you can click the pencil icon next to the menu to create your own custom settings.
- Sync - This determines how the song is played in the animation. *Event* will play the sound until it is finished. If the same sound is triggered again before the first one ends, the the original will keep playing until it finishes. *Start* works like Event, but stops if the sound plays again. *Stop* stops the sound in that frame. If you want to use this in conjunction with

other sound properties, create a new keyframe where you want the sound to stop and use this option. *Stream* will attempt to match the sound that is playing with the number of frames on other layers. This is best used for dialogue.

- Repeat - This setting allows you to set how long the sound repeats. You can set it to play only once, or have it loop as many times as you want. If your animation is a looping animation, you should set your music to loop infinitely.

7. Finish your project. When you are finally finished with your project, save it as an SWF file. This is the format used to play the movie. You can play it in virtually any web browser, or use a dedicated Flash player to watch it. There are also a variety of sites that you can upload it to for others to see, such as Newgrounds, Albino Blacksheep and Kongregate.

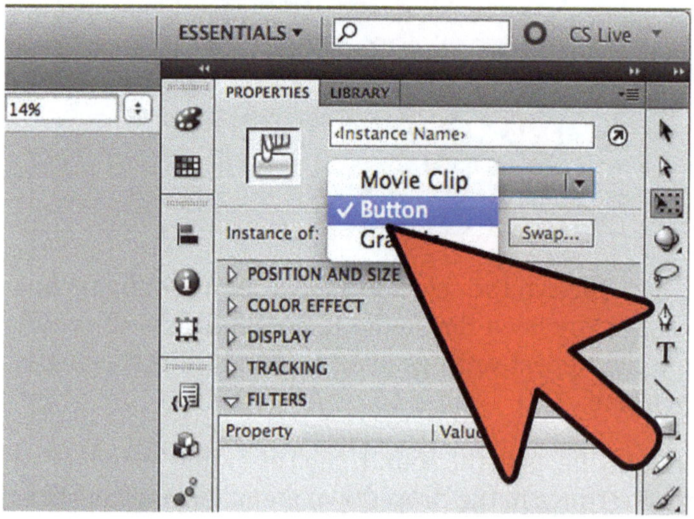

8. Take your future projects further. This guide addresses the basics of creating an animation, but there is so much more you can learn and do. Add a few buttons and branching paths, and you've got a choose-your-own-adventure game. You can take a crash course in ActionScript and gain much more control over the finer details of your animation. Keep experimenting, and you'll soon find yourself learning all kinds of tricks and implementations.

How to make a LEGO Animation

LEGO® bricks are one of the most classic, fun, and clever toys ever made. Advances in consumer electronics, such as affordable computers, camcorders and digital cameras have made it possible for to produce high quality Lego animations inexpensively.

Steps

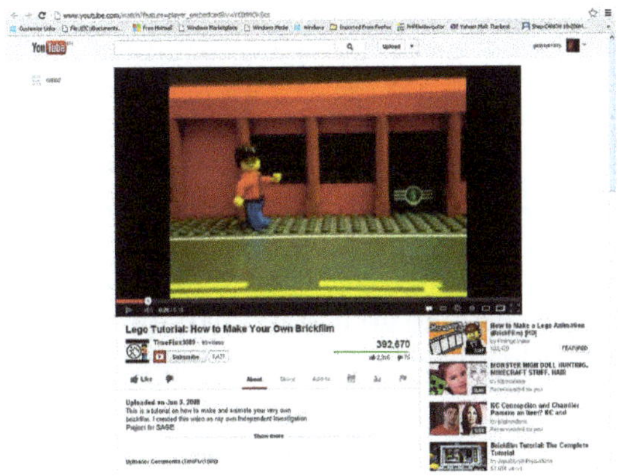

1. Go on a video sharing website like Youtube and search for LEGO movies, to get ideas. (Examples:LEGO Star Wars, LEGO Mario, LEGO Batman.etc.)

2. Make sure you have all of your materials.

3. Build and stage your set, this could be 100% Lego, a real world scene or a combination of the

two. Be sure to look through the camera you'll be using, to get a sense of how your video will look. While you're doing this you can check for unwanted elements that need to be covered up or camouflaged, especially in the background.

4. Next get the Lego minifigure actors ready. As the stock minifigure heads are very static you may want to have a few suitable heads ready to go if you'd like for your actors to be expressive. If you can't find heads that work you could always paint some yourself.

5. Position the starting scene of your movie and your camera keeping in mind that it is imperative that the camera be immobilized; otherwise your finished video will be jerky. Use a tripod or similar device to keep the camera still, then take the picture.

6. Now it is time to move the actors in your scene, but just a little bit. It is easiest to move the character about two paces on the platform or about half an inch on the floor. Continue this until you are done with your movie.

7. Use any stop motion application on your computer that can make variable fps time settings. preferably one that can set up to 15fps, It will give the best results.

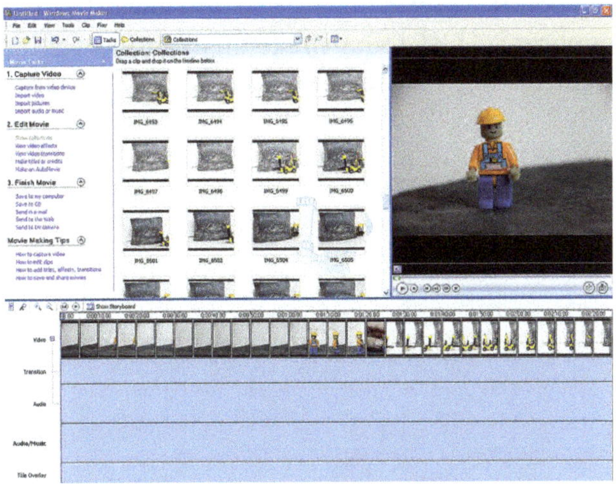

8. Go on iMovie, Windows Movie Maker or another movie making program and import your photos.

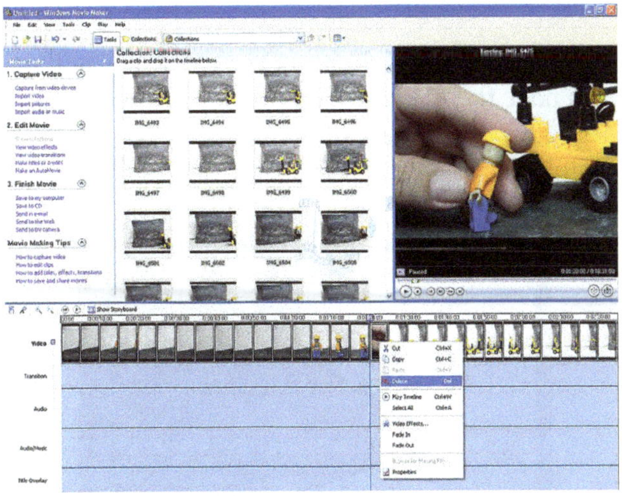

9. Delete any extra photos and put them in the correct order.

10. Watch your movie using the sideshow setting.

How to Convert a Video into a GIF Animation

GIFs are basically video flip books. Converting a video into a short GIF makes it smaller and easier to manage, and the popularity of GIF today make them perfect for blog posts, witty retorts, or simple jokes with friends. Converting GIFs to video is easy, and there are several ways to pull it off.

Method 1

Using Photoshop

1. Open your version of Photoshop without opening your video. You'll need a copy of the video to convert into a GIF. Once you have the file, open Photoshop, but do not select the video file just yet.

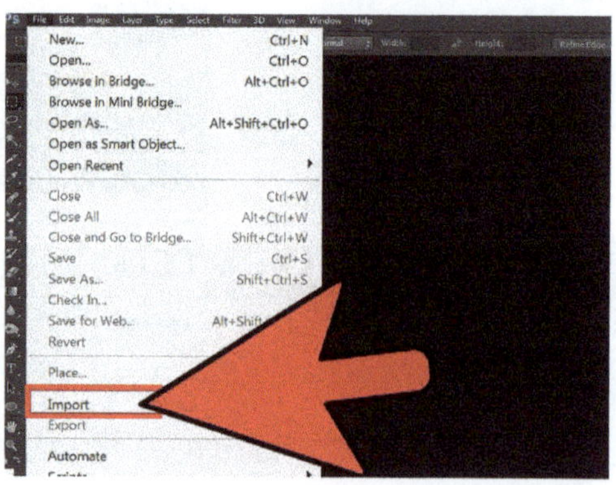

2. Click on "File," then "Import," and select "Video Frames to Layers." This will bring up a menu

box allowing you to change your settings when important the video. A GIF is basically a very fast slideshow. Photoshop takes your video and breaks it into these still images, allowing you to choose which ones are played together and turned into a GIF.

- If your file is already an .AVI movie file, skip ahead to the last step of the method.

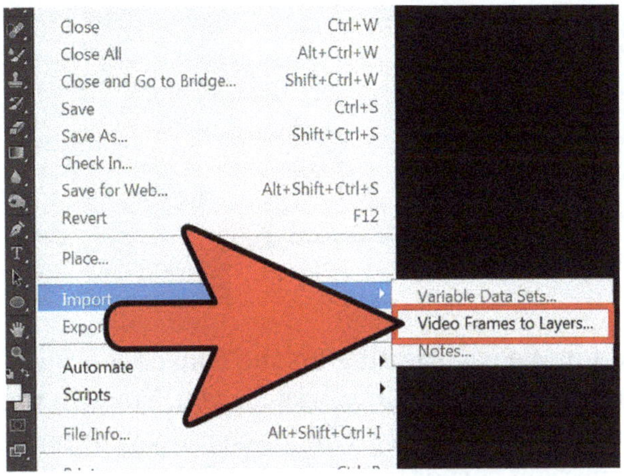

3. Choose the settings needed for your GIF. These will change from person to person, but the basics are easy to understand and adapt. The only crucial setting is that "Make Frame Animation" must be checked. Click "OK" when done to start your conversion.

- Selected Range Only allows you to move the sliders under the video preview to just the area you want to keep. The less video you use, the faster it will be.
- Limit to Every... allows you to cut out every other frame of the video, or more. The final GIF will be a bit choppy, but it will also be a smaller, faster file. The higher this number, the faster the final GIF will be and the easier it will be to work with. Uncheck it for the best, smoothest video quality.

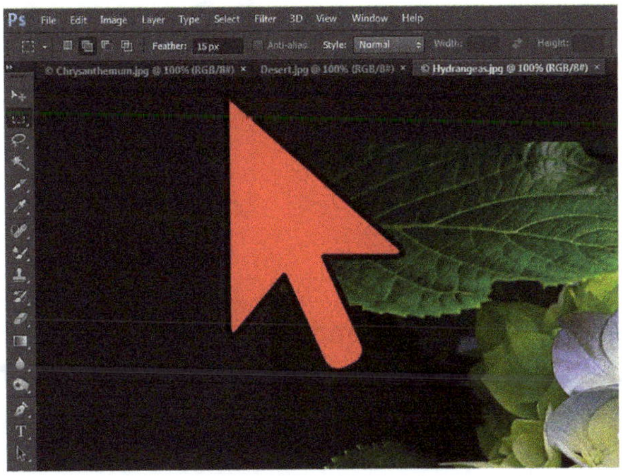

4. Edit or delete any frames you don't want in your final GIF. Each layer will be a frame of the final GIF. You can remove some, move the order around, or add text and other shapes and colors to the frames. You can recolor them, change to black and white, or add effects. Anything done to the layers now will be reflected in the final GIF.

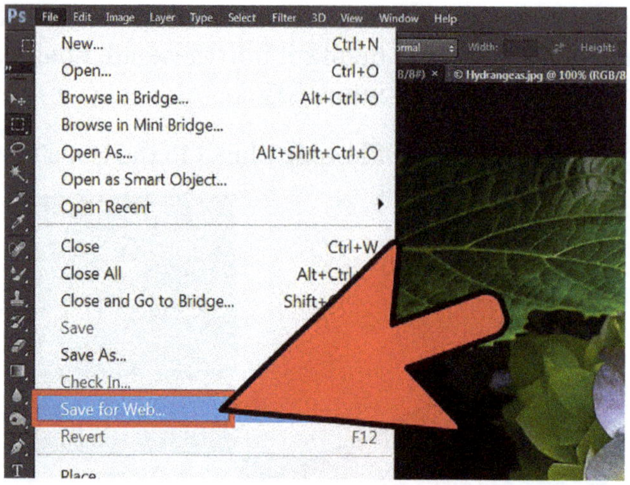

5. Click "File," then "Save for Web..." to bring up the conversion menu. Under "Presets" in the upper-right corner, choose a GIF option that works for you. You can then adjust everything from the transparency to the color mode, though sRGB is generally your best bet. After you've chosen a name, hit save in the bottom-right corner to finish your GIF.

- Before saving, you can use the "Optimize" button in the Timeline view (brought up by "Make Frame Animation" to slightly shrink the file size of the GIF. This is usually important for websites that want to stay fast and lean.

Method 2

Using Online Converters

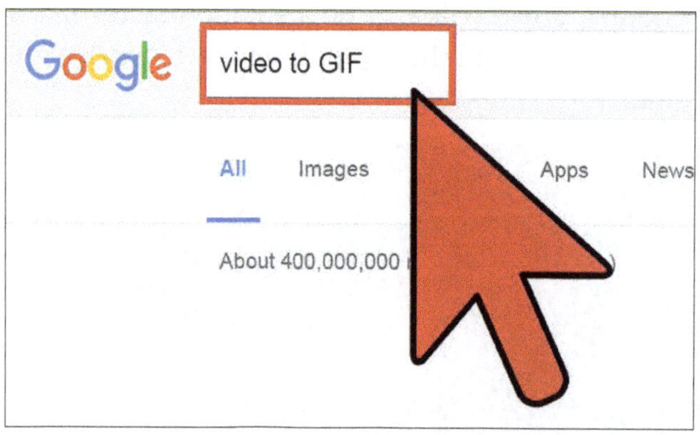

1. Search online for "Video to GIF" converter and find a site you feel comfortable using. There are hundreds of reputable, usable sites online for creating free GIFS. Use your favorite search engine to look one up -- there are plenty of viable options on the first page alone. While you can use any conversion site you like, some tested sites include:

- Imgur
- EzGif
- MakeaGif.com

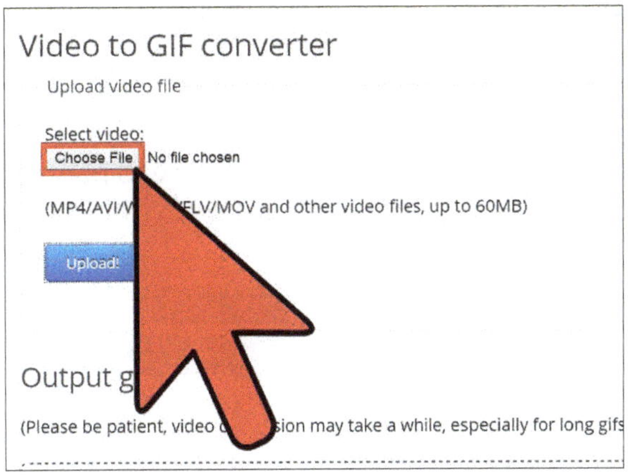

2. Find a video you want to make into a GIF online. You generally have two options -- you can either copy and paste the URL of the video from YouTube or Vimeo (Imgur), or drag and drop your video file from your computer (EzGif, MakeaGif).

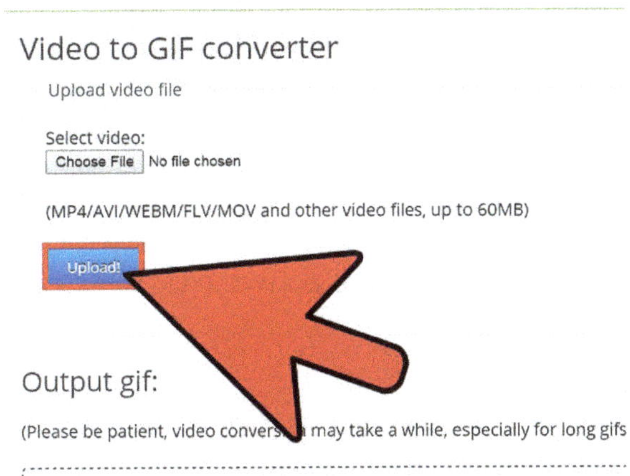

3. Locate the part of the video you want to convert. Find what part of the video you want to capture and pause it a few seconds before that position. Also, decide how big you want the GIF. In most web browsers, you can hold control and press plus and minus (+ -) to zoom in and out. If you're using a media player, you can re-size the window to change the size.

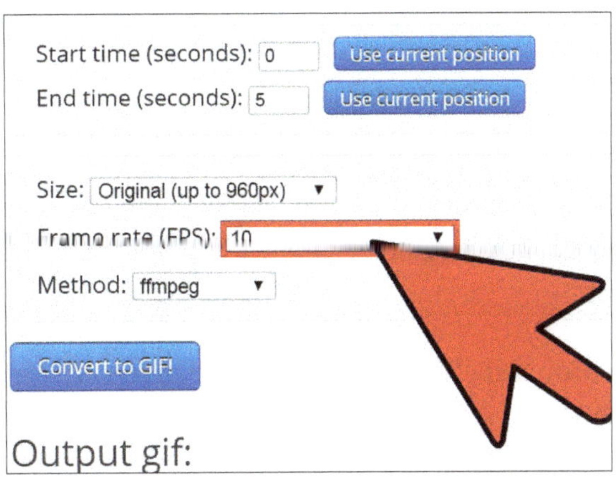

4. If offered, decide what frame rate you want to use. 12 FPS (frames per second) is a good frame

rate to capture faster movements. However, if your GIF is too big, your computer may not be able to run everything smoothly at a higher frame rate. Most videos are shot at either 30 or 60 fps, but GIFs are meant to be quicker, smaller, and a little jerky looking.

- The smaller the framerate, the faster the GIF will take to play and load. 10-15 FPS is usually perfect.

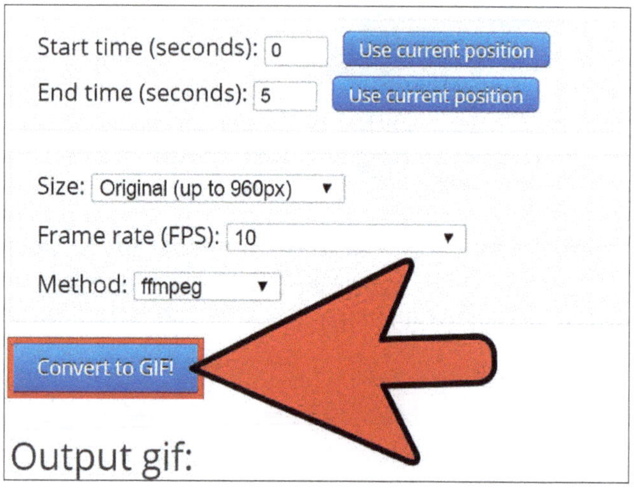

5. Press the record, review, or save button to convert your video. All of these sites are different -- still, the button used to save or convert your video should be easy to find. You'll likely be asked to select where to save your finished GIF when it is converted.

Method 3

Using Microsoft GIF Animator (.AVI Files Only)

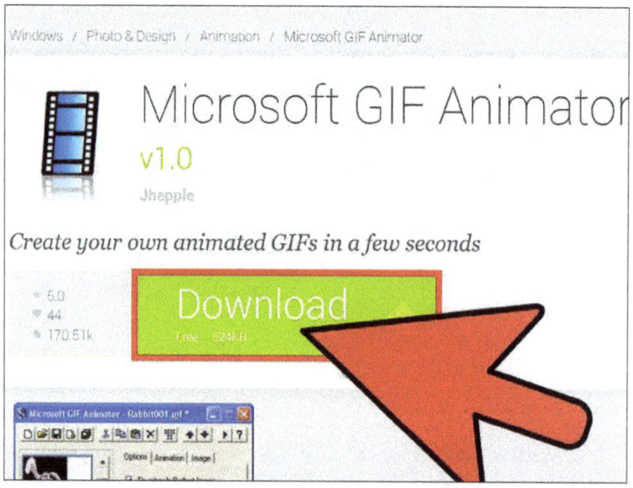

1. Open Microsoft GIF Animator and click the Open icon. This icon is of a folder being opened. This program comes standard on many Windows computers and is a quick and easy way to get a GIF. You must, however, use a .AVI movie file, which is a Microsoft-specific codec.

- If you don't have it, you can download MS GIF Animator for free online.

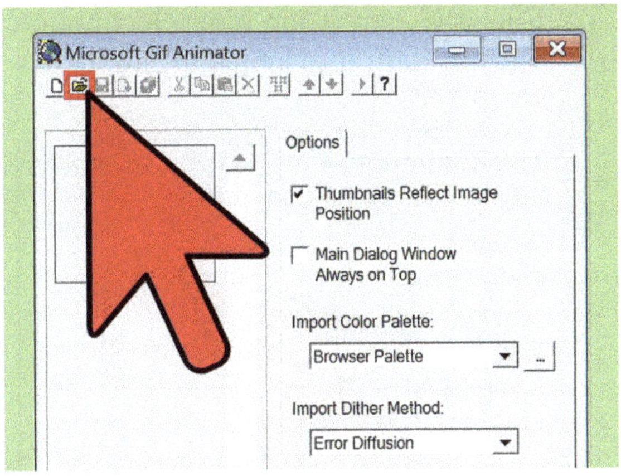

2. Navigate to the desired .avi video and select Open. The program will now read the individual frames from the video. This may take a while if you have a large video. If you are attempting to take a small part from a large video, cut the video to only that part before opening it in MS GIF Animator.

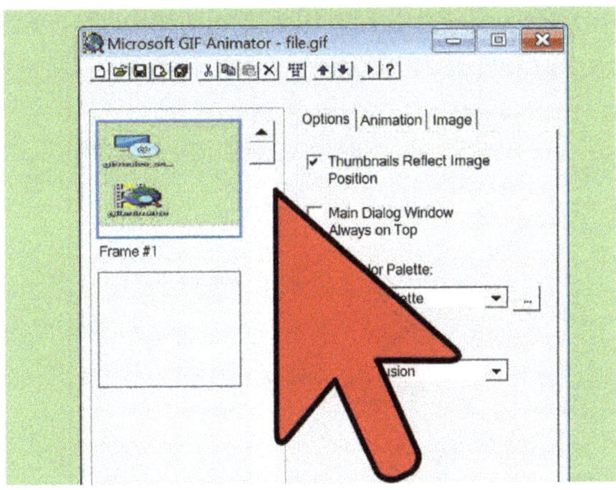

3. Edit, remove, or reorder the list of your frames along the side of the screen. These images show you the different frames of your video as you scroll down, like a flipbook. If you click the Play button, your video should play. It may not be the speed you'd like yet, but this can be changed.

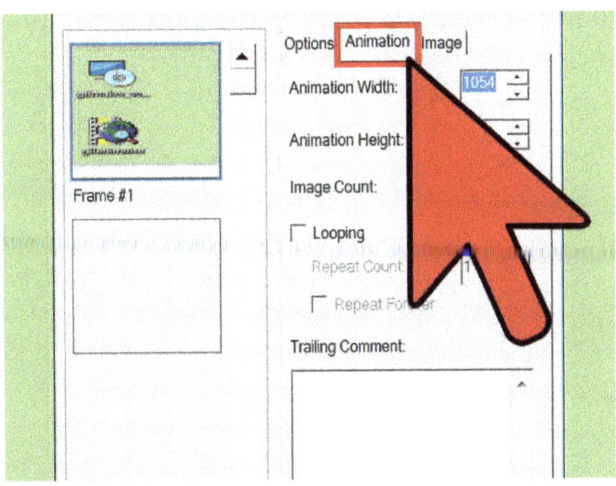

4. Loop your video like a real GIF. Select all frames by clicking the Select All button. This is the

button with three squares on it. Click the Animation tab, select Looping, and set how many times you want it to loop. Select forever if you want it to loop continuously.

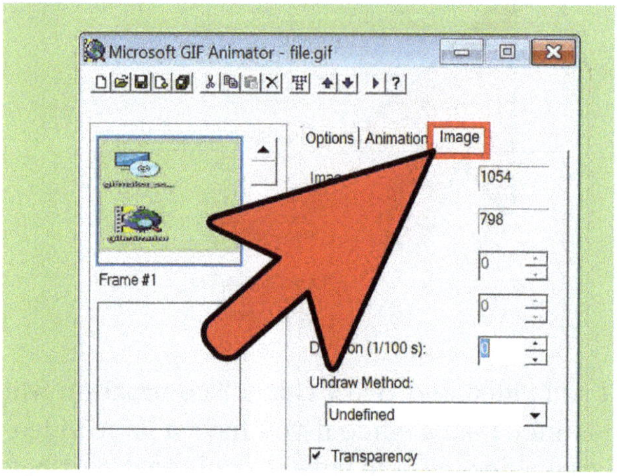

5. Click the Image tab and set the duration of each frame using the slider. Every time you change the duration, play it again and see what it looks like. Generally, 2-6 works well, but depending on the frame rate of your video you may need more or even less.

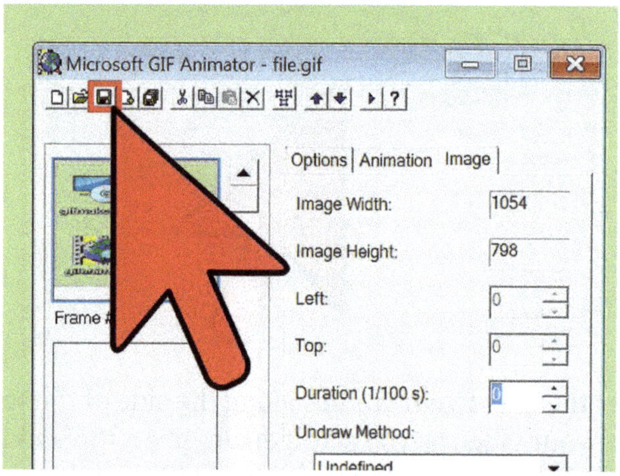

6. Click the Save As button to finish your GIF. This is the icon with multiple floppy disks. Save your GIF wherever you would like.

Chapter 6

Some Creative Designing Ideas

Digital design is applicable in almost all forms of visual communication that is practiced today. Digital flip books, invitations, logos, brochures, etc. are some of the items that are regularly made using desktop publishing and image editing software. The topics discussed in the chapter are of great importance to broaden the existing knowledge on digital design.

How to create a Digital Flip Book

As is implied by the name, traditional flip books are the kind of small books of sequential pictures. It's a development that could finally make true the illusion of animation when the pages are flipped. This novelty was once in the air among the children before being been superseded by television and video games. Be that as it may, technology has brought them back and you can make your own digital flip books for all your friends to share. Simply need a short time and the right software, you can make your still pictures come alive.

Steps

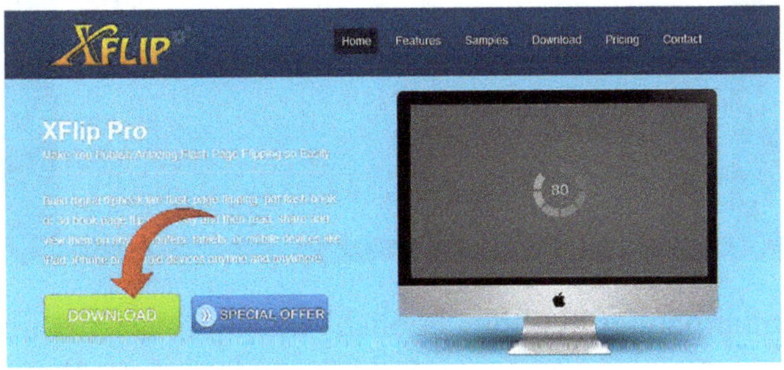

1. Find a Flip Book Software. There are many flip book making programs that can be downloaded including Flip Software, ncesoft, kvisoft, xFlip etc.

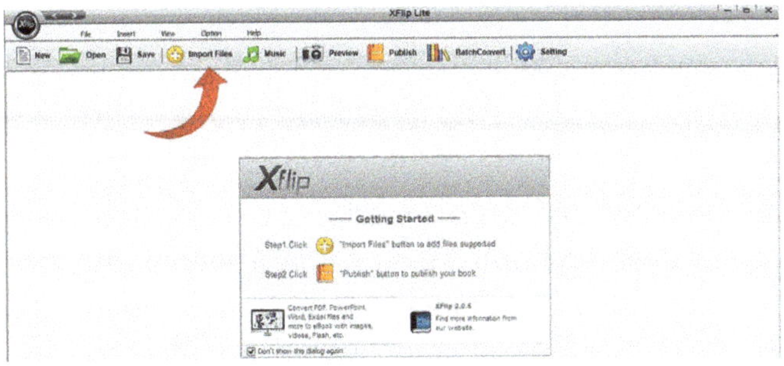

2. Run Flip Book Software and load files. Hit "Import" to browse your image files exactly as you

want it to appear in the flipping book. The powerful software also allows you to add many other files like PDF files, SWF files etc. You can upload as many image files as possible from your computer's hard drive into the software program.

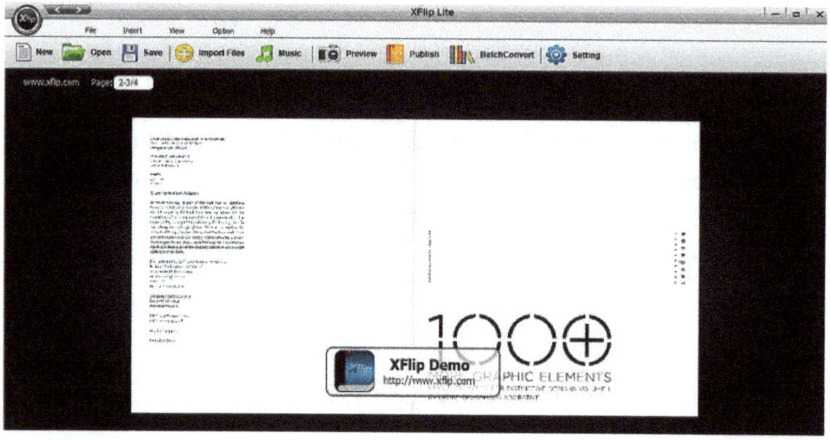

3. Select your desired output template. You may choose your desired template of flipping book that the software provides.

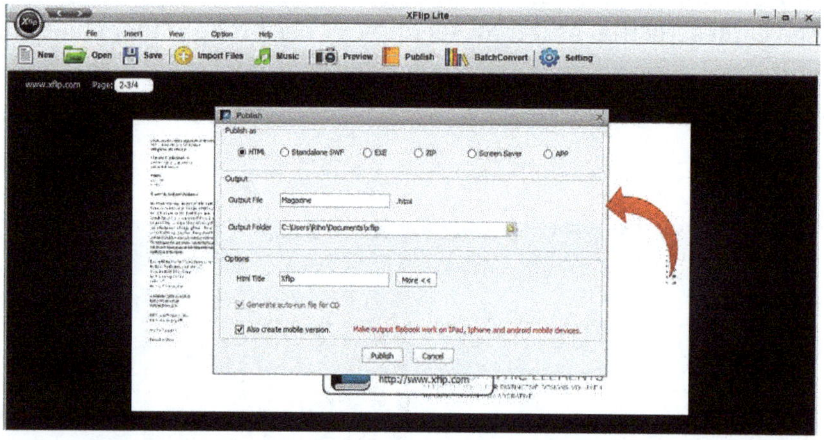

4. Start to publish your flip book. Click the "Publish" button to start converting your image files to flip page. Your files are uploaded and converted into a Flash. Save the output files to the folder created by the flip page software on your computer where you want to put the output files (may include HTML. XML, and SWF files).

How to create an Invitation in Microsoft Publisher

Once something that had to be ordered from a stationery shop, stylish invitations are things you can create yourself by using a desktop publishing program such as Microsoft Publisher. Publisher lets you produce invitations in either of 2 formats, traditional folded cards or a postcard format, using either its templates or your own designs. Following are instructions on how to create an invitation in Microsoft Publisher 2003, 2007, and 2010.

Method 1

Making a Folded Invitation Card

1. Select the design you want to work with. Microsoft Publisher organizes its invitation card templates according to the type of occasion you want to invite the card recipients to.

- In Publisher 2003, select "Publications for Print" in the New Publication task pane and then click the arrow to the left of Invitation Cards. Click one of the types of invitation listed to display the available designs in the Preview Gallery.
- In Publisher 2007, select "Invitation Cards" from the Publication Types list at the left edge of the screen. Invitation designs are grouped according to the type of event the invitation is for, followed by a section of common blank sizes, followed by blank sizes grouped by stationery manufacturer. You can highlight any design to see a larger version of it at the top of the Task Pane at the top right.
- In Publisher 2010, select "Invitation Cards" from the More Templates section under Available Templates. Invitation designs are grouped according to the type of event the invitation is for, followed by a section of common blank sizes, followed by blank sizes grouped in folders by stationery manufacturer. You can highlight any design to see a larger version of it at the top of the Task Pane at the top right.
- If you don't see the template you want, you can download additional templates from Microsoft if you have an Internet connection.

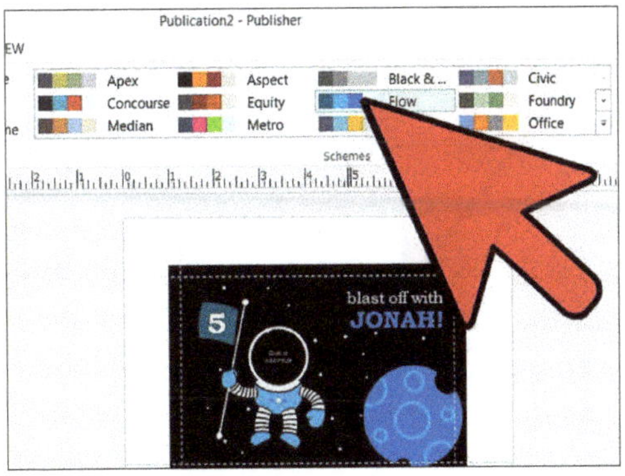

2. Choose the color and font scheme for your invitation. Each invitation card template comes with

a default color and font scheme, but if you wish to use a different color or font scheme, you can do so by selecting the appropriate new scheme. Choose a new color scheme from one of the named color schemes in the Color Scheme dropdown and a new font from the Font Scheme dropdown.

- You can also create your own custom color or font scheme by selecting the "Create new" option from either the Color Scheme or the Font Scheme dropdown.

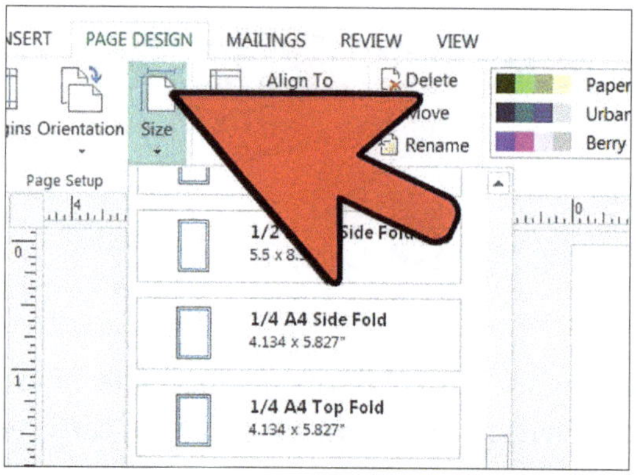

3. Decide how your card should be folded. Your invitation card will be printed on a single sheet of paper, but can be folded in 1 of 3 ways. You choose which way your card is folded from the Page Size dropdown in the Options section of the task pane. The available options are these:

- Quarter-page side fold. Your card pages will print on one side of the page, and when folded, will produce a card that opens on the left side.

- Quarter-page top fold. Your card pages will print on one side of the page, and when folded, will produce a card that opens at the top.

- Half-page side fold. Your front and back covers will print on one side of the page, and the card interior will print on the other. You can orient the contents so that the card will fold either on the side or at the top. A half-page card will fold to a larger size than a quarter-page card.

- These options are not available if you select one of the blank templates, as their page-folding schemes are pre-determined.

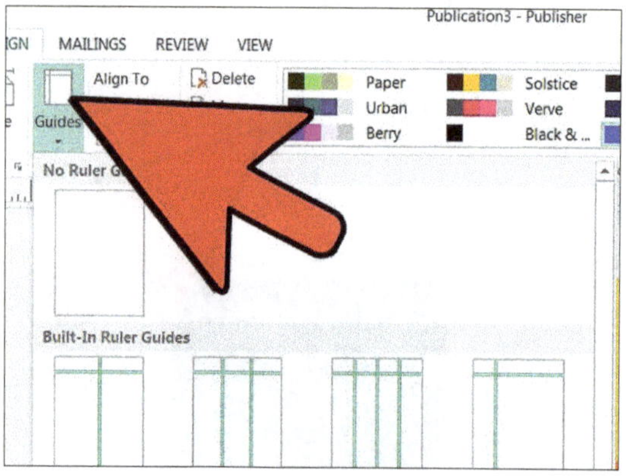

4. Determine the page layout. Although each of Publisher's invitation card templates has its own

default layout of the card's design elements, you can change the layout of those elements to your liking by selecting one of the options in the Layout dropdown on the task pane.

- These layout options are not available if you select one of the blank templates.

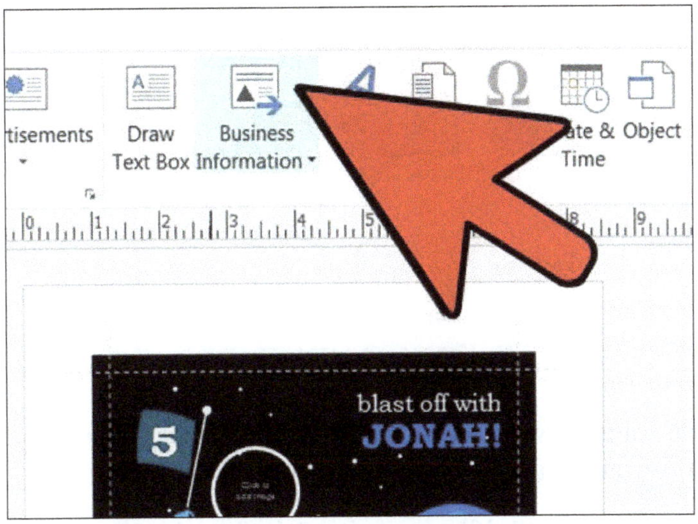

5. Insert your company or personal information, if desired. If you're using Publisher 2003, the program prompts you for this information the first time you use it. Afterwards, you select this information from Personal Information in the Edit menu to insert it in your invitation. In Publisher 2007 and 2010, you can select your company information set from the Business Information dropdown or select "Create new" to create a new information set. This information will be inserted into your invitation card.

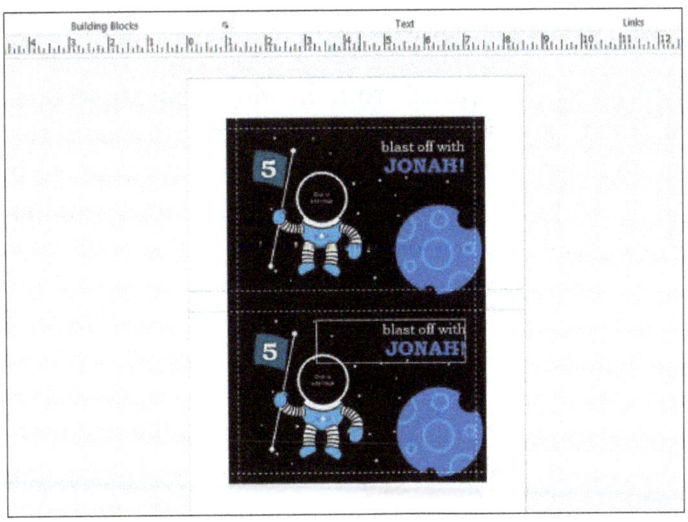

6. Create your invitation card. In Publisher 2007 and 2010, click the "Create" button at the bottom of the task pane to create your brochure. (Publisher 2003 automatically assumes at this point that you are creating a brochure and does not feature a "Create" button on its task pane.)

- At this point, you may want to print out the invitation to see if the design is what you want or create a PDF to email to others to get their input on the design.

Method 2

Making a Postcard Invitation

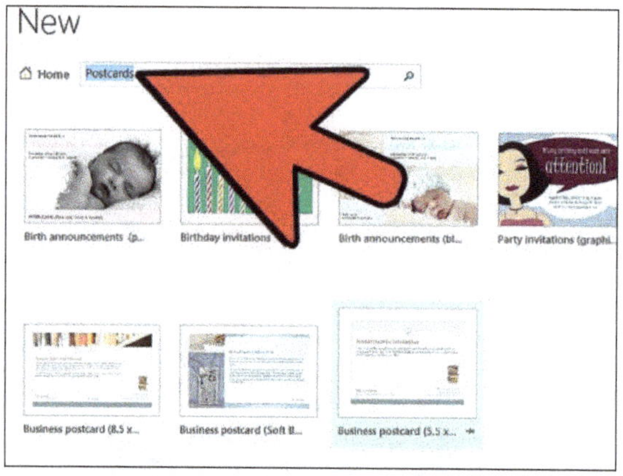

1. Select the design you want to work with. Microsoft Publisher organizes its postcard templates according to the purpose you plan to put the postcard to.

- In Publisher 2003, select "Publications for Print" in the New Publication task pane and then click the arrow to the left of Postcards. Click one of the types of postcard listed to display the available designs in the Preview Gallery.
- In Publisher 2007, select "Postcards" from the Popular Publication Types list at the center of the screen or from the Publication Types list at the left edge of the screen. Postcard designs are grouped according to the purpose of the postcard, followed by a section of common blank sizes, followed by blank sizes grouped by stationery manufacturer. You can highlight any design to see a larger version of it at the top of the Task Pane at the top right.
- In Publisher 2010, select "Postcards" from the Most Popular section under Available Templates. Postcard designs are grouped according to the purpose of the postcard, followed by a section of common blank sizes, followed by blank sizes grouped in folders by stationery manufacturer. You can highlight any design to see a larger version of it at the top of the Task Pane at the top right.

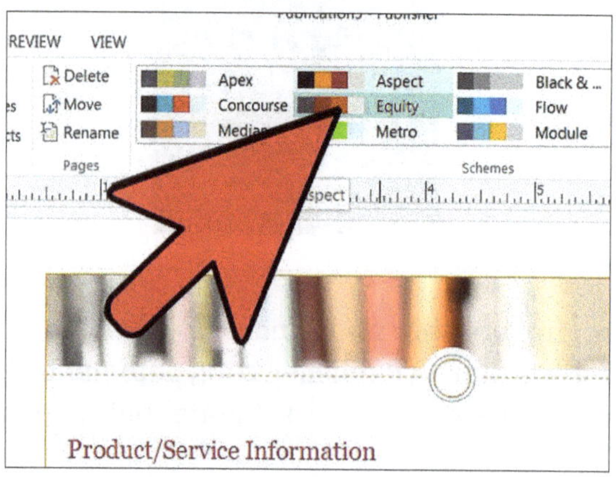

2. Choose the color and font scheme for your invitation. As with the invitation card templates, each

of the postcard templates comes with its own default color and font schemes that you can change to your liking by using the options in the Color Scheme and Font Scheme drop downs, either by selecting one of the listed options or selecting "Create new" to create your own.

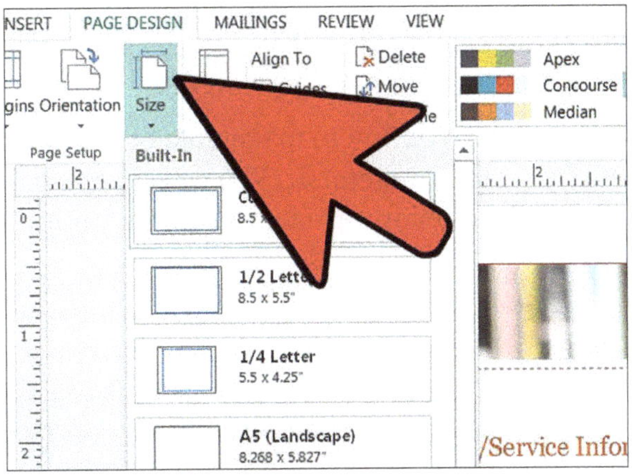

3. Decide how your postcard will be oriented when printed. Use the Page Size dropdown options to have your postcard invitation print as a quarter page or quarter sheet (4 cards to a regular sheet of paper or cardstock) or as a half page or half sheet (2 cards to a regular sheet of paper or cardstock).

- This option is not available when creating a postcard invitation from a blank template.

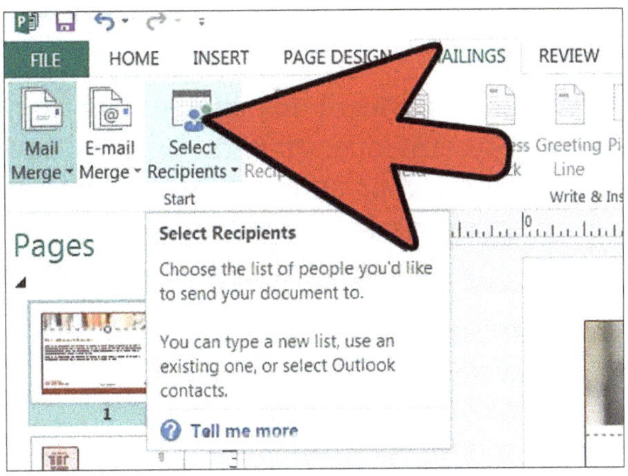

4. Decide what you want to include on the address side of the postcard invitation. You can choose to display only the mailing and return address on the mailing side of your postcard or to include supplemental information. You choose this option from the Side 2 Information dropdown list. A partial list of the options, those relevant to invitation postcards, are listed below:

- "Address only." Choose this option to display only the mailing and return address on the mailing side of the postcard invitation.
- "Map." Choose this option if your invitation is to an event and you plan to include a simple map to direct people to its location. This option is more commonly used for invitations to business events, but a map can help people find their way to the site of a wedding reception or graduation ceremony as readily as to a sale. (You'll need to replace the placeholder map with your own.)

- "Speaker notes." Choose this option if your invitation is to an event featuring a political, business, or motivational speakers to include a short list of the most important speakers.
- "Promotional text." Choose this option if the invitation is to a sales event and you want to list some of the major items for sale in a special offer that's explained in greater detail on the other side of the card.
- "Appointment text." Choose this option to make note of the time and place of an event. You can add your contact phone, fax, and email. (You can change or delete the line "To confirm or cancel appointment" if it's not appropriate to your invitation's purpose.)
- These options are not available when creating a postcard invitation from a blank template.

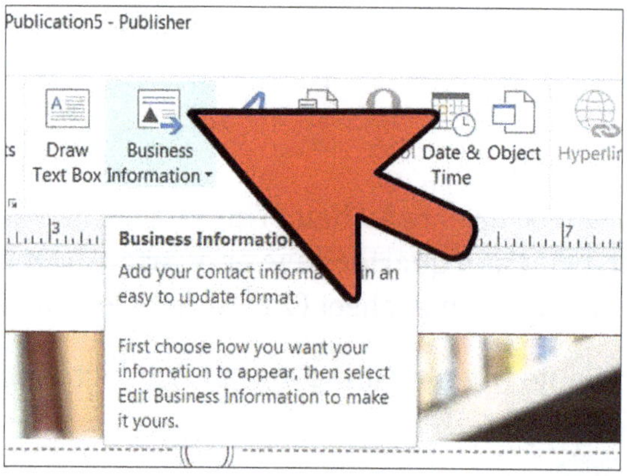

5. Include your address information. A postcard invitation differs from an invitation card in that the latter is enclosed in an addressed envelope, while the postcard invitation carries the mailing information on its back side. Including your information for the return address is handled the same way in Microsoft Publisher for postcard invitations as your version of Publisher handles your personal or company information if you choose to include it on an invitation card.

- To handle the mailing addresses, you can create a mail merge using a Microsoft Excel spreadsheet, an Access database, or a Word document.

6. Create your postcard invitation. As with invitation cards, click the "Create" button at the bottom of the task pane in either Publisher 2007 or 2010, while Publisher 2003 assumes the postcard is being created from the moment you choose "Postcards" from the New Publications task pane.

Method 3

Modifying, Saving, and Printing your Invitation

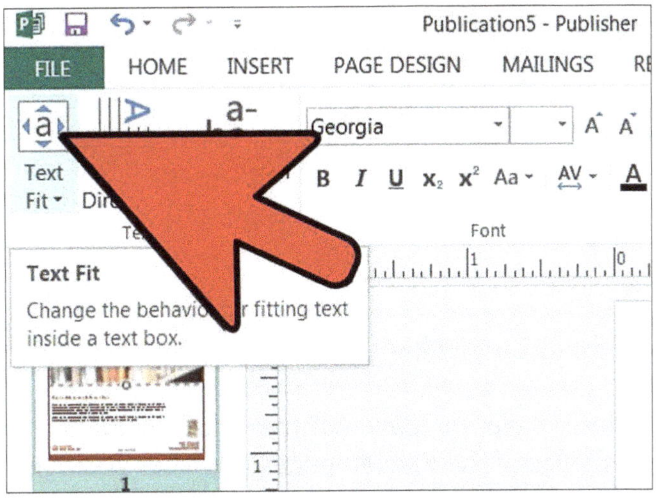

1. Replace any placeholder text with your own text. Click on the text you want to replace and type your new text in the text field.

- Text will automatically resize to fit the box in most cases. If you need to set the text to a certain size, either select "AutoFit Text" from the Format menu and then select "Do Not AutoFit" (Publisher 2003 and 2007) or select "Text Fit" in the Text group of the Text Box Tools Format ribbon and then select "Do Not AutoFit" (Publisher 2010). You can then manually select a new text size.
- Repeat this step for any other text you wish to replace.

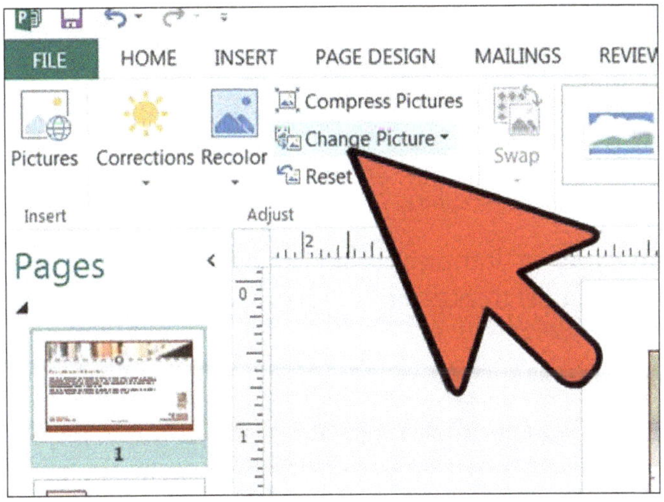

2. Replace any placeholder pictures with your own pictures. Right-click the picture you want to replace, then select "Change Picture" from the popup menu and choose where the new picture will come from. Repeat this step for any other pictures you wish to replace.

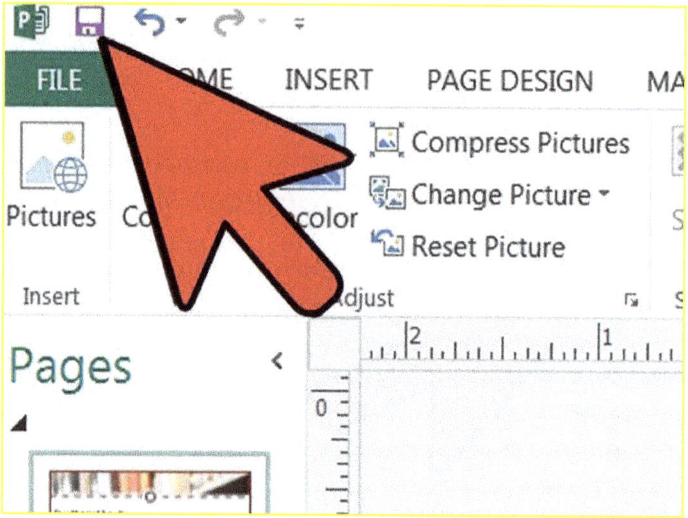

3. Save the invitation. Choose "Save" or "Save As" from the File menu (Publisher 2003 or 2007) or from the menu at the left edge of the File tab page (Publisher 2010). Give your invitation a descriptive name.

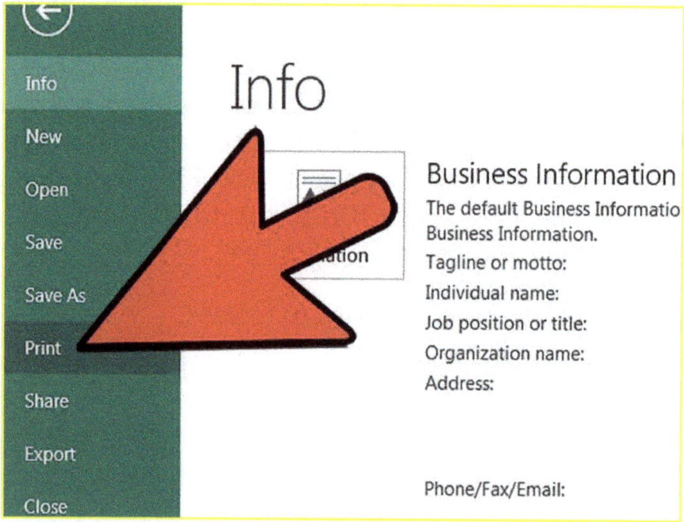

4. Print copies of your invitation as needed.

- If you plan to have your invitation printed professionally, you'll want to save or convert it to PDF format, as most printers prefer to receive documents in that format.

How to create a Logo in Microsoft Publisher

MS Publisher is a desktop publishing application included in some versions of the Microsoft Office suite. Publisher is designed to be user friendly and meet the needs of the average user with little or no design experience. This article provides step-by-step instructions on how to create a logo in Microsoft Publisher.

Steps

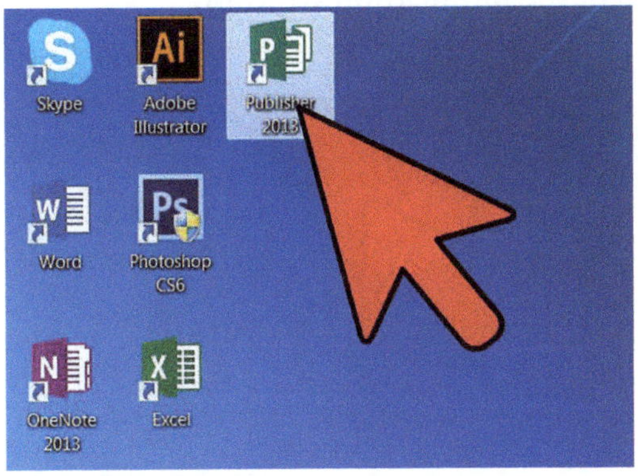

1. Open Publisher. Click the All Programs option from the Windows Start menu and select Microsoft Office. Select Publisher from the sub-menu. The application will open on the desktop. Choose a paper size for the work area. Select the Blank Page Sizes option from the Publication Types menu in the column on the left. Select the Letter (portrait) option from the available sizes. The work area has been prepared to design a logo in Microsoft Publisher.

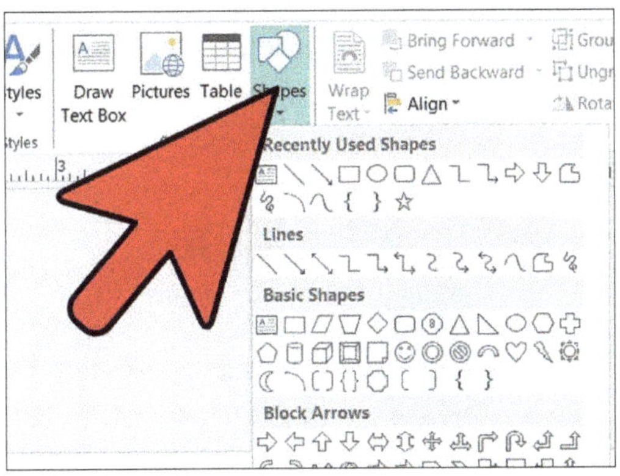

2. Choose a shape for the logo. Click the "AutoShapes" button located on the Objects toolbar and take note of the different submenus that appear in the "AutoShapes" menu. Browse the submenus to find a shape, line, banner, cutout or connector to use for designing your logo. Click any object to insert it into the document.

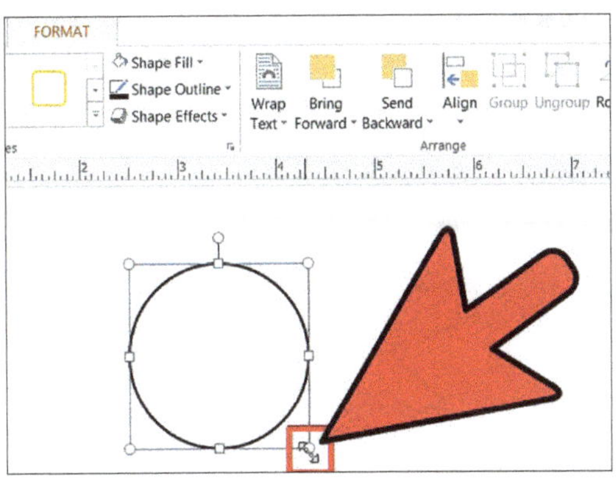

3. Resize the shape to fill the application window. Increase the size of the shape to improve the

resolution quality of the final product. Click and drag on an edge or corner to resize the shape. The shape should run to the edges of the application window.

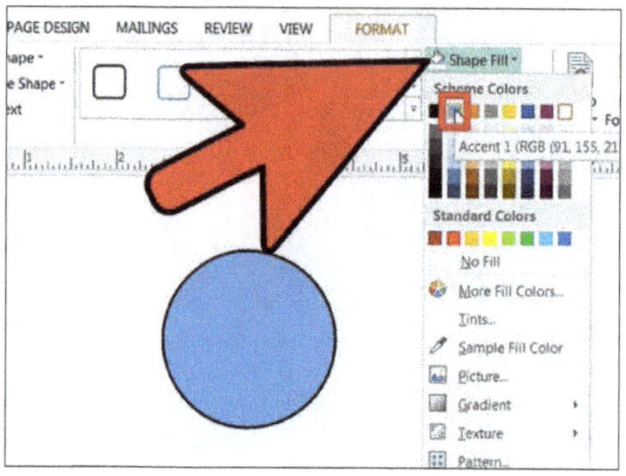

4. Choose a color for the shape. Click the Fill Color button on the toolbar. Select More Fill Colors to choose a color from the Standard color options, or click the Custom tab on the sub-menu to create a custom fill color.

- Choose a color that will contrast well with the color of the font used. Any possible shade or color can be created in the Custom Colors menu by adjusting the sliders in the color palette or by adjusting the RGB values. The fill transparency can also be adjusted.

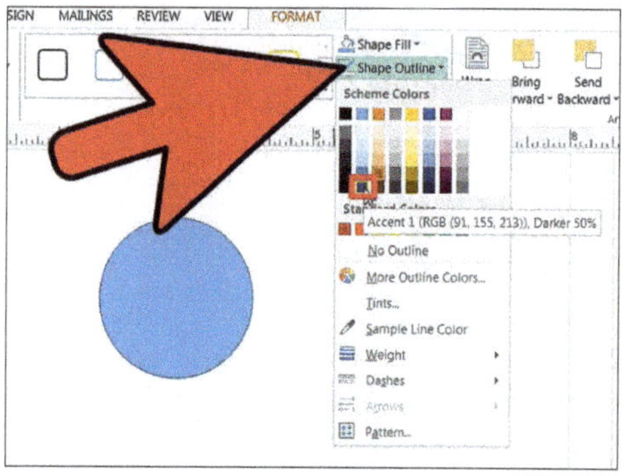

5. Choose a color for the shape outline. Click the Line Color button on the toolbar. Select the More Outline colors option from the sub-menu to view each of the available line colors or click the Custom tab on the sub-menu to create a custom line color. Any possible shade or color can be created in the Custom Colors menu by adjusting the sliders in the color palette.

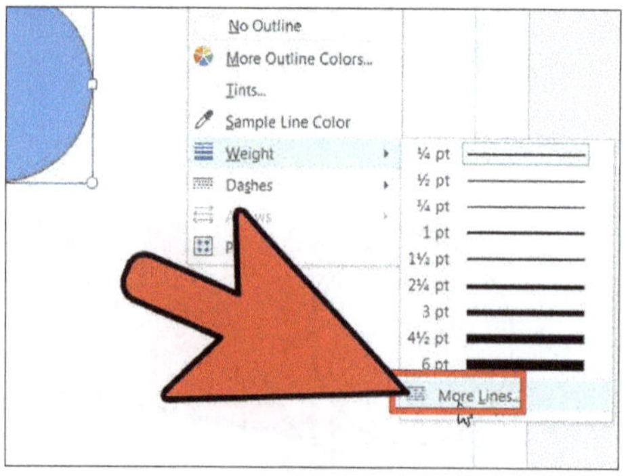

6. Choose a line style for the shape outline. Click the Border/Line Style button on the toolbar, and

choose the style and thickness of the shape outline from the options available. Choose from single, double or triple line styles, or choose the More Lines option located at the bottom of the pull-down menu. The shape outline can be adjusted to any width.

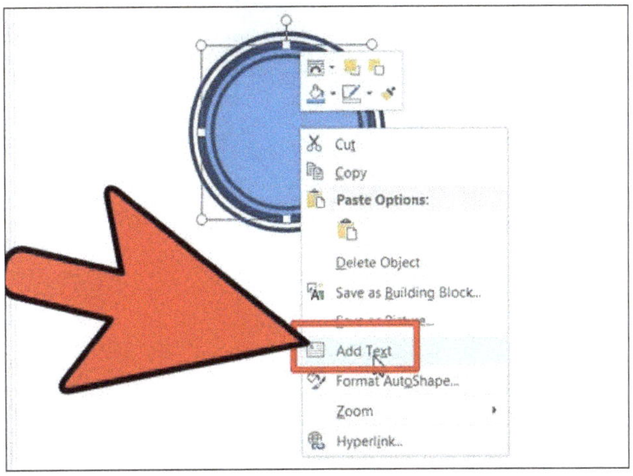

7. Add the logo text. Right-click the shape and select Add Text from the pull-down menu. A cursor will appear in the shape. Type the logo text.

- Change the font for the logo text. Right-click the design and choose the Change Text option. Choose a font for the text from the Font dialogue box. Choose a font that can be clearly read. Helvetica, Bodini, Garamond and Futura are among the most common fonts used by professional designers. Experiment with different fonts to find the one that most suits your project.
- Adjust the size of the text. Right-click the text again and choose Font from the pull-down menu. Choose the "AutoFit" Text option from the sub-menu and select Best Fit. The text will adjust to better fit the size of the object.

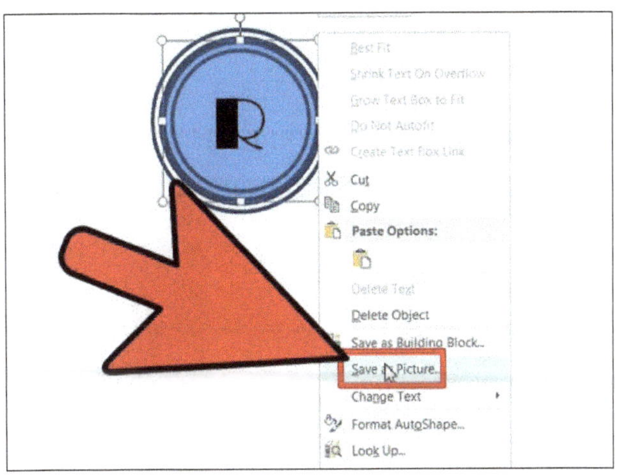

8. Save the logo as an image file. Right click the object and select the Save as Picture option from the pull-down menu. Click the Save as Type arrow and choose the Bitmap option from the pull-down menu. In the Save As dialogue box, select the 300dpi setting from the Print Resolution options. An image of the of the Publisher logo design has been saved to your computer.

How to create a Clipping Mask in Adobe Illustrator

This teaches you how to create a clipping mask in an Adobe Illustrator file.

Steps

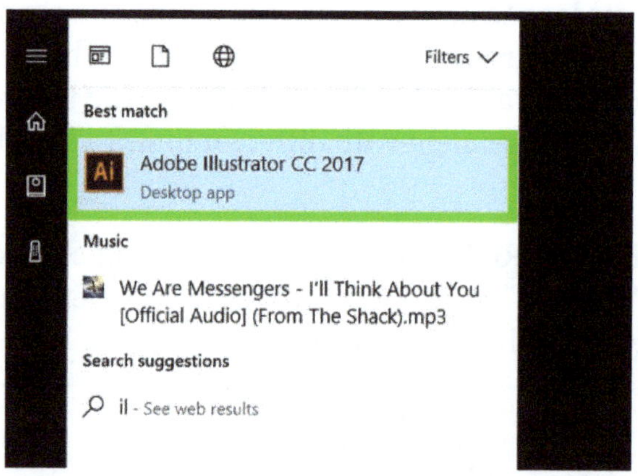

1. Open Adobe illustrator. It's a yellow and brown app that contains the letters "Ai."

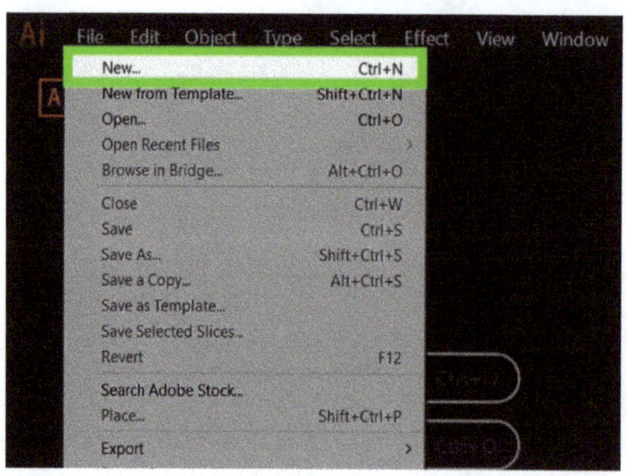

2. Click on File. It's in the menu bar in upper-left of the screen.

- Click New... to create a new file or image to mask.
- Click on Open... to open an existing file to mask.

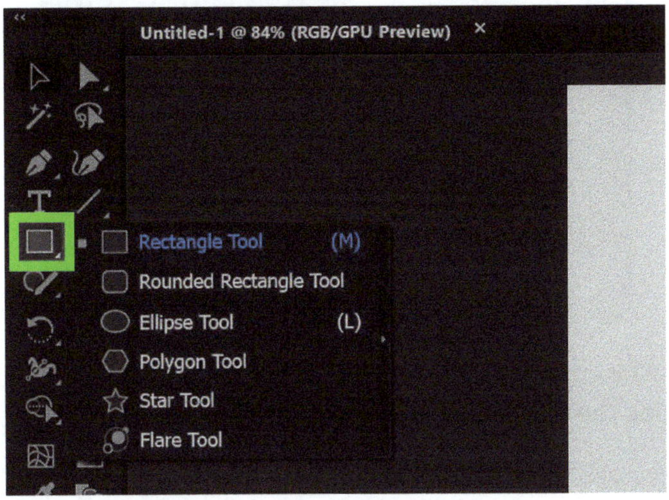

3. Long-click and release on the "shape" tool. It's just below the text tool (T) near the top of the toolbar on the left side of the screen.

- A drop-down menu will open to the right of the toolbar.

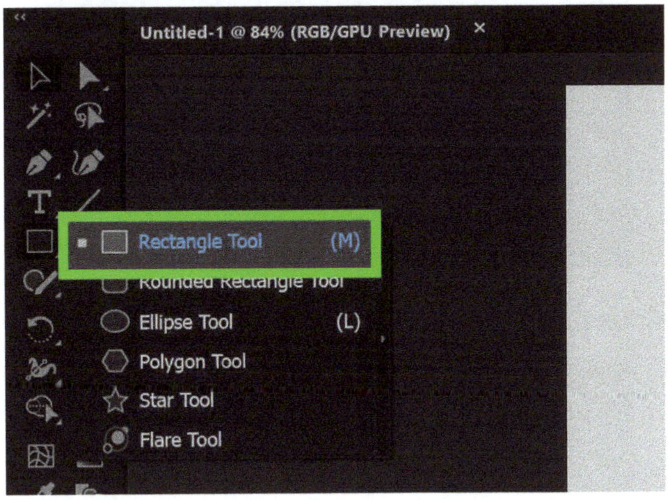

4. Click on a tool. Choose a tool to draw the shape of the mask you want to use on the image. Available tools, depending on the version of Illustrator, that can be used for a clipping mask include:

- Rectangle Tool
- Rounded Rectangle Tool
- Ellipse Tool
- Polygon Tool
- Star Tool

5. Draw the object you'd like to use as a mask. Do so by clicking on and holding somewhere on the screen, and then dragging the tool's crosshairs to create the size and shape you desire.

- The result is a vector shape that will act like a widow.

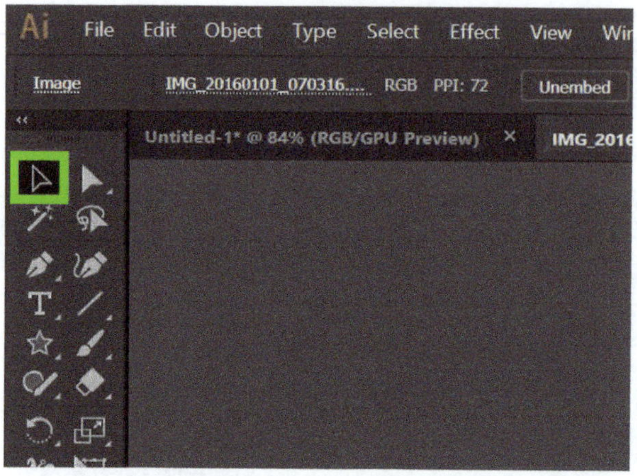

6. Click on the black pointer tool. It's in the upper-left corner of the tool bar.

7. Place the vector shape over the image. Do so by clicking on and dragging the vector shape until the portion of the image you want to remain visible is inside the shape you drew.

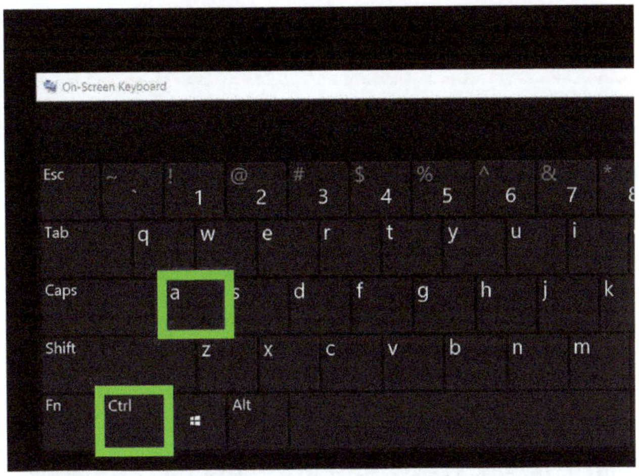

8. Press Ctrl + A (Windows) or ⌘ + A (Mac). Doing so selects all the objects in the window.

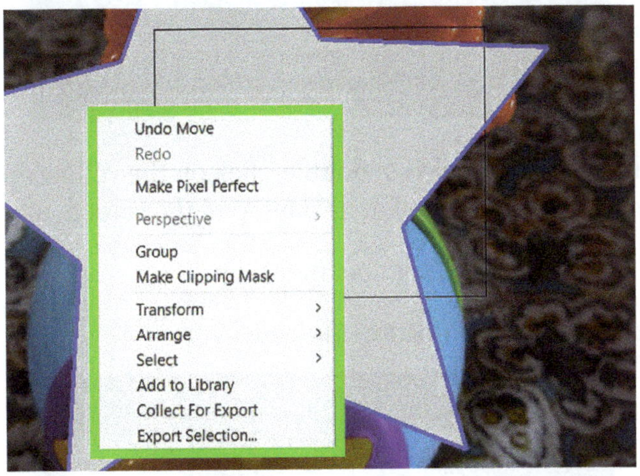

9. Right-click or Control-click on the image. A pop-up menu will appear.

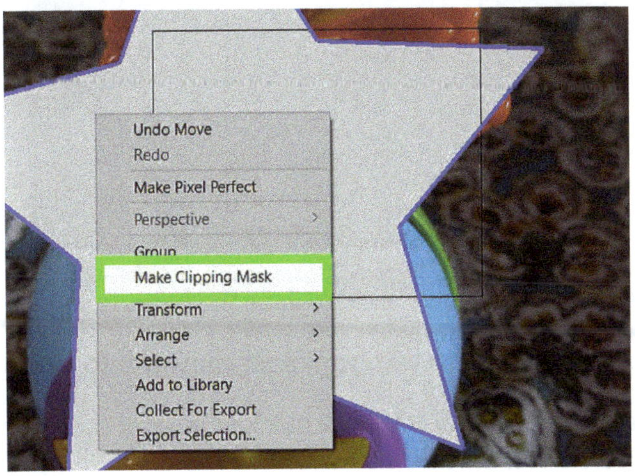

10. Click on Make Clipping Mask. It's near the middle of the menu.

- Your image will be clipped to the shape of the object you created.

How to add a Hyperlink in Illustrator

This teaches you how to add a hyperlink to a PDF document using Adobe Illustrator on Mac or PC.

Steps

1. Open or create an Illustrator file. To do so, double-click on the yellow app icon that contains the letters "Ai," then click on File in the menu bar at the top of the screen, and:

- Click on Open... to open an existing document; or
- Click on New... to create a new document.

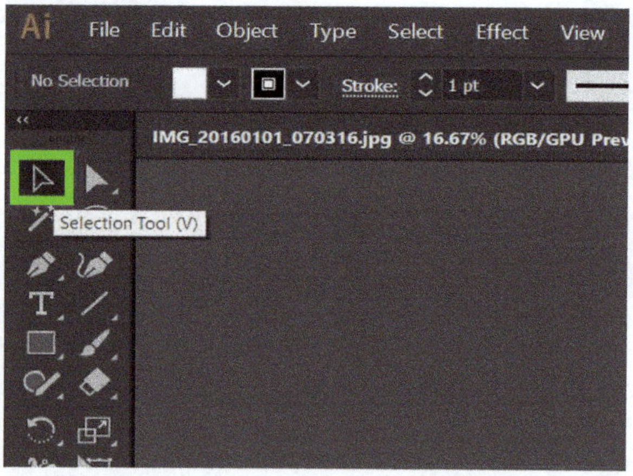

2. Create the object or text on which you'd like to place the hyperlink.

- If you want to add a hyperlink to text, you must convert it to outlines first. To do so:
    - Click on the Selection Tool. It's the black pointer in the upper-left part of the toolbar on the left side of the window.
    - Single-click on the text on which you're placing the hyperlink.
    - Click on Type. It's in the menu bar at the top of the screen.

- Click on Create Outlines. It's in the middle of the menu. Your text is now a series of individually-editable objects.
- Click on Object. It's in the menu bar at the top of the screen.
- Click on Group. It's near the top of the menu. Your text outlines can now be moved as a group.

3. Arrange your text or object. Use the Selection Tool to select your text or object and place it where you want the hyperlink to appear on your page.

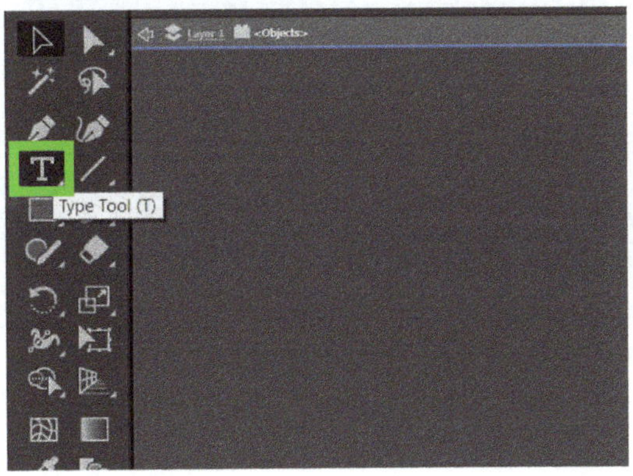

4. Click on the Type Tool. It's the T icon at the upper-right of the toolbar on the left side of the window.

5. Click anywhere on the document. Doing so creates a text box.

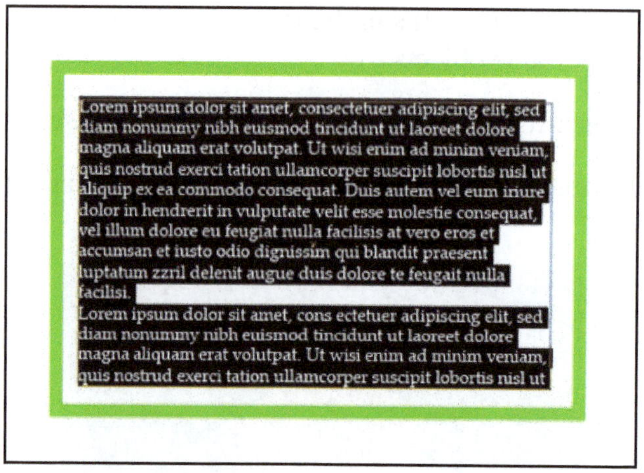

6. Type the URL for the hyperlink. Start with "http://" so PDF reader apps will recognize it as a live link, then type the web address to which you want to link.

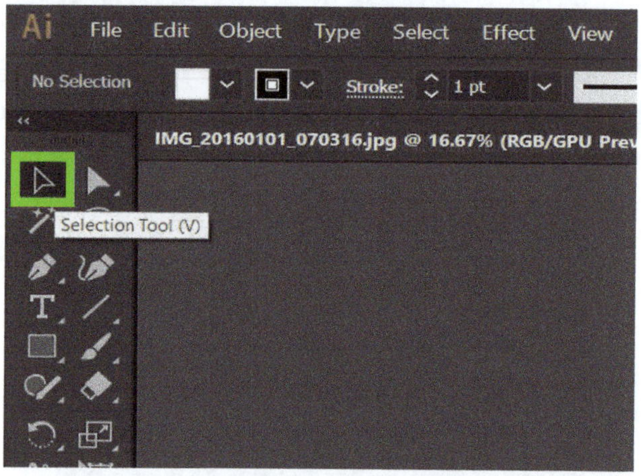

7. Click on the Selection Tool. It's the black pointer in the upper-left part of the toolbar on the left side of the window.

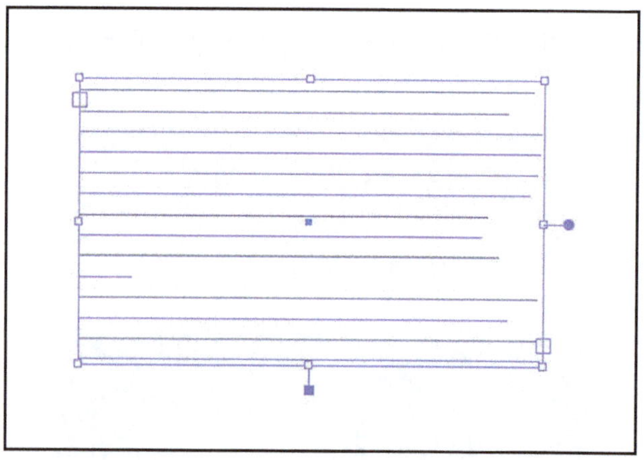

8. Move the URL over the text object you want to link from. Use the Selection Tool to do so.

- If you wish, you can resize the URL so it fits directly over the text or object. Do so by clicking and holding on the small squares of the selection box that surrounds the text, and stretching or condensing the URL text to the dimensions of the object or text from which you're linking.

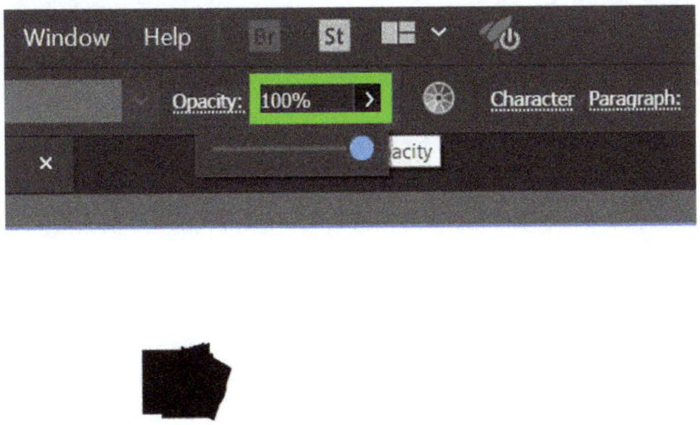

9. Click on the "Opacity:" drop-down menu. It's at the top of the Illustrator window.

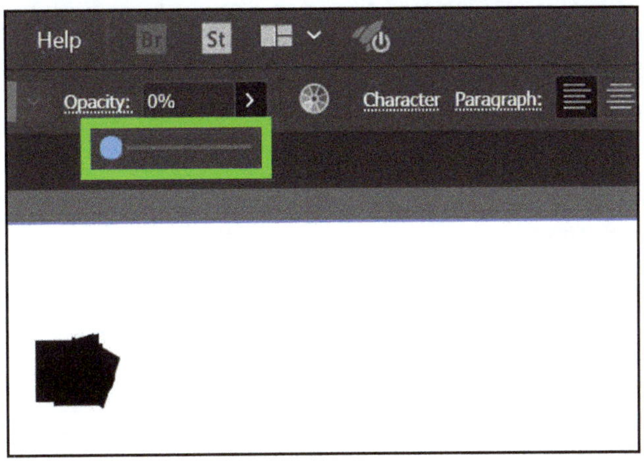

10. Click on 0%. The hyperlink on top of your text or object is now invisible.

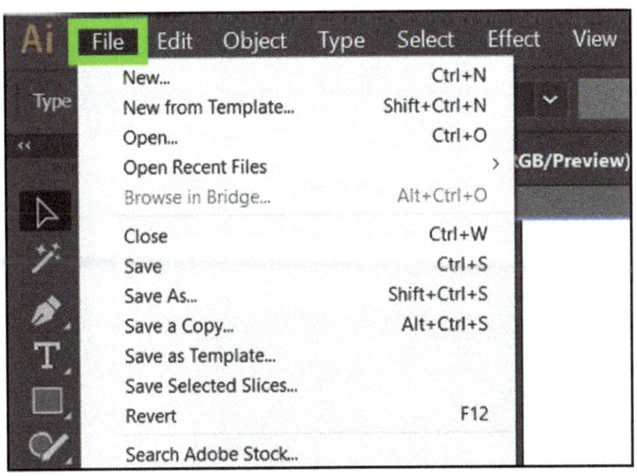

11. Click on File. It's in the menu bar at the top of the screen.

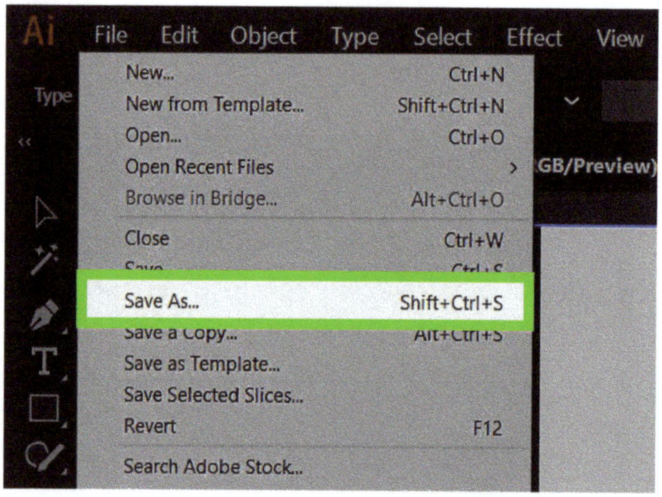

12. Click on Save As.... It's near the middle of the drop-down menu.

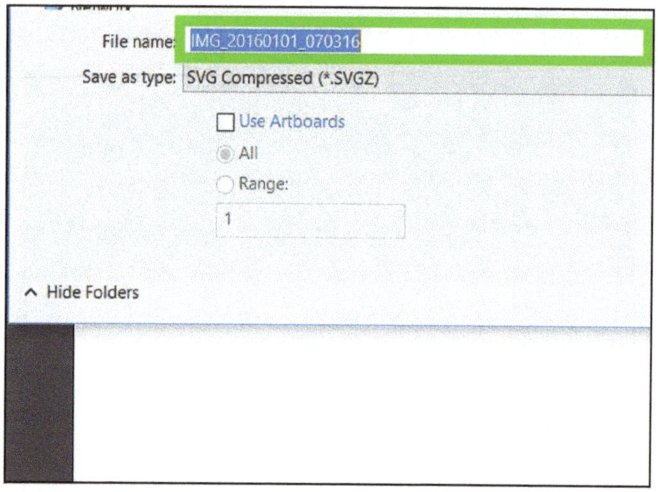

13. Name your file. Do so in the "Save As:" field at the top of the dialog box.

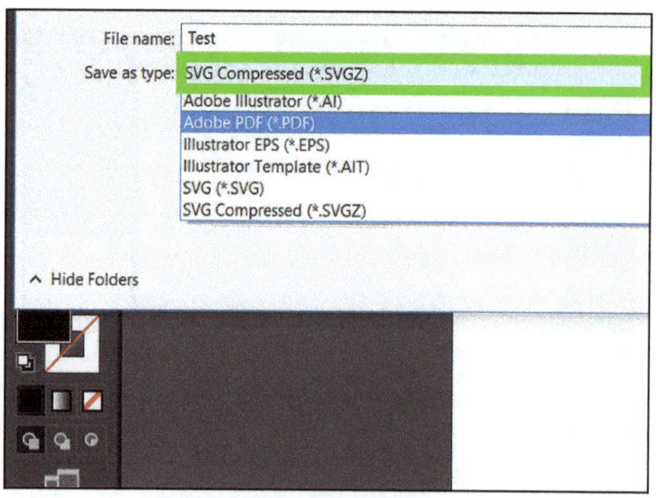

14. Click on the "Format:" drop-down menu. It's at the lower-left of the dialog box.

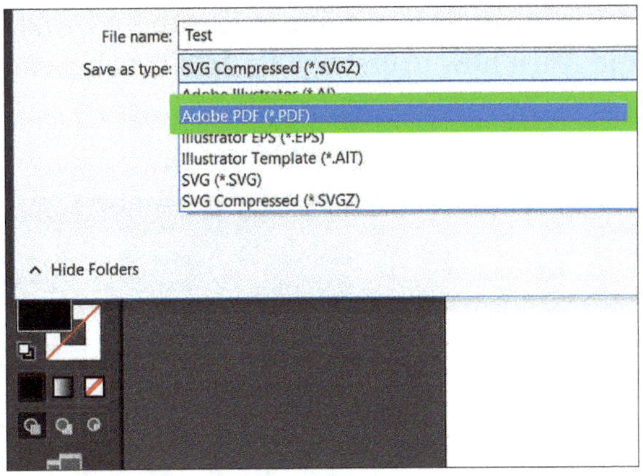

15. Click on Adobe PDF.

16. Click on Save. It's in the lower-right corner of the dialog box.

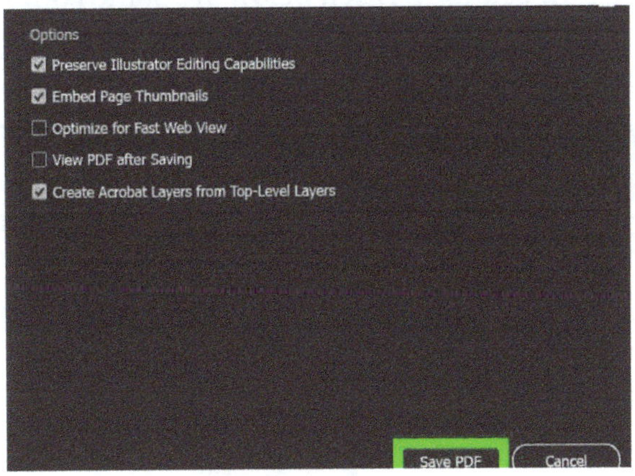

17. Click on Save PDF. It's in the lower-right corner of the dialog box. When your document is opened in a PDF reader, the app will recognize your text or object as a hyperlink.

How to make a Brochure in Adobe Illustrator

A brochure is a piece of paper that includes photos, graphics and information. There are many types of brochures such as the Z-fold which has 4 - 6 panels, a bi-fold which has 4 panels and a tri-fold which has 6 panels. For this tutorial were going to create a tri-fold brochure and make it print ready. Follow this tutorial and learn how to create a tri-fold brochure using Adobe Illustrator CS5.

Steps

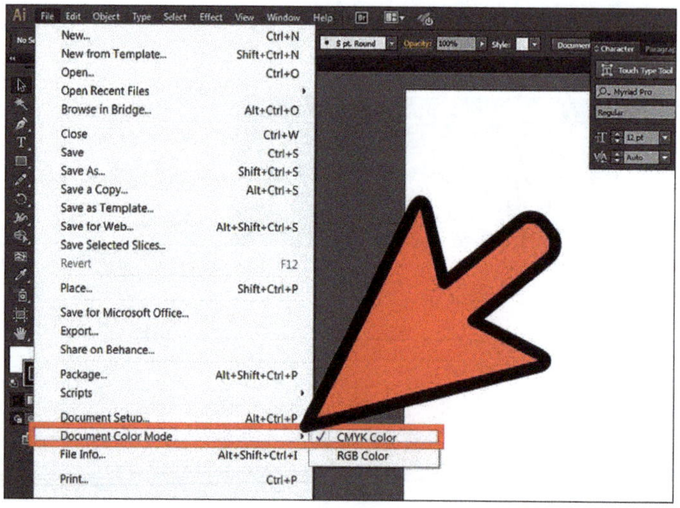

1. Prepare your file by making it print ready.

- Create a letter size document (11x8.5 inches) and change the document color mode to CMYK. You can do this by going to file > document color mode > CMYK Color.
- Add color swatches such as red, pink, green, yellow and dark yellow. Keep in mind that you can also choose your own colors. Written below are some combinations of the colors used on the tutorial. Red: C=0, M=67, Y=50, K=0; Pink: C=0, M=31, Y=37, K=0; Green: C=59, M=0, Y=33, K=0; Yellow: C=0, M=0, Y=51, K=0; Dark Yellow: C=0, M=7, Y=66, K=0.

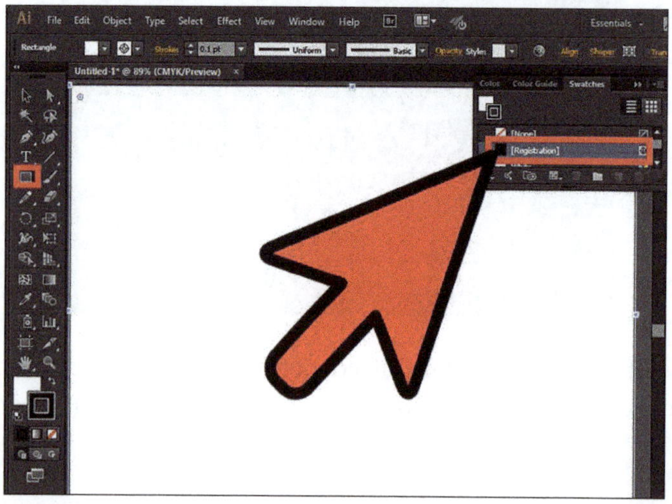

2. Now you need to create a crop guide by using a rectangular shape. A crop guide is a guide used by printers to know where to trim your brochure once printed. Create the shape with a size of 11x8.5 inches and color the stroke using the registration swatch. Change also the weight of the stroke to a 0.1 pt.

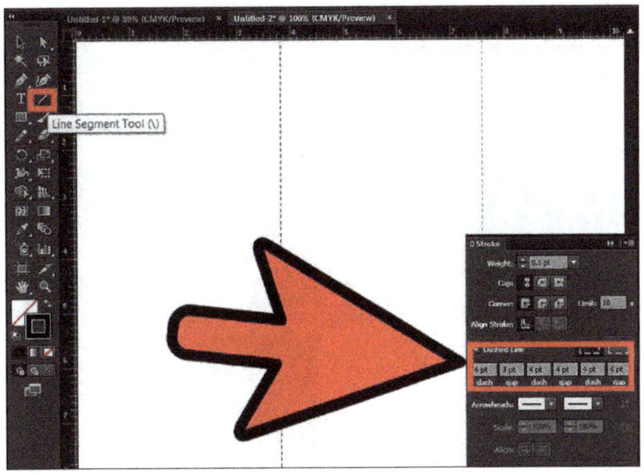

3. Then divide your 11 inches (27.9 cm) width-space into 3. Mark your division using guides and then place dashed lines on them. To create your dashed line use the line segment tool to create a line then click dashed line on your strokes panel or window.

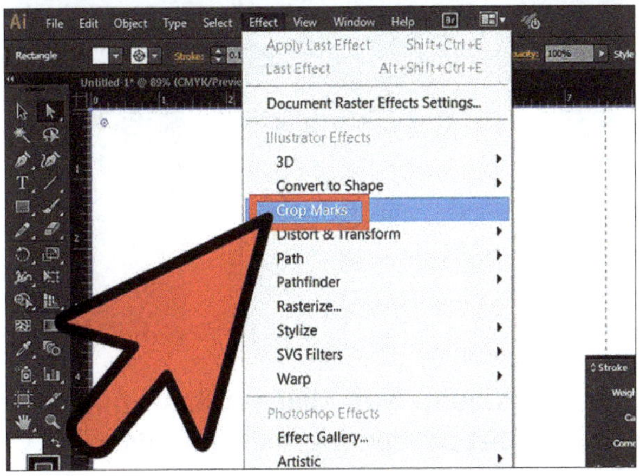

4. Add crop marks on your document. To add crop marks, select your crop guide or rectangular shape and then go to effect and click on crop marks.

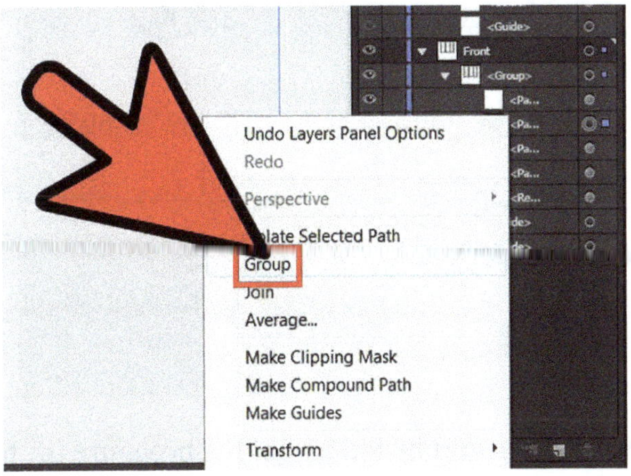

5. Group everything together. Select all (or Ctrl+A), right-click and click on group.

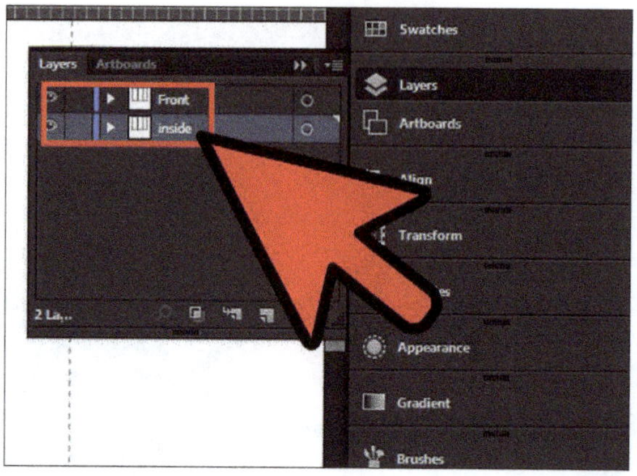

6. Make a copy of the group and rename them "FRONT" and "INSIDE." To make a copy drag the group to your create new layer icon.

7. Create the contents of your document. Now that you have finished preparing your brochure, it's time to add editorial content. Start by creating backgrounds using your rectangular shape and selecting colors on your color swatch. Make sure that your rectangular shape is extended and not exactly fitted on your crop guide.

8. Create content for the front, back and inside flap of the brochure (or the "FRONT" group). Create your content by combining photos, graphics and texts. You can follow the layout on the accompanied illustration or create your own also.

9. And finally, it is time to add content on the left, middle and right inside panels of your brochure (or your "INSIDE" group). Once you do that, you are done.

10. Here's a sample of the final artwork when folded.

Permissions

All chapters in this book are published with permission under the Creative Commons Attribution Share Alike License or equivalent. Every chapter published in this book has been scrutinized by our experts. Their significance has been extensively debated. The topics covered herein carry significant information for a comprehensive understanding. They may even be implemented as practical applications or may be referred to as a beginning point for further studies.

We would like to thank the editorial team for lending their expertise to make the book truly unique. They have played a crucial role in the development of this book. Without their invaluable contributions this book wouldn't have been possible. They have made vital efforts to compile up to date information on the varied aspects of this subject to make this book a valuable addition to the collection of many professionals and students.

This book was conceptualized with the vision of imparting up-to-date and integrated information in this field. To ensure the same, a matchless editorial board was set up. Every individual on the board went through rigorous rounds of assessment to prove their worth. After which they invested a large part of their time researching and compiling the most relevant data for our readers.

The editorial board has been involved in producing this book since its inception. They have spent rigorous hours researching and exploring the diverse topics which have resulted in the successful publishing of this book. They have passed on their knowledge of decades through this book. To expedite this challenging task, the publisher supported the team at every step. A small team of assistant editors was also appointed to further simplify the editing procedure and attain best results for the readers.

Apart from the editorial board, the designing team has also invested a significant amount of their time in understanding the subject and creating the most relevant covers. They scrutinized every image to scout for the most suitable representation of the subject and create an appropriate cover for the book.

The publishing team has been an ardent support to the editorial, designing and production team. Their endless efforts to recruit the best for this project, has resulted in the accomplishment of this book. They are a veteran in the field of academics and their pool of knowledge is as vast as their experience in printing. Their expertise and guidance has proved useful at every step. Their uncompromising quality standards have made this book an exceptional effort. Their encouragement from time to time has been an inspiration for everyone.

The publisher and the editorial board hope that this book will prove to be a valuable piece of knowledge for students, practitioners and scholars across the globe.

Index

CPSIA information can be obtained
at www.ICGtesting.com
Printed in the USA
LVHW060856030122
707669LV00002B/185